BIAS IN THE WORKPLACE AND SOCIETY

T0291408

Bias in the Workplace and Society looks at the causes and management of the biases that underpin all behaviour inclusive of discrimination, prejudice, and stereotyping that can occur in the workplace and in everyday contexts. It considers how such biases are developed in relation to societal and global issues and explores the manifestations of bias that are illustrated across a variety of situations. The book is based on the premise that everyone is biased and there is no such thing as an unbiased person. We cannot eliminate bias, but we can manage it.

Grounded in the latest research, the book focuses on the impact of biases as they are manifested in everyday life. The first three chapters look at the reality of bias, how it develops, and how it is then reinforced by four forces – politics, business, religion, and social media. From this point it moves to explore the impact of bias across ten different areas, and, for each, it encourages discussion and debate as to the reality of impact. It asks the reader to consider the possibility that they are personally impacted by unconscious and conscious biases.

The final two chapters then draw everything together, challenging the reader to assess the reality of both unconscious and conscious biases in their life before moving to provide guidelines as to how biases can be managed. The point is made that behavioural change as a result of this self-examination is optional – it is a personal decision.

This book is suitable for all persons concerned about the impact of bias and, particularly, students of management, leadership, HRM, diversity and decision making.

Douglas G. Long was born in New Zealand but has lived in Australia for most of his adult life. Since 2012 he has taught in the School of Management and Governance at the University of New South Wales Business School in Sydney.

BIAS IN THE WORKPLACE AND SOCIETY

Douglas G. Long

Routledge
Taylor & Francis Group

LONDON AND NEW YORK

Designed cover image: ©GettyImages Credit: designer491. Creative #: 1272410872

First published 2025
by Routledge
4 Park Square, Milton Park, Abingdon, Oxon OX14 4RN

and by Routledge
605 Third Avenue, New York, NY 10158

Routledge is an imprint of the Taylor & Francis Group, an informa business

© 2025 Douglas G. Long

British Library Cataloguing-in-Publication Data
A catalogue record for this book is available from the British Library

ISBN: 978-1-032-86623-9 (hbk)
ISBN: 978-1-032-86620-8 (pbk)
ISBN: 978-1-003-52834-0 (ebk)

DOI: 10.4324/9781003528340

Typeset in Sabon
by Taylor & Francis Books

Biases are universal: Bias impacts everyone no matter who, no matter where. Bias is the impact on our behaviour (the decisions and judgments that we make) that occurs when our (often unconscious) world view controls how we process and interpret information in the world around us. It is a situation in which, based on our unique mental frameworks, we create and respond to the "subjective reality" arising from our perception of the input.

CONTENTS

ILLUSTRATIONS

Figures

Table

ABOUT THE AUTHOR

Douglas G. Long was born in New Zealand but has lived in Australia for most of his adult life. His tertiary education was in New Zealand, Australia, England and the United States, culminating in 1985 with a PhD in Organisational Psychology. His earlier studies were in history, religious studies, and economics.

For many years he taught in universities in Australia and the United States, including in Melbourne, Preston Institute, David Syme Business School, RMIT Graduate School of Management and, in the USA, Drexel University. From 1988 to 2001 he was associated with Macquarie Graduate School of Management in Sydney where he researched, designed and delivered the programme Leadership in Senior Management. 2002–2012 he was with Australia's Southern Cross University Graduate College of Management where he supervised doctoral candidates. Since 2012 he has taught in the School of Management and Governance at the University of New South Wales Business School in Sydney.

He is the author of 4 previous books published by Routledge-Gower.

INTRODUCTION

On October 14, 2023 Australia held a referendum to insert a new clause into its Constitution. The question being asked was: "*A Proposed Law: to alter the Constitution to recognise the First Peoples of Australia by establishing an Aboriginal and Torres Strait Islander Voice. Do you approve this proposed alteration?*". Respondents needed to write "yes" or "no" in the box provided. Campaigning was fierce and, as the voting day approached, supporters of both the "yes" and the "no" case became increasingly polarised, and accusations of prejudice were rife. Voting (as in all elections and referendums in Australia) was compulsory for all Australian citizens aged 18 and over. Across Australia the majority vote (around 60%) voted "no" and the move to insert the clause was defeated.

The referendum had its genesis in an initiative supported by the Australian Government in 2017 – a constitutional convention that brought together over 250 Aboriginal and Torres Strait Islander leaders at the foot of Uluru in Central Australia on the lands of the Anangu people. The majority resolved, in the "Uluru Statement from the Heart", to call for the establishment of a "First Nations Voice" in the *Australian Constitution* and a "Makarrata Commission" to supervise a process of "agreement-making" and "truth-telling" between governments and Aboriginal and Torres Strait Islander peoples.

Given that most Australians would claim that they are not racist and that they believe that the Indigenous peoples should be recognised and respected, it is not surprising that those claiming the referendum result is evidence of a racist society are vehemently opposed. This is particularly the case when attempts are made to argue that racism is deeply entrenched in Australia's DNA. The point is made that many of those voting "no" were themselves Indigenous and at least two of the most vocal opponents were prominent Indigenous leaders. Doubtless the debate and recriminations will continue for some time and each side will find arguments to support their views.

DOI: 10.4324/9781003528340-1

What is clear from this event is that the making of major decisions is a very complex process in which emotions can be massaged in such a way that factors such as the statement not being sufficiently strong, or fear of the unknown, can be weaponised. It is an example of national (probably) unconscious bias in decision making.

On Tuesday August 31, 2021, the Australian Broadcasting Corporation (ABC) programme "Catalyst" showed a documentary entitled "Magic and the Brain"[1] in which it was clearly demonstrated that what we understand as "reality" is, in fact, our brain's interpretation of some external stimulus – something we have seen, heard, or otherwise experienced. The programme showed that, from our birth, we each develop our own particular framework for making sense of what we see. By the time we are adults, we each have our own, individual mental framework.

Although we are mostly unaware of our individual mental frameworks, there are indicators available should we want to use them. If, in our interactions with other people, we notice behaviours such as the following (either in ourselves or others) it may indicate that a mental framework has caused bias:

- Heavily opinionated or one-sided arguments
- Reliance on unsupported or unsubstantiated claims
- Presentation of highly selected facts that lean to a desired outcome
- Pretending to present facts but offering only opinion
- Use of extreme or inappropriate language
- Trying to persuade others to think a certain way regardless of any factual evidence
- Lack of knowledge and/or experience when commenting on unrelated topics

Clearly many of us have very similar mental frameworks but none are identical. For example, three people may see the same car yet describe its colour as ranging from green, through teal, to blue; two people may witness the same event yet, when asked, report it quite differently because their framework may have focused on different elements, or several people may listen to the same piece of music yet respond to it quite differently.

In most cases these differences occur without any value judgement. I may see my car's colour as being "teal", but I am perfectly happy to let you describe it as being "blue" or "green" – I am not going to argue as to whether either description is "good" or "bad": our opinions of the colour are simply "different", and I will readily understand them as being influenced by the lighting under which the car is seen. All I am really concerned about is whether my car will perform satisfactorily when I need to use it. As a matter of personal satisfaction, I might like the fact that it is "teal" because I like that colour, but I will readily admit that even if it was "blue", "green" or anything else it would still be basically the same car and would be expected to perform in exactly the same fashion.

Yet inherent in this "different" lies the potential for serious social problems.

If my mental framework is formed in a western society, growing up in a family and society with primarily European characteristics, I may more easily recognise individuals with similar characteristics to me than will I recognise individuals with, for example, Asian characteristics (and vice versa). While, in the majority of cases this is not a problem, as we know from both history and current experience, this "different" can easily degenerate into discrimination, segregation, and oppression. Whatever our mental framework, it is only a hair's breadth from contributing to us showing "bias" in some or another fashion. Our mental models, i.e. our perspectives of how something works, carry with them an inherent bias. We cannot keep all of the details of the world in our brains, so we use models to simplify the complex into understandable and organisable pieces. They give us a framework for dealing with the variety of events, situations, and challenges that we face on a daily basis and, all too often, the model we choose is impacted by biases of which we are unaware.

An illustration of this is found in a study that explored the phenomenon of perceiving illusory faces in inanimate objects. Wardle et al discovered that illusory faces in inanimate objects are readily perceived to have a specific emotional expression, age, and gender. They observed a strong cognitive bias to perceive illusory faces as male rather than female. This male bias could not be explained by pre-existing semantic or visual gender associations with the objects, or by visual features in the images. The illusory images were non gender specific and age neutral – they were simply graphics of the sort that may be used, for example, by a machinery manufacturer to illustrate parts of some equipment. Despite this, people were able to attribute human age and gender. The researchers argue, "this robust bias in the perception of gender for illusory faces reveals a cognitive bias arising from a broadly tuned face evaluation system in which minimally viable face percepts are more likely to be perceived as male."[2] We see what our unconscious bias guides us to see. Our mental model controls, or at least heavily impacts, our perceptions.

It is this issue of bias's impact that needs to be addressed. As I do so, it is certain that many of my own biases will be revealed – even if I have no intention of making such revelations nor even know that I have that bias. I will try to be neutral. Using recent research, this book explores both the ubiquity and complexity of bias as well as issues impacting our attempts to limit the negative manifestations of such biases.

As every intelligence services analyst knows, the task of an analyst is to find similarities across disparate units of data in order to ascertain patterns and connections. They seek to "connect the dots" across a wide variety of seemingly unconnected pieces of data. This is then followed by providing a report that can inform those who are responsible for making decisions. The analyst is always well aware that their job is to provide a report that others can use. Although the analyst makes decisions as to what data are relevant, they are not the ones to make the decision on how to use the report. Often times the analysts "get it right". Sometimes they get it wrong. Sometimes "getting it wrong" is because of pressure applied to find data that supports a preconceived idea (such as in the case of the weapons of mass destruction that were claimed to be possessed by Iraq and which lead to the 2003 invasion of Iraq by the USA and "the coalition of the willing"). Most times, however, when the analysts "get it wrong" it is because there is inadequate data available although, usually, in such cases, the analyst is honest as to their doubts. Although the analyst will make decisions as to the data to be used and how it is used, for use of the final report, the analyst is an "advisor" rather than a "decider". This approach of considering widely diverse data on bias and "joining the dots", is the one taken in this book. The book provides a report. The reader determines what and how and if the information provided is used.

This book draws together an extensive, 20 plus year body of research into bias and presents both the findings and their potential implications in a way that is designed to facilitate personal responsibility for managing one's biases. As stated, rather than being a work based on new research, this is a work that seeks to "join the dots" between a variety of studies from across the globe to provide a cohesive discussion on the universal reality of biases, how they are formed and reinforced, and of their impact. It is for the reader to decide *what* and *how* this is used. However, it is anticipated that this book will best be used as a platform from which to launch discussions that can facilitate awareness and behavioural change in relation to the prejudices, stigma, biases, and discrimination that impact individuals' lives, organisational performance, and societies at large, across the world today. In many cases the original author's words are used to ensure accuracy in their message.

The book is divided into three sections. Chapters 1–3 explain that the decision-making process provides context and then explore the concept of bias itself and how it is developed and reinforced. Chapters 4–14 explore the impact of bias across a variety of areas, and Chapters 15–16 explore how bias can be managed so as to minimise its undesirable impacts.

Notes

1 https://iview.abc.net.au/video/SC2002H010S00
2 https://www.pnas.org/content/119/5/e2117413119

1

DECISION MAKING

The Context for Bias Impact

It had been a long day in a city in mid-west USA. I had been back in the USA for just three days and, today, I had been in several meetings but was now on my way back to where I was staying. Seeing a small shopping centre, I pulled into the parking lot and then went to buy some food. Returning to the car, I pulled out to the road and turned immediately left to continue home. Within seconds I realised I had made a mistake. Ahead of me was a set of traffic lights with all the stopped cars being on the same side as me – but facing me! An urgent "U-turn" quickly remedied the situation without anyone or anything being damaged, but the situation could have been very bad. I could have provoked a "head-on" collision in which people and vehicles were seriously damaged. My tiredness had activated a decision-making heuristic in which one always drove on the "left" side of a road – the status quo in Australia and many other countries. In the USA, as I well knew, one drives on the "right" side of the road. Instead of consciously reminding myself of the different road standards, my tiredness had triggered an unconscious bias developed over many years living in Australia and other "keep to the left when driving" countries.

My experience was reasonably benign. However other instances where bias impacts can be tragic. In February 2024 Australian media reported that "A doctor who incorrectly diagnosed an Aboriginal man with a condition related to illicit drug use has said it was 'just pattern recognition,' an inquest has heard".[1] At an inquest, the doctor stated his first impression led him to assume the man was suffering from cannabinoid hyperemesis syndrome (CHS). "There is a lot of marijuana use in the community," the doctor said. "It's just pattern recognition." ... "You make a decision, you make an impression, and you just hang to it," he said. "That's what the basis of cognitive bias [is]." The doctor made clear his bias was due to the 36-year-old's clinical symptoms, not his ethnicity.

DOI: 10.4324/9781003528340-2

No matter who we may be, our status in life, or where in the world we live, all of us make myriad decisions on a daily basis. For most of us, the majority of these decisions are relatively minor but for all of us our decisions, whether minor or major, can have impact on both us and others. For this reason, over the years much academic attention has been given to how people make decisions although, for the majority of people, the process of decision making and decision-making models seem to have little relevance in their everyday activities. Even in the making of major decisions by people who are well versed in decision-making theory and models, anecdotal evidence indicates that these tend to be used mainly "post facto" (after the decision has been made and implemented) in order to ascertain possible reasons why "the wrong decision" was made. Seldom, it seems, do we conduct a similar post facto analysis when the results we desire eventuate – "the right decision" was made! It's a little similar to the golfer who, after playing a poor shot, practices what should have been done yet scarcely ever practices what was done "right" after playing a good shot!

It is generally agreed that the decision-making process comprises a series of discrete steps. These can be summarised as: define the problem, identify limiting factors, develop potential alternatives, analyse the alternatives, select the best alternative, and implement the decision. Clearly this is a time-consuming process – especially if any or all of these steps have sub-steps. Accordingly, we all develop short-cuts that facilitate decisions being made in a timely manner. These short-cuts tend to be where our emotions and world views have significant influence. They are "heuristics" that we all employ in decision-making – far too often without considering whether they are actually the right ones.

While this book does not seek to be a work on judgement and decision making (JDM) per se, immediately one starts discussing the impact of biases across broad areas of human activity there is automatically an association with JDM theory and practice and hence a need to discuss some of the underpinnings for current approaches to the topic.

Etzioni in the 1980's[2] explored the issue of our limited capacity to handle complexity in decision making. The researcher said:

> ... Psychologists argue compellingly that even before our present troubles began, human minds could not handle the complexities that important decisions entailed. Our brains are too limited. At best, we can focus on eight facts at a time. Our ability to calculate probabilities, especially to combine two or more probabilities – essential for most decision making – is low. And the evidence shows that we learn surprisingly slowly. We make the same mistakes over and over again, adjusting our estimates and expectations at an agonizing crawl, and quite poorly at that.
>
> Moreover, we are all prone to let our emotions get in the way – fear, for one. Since all decisions entail risks, decision making almost inevitably evokes anxiety. ... Political factors are another complicating consideration, partly because we try to deny their importance. ... even before the world

turned ultracomplex and superfungible, our intellectual limitations were such that wholly rational decisions were often beyond our grasp.

The situation has not changed since 1989. If anything, decision making is more complex today than ever before because of the internet, mobile telephony and the impact of social media with their immediacy of criticism (and praise) from multiple sources – some of which may even be relevant. No matter who we are or the context within which we live, we all need appropriate short cuts (heuristics) that can facilitate timely decision making. Cognitive psychology defines heuristics as "useful shortcut, an approximation, or a rule of thumb for searching through a space of possible solutions".

The interplay of emotion and cognition dominates all decision making[3]. Norbert argued that

> affective states influence which strategy of information processing individuals are likely to adopt. As a large body of experimental research documents, individuals who are in a happy mood are more likely to adopt a heuristic processing strategy that is characterised by top-down processing, with high reliance on pre-existing knowledge structures and relatively little attention to the details at hand. In contrast, individuals who are in a sad mood are more likely to adopt a systematic processing strategy that is characterised by bottom-up processing, with little reliance on pre-existing knowledge structures and considerable attention to the details at hand. ... In a nutshell, we usually feel bad when things go wrong and feel good when we face no particular problems. Hence, negative affective states may signal that the current situation is problematic and may hence elicit a processing style that pays close attention to the specifics of the apparently problematic situation. In contrast, a positive affective state may signal a benign environment that allows us to rely on our usual routines and pre-existing knowledge structures.
>
> This means that the relationship between emotions and decision making is bidirectional, and the positive or negative outcome of a decision can profoundly affect the decider's feelings. This is important because whatever the heuristics we choose at any time can be impacted by previous decisions. We need to ensure that such influence is understood and assessed rather than simply accepted as being appropriate.

In making decisions we are often confronted with uncertainty as to whether one's choices will lead to benefit or harm[4]. It is pointed out that a decision can be regarded as an outcome of the mental processes leading to the selection of a course of action among several alternatives. Such selection is impacted by affect. This raises the issue of regret theory in which the central idea is that, when making decisions individuals take into account not only the consequences that might be obtained as a result of the action chosen but also how each consequence compares with what they would have experienced under the same state of the world, had they chosen differently. Therefore, the consequence and expected utility of alternative outcome that could have obtained are dependent on one another. However, people maximise utility in a sense that they aspire to avoid regret or disappointment. A decision maker under such influences might opt for what appears to be a suboptimal choice to avoid future regrettable situations.

There are two types of affective influences: those of relevant emotions and those of irrelevant emotions. Relevant emotions are the ones which originate from the decision-making task at hand. It has its source in the consequences of the decision itself and is felt during the time of making decision (also called pre-dicted emotions) or when the consequences are experienced (i.e., after the out-come is given). These emotions might be reflected through changes in the nature or depth of processing or visceral influences on behaviour. Examples of these emotions include regret, disappointment, etc. Irrelevant emotions are the ones which come from any source other than the decision-making task at hand. These are called incidental emotions. The sources for these emotions are usually present in the environmental stimuli (e.g., good smell, beautiful sights and scenes, good music, etc.), or it may also include a person's mood or temperamental disposi-tion. It is argued: "In addition to mood, incidental emotional information from stimuli present in the environment can and does influence decision making." Most people in marketing and sales functions are very aware of this!

This matter of emotions impacting decision making is important[5]. The field of judgment and decision making (JDM) long neglected the influence of "hot processes" on decision behaviour in favour of a focus on "cold," deliberative, and reason-based decision making. Historically, this was due at least in part to hot processes being viewed primarily as biased, leading to irrational choice behaviour. However, over recent years the attention has increasingly considered how affective feelings influence judgments and decisions.

It is now widely recognised that integral affect (experienced feelings about a stimulus) and incidental affect (feelings such as mood states that are indepen-dent of a stimulus but can be misattributed to it or can influence decision pro-cesses) can be used to predict and explain a wide variety of judgments and decisions. First, affect can act as information: at the moment of judgment or choice, decision makers consult their feelings about a choice and ask, "How do I feel about this?" Second, affect appears to serve as a common currency in judgments and decisions, allowing us to compare the values of very different decision options or information (e.g., compare apples to oranges). By translat-ing more complex thoughts into simpler affective evaluations, decision makers can compare and integrate good and bad feelings rather than attempt to make sense out of a multitude of conflicting logical reasons. This function is thus an extension of the affect-as-information function into more complex decisions that require integration of information. It implies that affective information can be more easily and effectively integrated into judgments than less affective information.

Returning to the matter of heuristics or "mental shortcuts" in decision making, simple heuristics can be efficient ways of decision making and literature has shown that they are widely used in actual decision situations. This creates a choice problem, in which different heuristics are likely to lead to different choices. "A person makes a decision (and possibly uses a heuristic for decision making) in a certain situation. The use of a heuristic could thus be triggered both by situational factors such as task and context, and by personal factors."[6]

One of these situational factors is time because the shorter the available time in which a decision is needed, the less consideration will be given to the heuristic used – we will revert to what is comfortable. The researchers employed this factor to create a situation in which decision makers were more likely to rely on familiar heuristics, and then studied the type of heuristics subjects with different decision-making styles employed. They focused their research on retail purchase decisions and concluded "… that time pressure leads to a considerable decline in choosing the cognitively complex product". In other words, time pressure was more likely to trigger decisions that were based on "avoiding cognitive complexity. … a [greater time demanding] rational decision style could be much stronger for more important purchase decisions."

Although the above-mentioned works provide no discussion of bias per se, it would appear reasonable to extrapolate that factors such as mood, incidental emotional information from stimuli present in the environment, and time pressure in decision making impacts the selection of heuristic (ie. the shorter the available time frame, the greater the probability of an inappropriate heuristic being selected). Accordingly, these strongly influence the decision-making process and the outcome achieved.

The concept of cognitive bias in decision-making was first introduced by researchers Amos Tversky and Daniel Kahneman in 1974[7]. Today the role of cognitive bias in decision-making is primarily considered to be relevant in the context of JDM under conditions of uncertainty – ie in situations where solutions are more in the realm of probability rather than in mathematical certainty. Current thinking about JDM largely follows from the "heuristics and biases" framework proposed by Kahneman and Tversky – a model which is now widely regarded as the most defensible, descriptive model of human decision-making under uncertainty.

In decision-making, the three critical aspects are "what" decision is to be made, "who" makes the decisions and "how" the decisions are made. Kahneman and Tversky focused on "how" decisions are made and argued that the three key processes were: "(i) representativeness, which is usually employed when people are asked to judge the probability that an object or event A belongs to class or process B; (ii) availability of instances or scenarios, which is often employed when people are asked to assess the frequency of a class or the plausibility of a particular development; and (iii) adjustment from an anchor, which is usually employed in numerical prediction when a relevant value is available." They saw these as being "… usually effective, but they lead to systematic and predictable errors. A better understanding of these heuristics and of the biases to which they lead could improve judgments and decisions in situations of uncertainty."

A 2003, study[8] discusses the contribution of Kahneman and Tversky to the field of behavioural economics. It argues that "Kahneman and Tversky's work provides fundamental insights into the psychology associated with [the concepts of risk and return]. Their work is comprised of two strands, prospect theory and heuristics and biases. Prospect theory describes how people make decisions when facing risky (or risk-free) alternatives, while heuristics and biases describe, among other things, how people assess risk." More recently[9] it has been has argued that Kahneman and Tversky made a distinction between the normative theory, which describes the judgements that should be made, and what people actually do. People are systematically biased in these cases. Later research (published in 2017)[10] makes the point that "Tversky and Kahneman discovered that humans make predictable errors of judgement when forced to deal with ambiguous evidence or make challenging decisions. These errors stem from 'heuristics' and 'biases' – mental shortcuts and assumptions that allow us to make swift, automatic decisions, often usefully and correctly, but occasionally to our detriment."

The literature is in general agreement that the decisions we make are for resolving problems we encounter. These problems largely fall into one of four categories: simple, complex, complicated, and chaotic (or "wicked").

Decisions around simple problems are straightforward. We can identify the key stakeholders and how they are impacted by a decision. We can identity the economic and legal issues that we must consider when making the decision. And we can see that the normative aspects of the decision are aligned with our instrumental considerations. We are confident in our decision because the knowledge we applied to the decision converge around a single answer – despite multiple issues considered across multiple stakeholder groups.

This is not the case for decisions that address the remaining three categories. With complex, complicated, and chaotic problems we need to resolve matters having, for example, complexity in the environment and/or complexity involving incomplete information. In these there is a need to resolve contradictions arising from the paradoxical nature of managing competing demands from various sources. In some of these cases, decisions can often impact each party differently, and a key element of decision-making is recognising when these contradictions arise. When we uncover contradictions, we are acknowledging the complexity of the decision, and forcing ourselves to come up with creative solutions. In other cases, normative and instrumental considerations of the same decision may be contradictory. For example, a decision that can be deciphered as responsible may also be deciphered as illegal or economically unviable. In yet others, many decisions are more complex because we cannot coalesce around a single answer. Instead, we may find that addressing one aspect of the decision contradicts addressing another aspect of the decision.

This may feel like we are holding a rope with others pulling us in opposing directions. Dilemmas present choices with no clear answer and it is difficult to be comfortable with the paradoxical nature of the decision – we are expected to pull ourselves into two different opposing directions while finding common ground between the two.

We are typically not given a set of formulas to calculate. We are not given a set of answers to choose from. We are not even given all the information needed to answer the questions. We must process information from what is available, construct the decision we must make, and use the limited information available to make a decision. We may not be able to know what changes lie ahead and so, when we make decisions, we must recognise that there is uncertainty in the outcomes of our decisions. In some cases, we can model the uncertainty. In other cases, we must include contingencies into our decisions.

The more complicated the problems we encounter, the more difficult our decision making becomes. For this reason, as already indicated, we develop our own set of short cuts or heuristics in order to manage the complexity and enable us to move forward. And, again as already indicated, the heuristic we choose will be heavily influenced by our world view – our biases.

A 2012 doctoral dissertation adds another layer to this[11]. Stephenson explored issues contributing to poor strategic decisions by top management teams (TMT) and, citing earlier research, makes the point that "a group under stress will exhibit a greater desire for consistent opinions and preferences among members to provide uniformity, which satisfies a need for closure on issues. ... a stressful situation will tend to amplify the influence that more powerful members have and may lead to a yielding-behaviour by others to accept majority views on issues. ... Stressful conditions lead to a 'closing of the group mind', resulting in dismissing unpopular options and acceptance of autocratic leadership by other team members. ... This means that not all alternative options that are viable may be considered during decision making in stressful situations." He continues:

> Stress is not the only reason why alternative decision options may not be considered especially when the TMT already shares ideas on potential solutions to a problem. Research has shown that shared ideas are given much greater weight in discussions when compared to dissenting ideas. The difference in weight is thought to be approximately an exponential reduction in appeal for dissenting ideas when compared to the weighting for popular ideas. ... This means that TMT members will give more weight to ideas similar to their own and less weight to those that differ from their own. The net result is that different ideas are often ignored to varying degrees depending on their distance from the median and the rest of the team clusters around popularly shared ideas. ... The implication for decision making is that there will be a tendency to restrict consideration of strategic alternatives to only those ideas that are most shared.

As will be discussed later, the "in-group" impact on bias is significant.

There is a natural tendency to rely on the heuristics with which we are most familiar and comfortable – those we do not have to struggle to use – but, for optimal decisions, it is crucial to realise that the more complex the problem or issue encountered, the more important it is to check we are using the best possible heuristic. Very often this will necessitate a total rethink of our underlying world view and so be very challenging. Such an approach is particularly important when addressing "chaotic" (or what are also known as "wicked") problems. A "wicked problem" is a one that is difficult or impossible to solve because of incomplete, contradictory, and changing requirements that are often difficult to recognise.

We need now to explore how our biases develop and are reinforced as well as how biased decisions we make impact on every aspect of life in every community across the globe. This will lead us to consider how we can manage our biases in order to minimise undesirable (and usually unintended) consequences.

As we grapple with this consideration on managing our biases, it is important to remember that a heuristic is not a cognitive bias. A *heuristic* is a rule, strategy or similar mental shortcut that one can use to derive a solution to a problem. It is important also to note, however, that while the use of heuristics can reinforce existing biases, not all biases are reinforced by the heuristics used. It is the choice of heuristic that determines the action: our biases are what impact our choice of heuristic. And it is our underlying value systems that, through our world view (our bias), ultimately drive our choice of heuristic.

Questions for group discussion:

1. "The interplay of emotion and cognition, dominates all decision making." What is your response to this statement? Why?
2. In decision-making, "There are two types of affective influences: those of relevant emotions and those of irrelevant emotions." In your own experience, which of these tends to be dominant? Why? How can you distinguish between "relevant emotions and irrelevant emotions"?
3. "The literature is in general agreement that the decisions we make are for resolving problems we encounter. These problems largely fall into one of four categories: simple, complex, complicated, and chaotic." Discuss the differences between these. Why do we have a preference for seeking to reduce all problems to "simple" without realising that this risks attempting a simplistic solution that will resolve only symptoms?
4. "A group under stress will exhibit a greater desire for consistent opinions and preferences among members to provide uniformity, which satisfies a need for closure on issues." What is the connection between this and the "groupthink" scenario? How can we avoid falling into this trap?
5. "Research has shown that shared ideas are given much greater weight in discussions when compared to dissenting ideas. The difference in weight is

thought to be approximately an exponential reduction in appeal for dissenting ideas when compared to the weighting for popular ideas. ... This means that TMT members will give more weight to ideas similar to their own and less weight to those that differ from their own. The net result is that different ideas are often ignored to varying degrees depending on their distance from the median and the rest of the team clusters around popularly shared ideas." To what extent do you allow group pressure rather than independent assessment to influence you decisions? How can you manage the values conflicts that this can engender?

Notes

1 https://www.theguardian.com/australia-news/2024/feb/27/ricky-hampson-jr-aborigina l-man-death-doctor-diagnosed-drug-illness-cognitive-bias-cannaboid-hyperemesis-ma rijuana-use
2 Etzioni, Amitai, (2001). "Humble Decision Making." Harvard Business Review on Decision Making, (Harvard Business School Press: Boston, MA, 2001), 45–57., Available at SSRN: https://ssrn.com/abstract=2157020 (Originally published in July-August 1989. Reprint 89406)
3 Schwarz, Norbert, 2000, *Emotion, cognition, and decision making,* Cognition and Emotion *Volume 14, 2000 – Issue 4,*https://doi.org/10.1080/026999300402745
4 Debarati Bandyopadhyay, V.S. Chandrasekhar Pammi1, Narayanan Srinivasan, 2013, *"Role of affect in decision making",* Progress in Brain Research, 2013, Vol.202, p.37–53
5 Peters, Ellen, Vastfjall, Daniel, Garling, Tommy, & Slovic, Paul, 2006, "Affect and decision making: a 'hot' topic" Journal of Behavioural Decision Making, https://doi.org/10.1002/bdm.528
6 Cristina del Campo, Sandra Pauser, Elisabeth Steiner, and Rudolf Vetschera, 2016, "Decision making styles and the use of heuristics in decision making", J Bus Econ (2016) 86:389–412 DOI 10.1007/s11573–016–0811-y
7 Amos Tversky and Daniel Kahneman, 1974, "Judgment under Uncertainty: Heuristics and Biases", Science 185, no. 415 (1974): 1124–1131. DOI: 10.1126/science.185.4157.1124
8 Hersh Shefrin & Meir Statman (2003) The Contributions of Daniel Kahneman and Amos Tversky, Journal of Behavioral Finance, 4:2, 54–58, DOI: 10.1207/S15427579JPFM0402_01
9 Baron, Jonathan, 2014, "Heuristics and Biases", Ch.1 in The Oxford Handbook of Behavioral Economics and the Law, Eyal Zamir and Doron Teichman, eds
10 Morvan, Camille & Jenkins, William J, 2017, "An Analysis of Amos Tversky and Daniel Kahneman's Judgment under Uncertainty Heuristics and Biases", DOI https://doi.org/10.4324/9781912282562
11 Stephenson, Christopher B, 2012, "*What Causes Top Management Teams to Make Poor Strategic Decisions?*", A thesis submitted in fulfilment of the requirements for the degree of Doctor of Business Administration (DBA), Southern Cross University, Australia

2

UNDERSTANDING BIAS

The Oxford Dictionary defines bias as "predisposition, prejudice, influence" and uses the example of lawn bowls as an illustration of how the weights within a bowl will cause it to veer in a particular direction rather than to roll in a straight line. Bias per se is neutral as, depending on how you actually use the bowl, it will run to left or to right depending on what you intend. The same is true in how we use bias impacts us in everyday life. Bias in social interactions is veering away from treating all people with the same degree of equity. We are biased either in favour of (a positive bias) or against (a negative bias). Ultimately any bias in human interactions risks moving us away from treating every individual with the unconditional respect that ought to be the inherent right for everyone to receive. "Unconditional respect" requires that we distinguish the person from the behaviour. We may be vehemently opposed to what a person is doing or has done but, in addressing the behaviour, we need to so in a manner that is respectful of the person. This matter of "unconditional respect" is explored further later in this book.

"Bias" is the catch-all phrase that summarises impacts on our social interactions – it is a situation in which individuals create and respond to their own "subjective reality" from their perception of the input. This subjective reality then has the potential to dictate my behaviour as it impacts on the situation or on another person(s). If my subjective reality sees others as being "superior" to me then I will readily defer to them: if my subjective reality sees others as being "inferior" to me then I will expect deference from them. The door is open to stereotyping, prejudice and discrimination. Unless I am aware of my biases and am prepared to take control of them, they are highly likely to insidiously control me because they are an integral part of what I consider to be "normal".

The reality and implications of bias have been the subject of research for many years. There is no doubt as to the reality of discriminatory behaviour in

DOI: 10.4324/9781003528340-3

every society and across every hierarchical, educational, and societal level. Because of this, it is important to examine questions relating to the causes and management of the biases that underpin all discrimination, prejudice, and stereotyping. It is not surprising, then, that in just the first 23 years of the 21st century, across the globe, institutions and disciplines, there have been around 200 general academic studies relating to bias. It is these studies that comprise the research base for this book.

Dovidio et al[1] explored the history of psychological research into understanding prejudice, stereotyping and discrimination. It shows how today's analysis of bias, and its associated phenomena, has become far more nuanced over the past 50 or so years. This more nuanced understanding has impacted the fields of law, medicine, business, and education. Where earlier studies tended to focus on individual differences, it is now recognised that group processes (i.e. the impact on us of others in the same group – our "in-group" of the moment) are also involved and that both group processes and social identities foster and maintain prejudice and stereotyping. This is because group process refers to how any group of people work together to get things done. In formal organisations it is common for a great deal of time and energy to be spent setting and striving to meet goals, but, in the main, very little time is spent considering what is happening between and to the organisation's people. Current studies make clear that this interactions process is just as important as the result because, to a very great extent, it is the quality of the process that determines the result. (As an aside, this lack of seriously considering what is happening between and to the organisation's people is a major reason why "teams" so often fail to produce the synergy of which they are capable.)

It is now understood that any work on bias needs to not only consider how specific emotions, unconscious processes and fundamental neural processes contribute to biases, but also the socio-cultural aspects. We need to consider how social structure impacts biases across social institutions including those of the legal and health-care systems. It was certainly pertinent with the entry of Donald Trump into the political arena when this sociocultural-individual interaction was seized upon by the media. It can also be seen in the increasing incidence of political and social polarisation across traditional liberal western democracies.

Although, at least since the US Civil Rights movement of the 1950's and 60's it has been largely recognised that this link between individual behaviour and one's socio-cultural environment exists, over the years the link has been largely downplayed and ignored by dominant sectors of the community. Many, including the filmmaker activist Michael Moore with his 2001 book "*Stupid White Men*", had attempted to maintain focus, but it was not until the 21st century rise of the Black Lives Matter (BLM) movement that the link was again forced into the forefront of global consciousness.

For many years there has been disquiet about the disparity between treatment of blacks and whites in police stops, arrests, incarceration and police shootings in the USA. The records show that seldom are police officers held to public account by the media or face an investigation by an independent authority rather than one by their own or an external police force. The record shows that it is extremely rare for a police officer to be prosecuted for a fatal shooting (and not only in the United States!). This also flows over to the disparity in treatment of whites who are involved in violence against blacks[2].

In February 2012 an African American teen in Sanford, Florida, USA, Trayvon Martin was shot and killed by George Zimmerman. Zimmerman was the neighbourhood watch coordinator in his gated community and Martin was, totally legitimately, temporarily staying there at the time. Martin was later found to be unarmed but Zimmerman claimed that the shooting was an act of self-defence and that he was acting within the constraints of Florida's "stand-your-ground" legislation. Although initially arrested, the local police argued that Zimmerman had a right to defend himself with lethal force and he was released without charges being laid. Six weeks later, after considerable community pressure, a special prosecutor appointed by the Governor of Florida, charged Zimmerman with murder. The trial was held in June 2013 and resulted in an acquittal on all murder and manslaughter charges. The Black Lives Matter (BLM) movement then came into being. However, it was not until the 2014 deaths of two more African American men – one in Missouri and one in New York – that the movement attracted widespread national and international media attention in highlighting racism, discrimination, and inequality experienced by black people. BLM has made clear the link between individual actions and the environments within which we live – and the bias by which we are all impacted.

As already indicated, for most people, bias is a human construct of disproportionate weight *in favour of* or *against* an idea or thing, usually in a way that is closed-minded, prejudicial, or unfair. A bias can be consciously or unconsciously learned. What we see and experience from birth provides unconscious conditioning that becomes ingrained and further developed through our society – it is our social conditioning. People may develop biases for or against an individual, a group, or a belief. It is this concept of bias that most of us have in mind when we describe a person as being "biased". In this understanding, all "bias" is seen through a value lens. Depending on how this lens resonates with our own mental framework we will regard a person's words and/or actions as being somewhere on the good-bad spectrum or we may even claim that those claiming bias are mistaken because, clearly (in our view) the person is unbiased.

Bias, like prejudice, is an attitude. Biases tend to be the attitudes held by others but which we do not share. They are, therefore, often labelled "good" or "bad", "positive" or "negative". They have an important impact on all of us and on our interpersonal relations. Almost everyone claims to be in favour of removing bias and reducing prejudice, but not everyone is willing to admit that any specific attitude held by them *is* possibly bias or prejudice. Invariably a questioner will be met with material to "prove" that bias or prejudice is not present and that the individual's attitudes are supported by "fact". Those arguing that bias is not present frequently use examples that are individually specific in an attempt to counter any claims of widespread reality.

Regardless of the level of intelligence or education, most individuals hold attitudes on most topics. High intelligence and extensive education do not necessarily release people from bias, nor do they automatically cause people to launch a full and objective enquiry before forming opinions. The same biases are shared to the same intense degrees across varying intelligence levels and social strata – something that was highlighted in the events following President Trump's loss in the 2020 US Presidential elections: the events in Washington of January 6, 2021 were attended by, and actively involved, people from all backgrounds, educational status, societal status, etc. Attitudes are not necessarily a function of degree or amount of knowledge about the object of the attitude. Justifications of the attitudes we hold tend to be a function of the rationalisations we use to justify the knowledge we have, or lack of it, on almost any topic.

All our attitudes impact on our behaviours. They provide us with frames of reference within which all input is assessed and processed. They are a general background of feeling against which factual events can be viewed. They provide us with sets of heuristics that enable us to function in our day to day lives. For this reason, they supply us with the unique loading of feeling and emotion to our perceptions of things and events. They can rapidly morph to become the base for our opinions – our evaluations (not descriptions) of the factual evidence. And this is regardless of age, experience and/or education – our world view impacts our thinking and our behaviour.

The science blogger, Jonah Lehrer says[3],

> … The expansion of the frontal cortex during human evolution did not turn us into purely rational creatures, able to ignore our impulses. In fact, neuroscience now knows that the opposite is true: a significant part of our frontal cortex is involved with emotion. David Hume, the eighteenth-century Scottish philosopher who delighted in heretical ideas, was right when he declared that reason was "the slave of the passions".
>
> *(p.24)*

It is generally accepted that bias exists in two main forms – conscious bias and unconscious bias. Conscious bias is those biased attitudes about an individual, group or society about which we are aware, while unconscious bias operates outside our awareness and control. Unconscious bias is difficult to access or be aware of, yet such biases influence us to a greater extent than do conscious biases. Such lack of awareness can blind us to inappropriate behaviour even though others recognise that it is inappropriate. A tool developed in 1955 by psychologists Joseph Luft and Harrington Ingham (the Johari Window)[4] is today a widely used heuristic exercise for helping people reduce this blind spot. The Johari Window model posits that others learn about us from what we consciously and unconsciously disclose through our behaviour (our words and our actions). Accordingly, others develop their perceptions of us and, because "perception is reality", at times, this can mean they react differently from what we expect when responding to what we say or do. By actively seeking both deliberate (i.e. what we have specifically requested) and accidental (i.e. what we see in how others act towards us) feedback from others, we are able to learn more about ourselves and that feedback is capable of helping us identify our unconscious biases as well as helping us challenge our conscious biases.

However, despite tools such as this, bias remains rampant across society. Even casual observation provides evidence that specific bias is highly dependent on variables like a person's socioeconomic status, race, ethnicity, educational background, and similar. In later chapters the reasons for this will be explored.

Questions for group discussion:

1. "Bias in human interactions risks moving us away from treating every individual with the unconditional respect that ought to be the inherent right for everyone to receive." What is your reaction to this statement? Why? What does it mean to you regarding dealing with inappropriate behaviour?

2. "Subjective reality has the potential to dictate my behaviour as it impacts on the situation or on another person(s)." What is your understanding of "subjective reality" and what realistic and readily available actions can be taken to test it?

3. "Where earlier studies tended to focus on individual differences, it is now recognised that group processes (i.e. the impact on us of others in the same group) are also involved and that both group processes and social identities foster and maintain prejudice and stereotyping." When the group's subjective reality and my subjective reality disagree, how can this be managed?

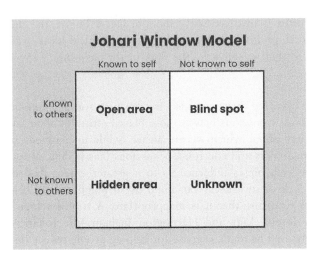

FIGURE 2.1 Luft & Ingham's Johari Window

4.   "Unconscious bias is difficult to access or be aware of, yet such biases influence us to a greater extent than do conscious biases." What is your reaction to this statement? Are unconscious biases really a danger? How can we manage them?
5.   Of the biases listed above, which ones do you recognise as impact on your behaviour? What behaviours of yours lead you to recognising you have these biases? If you consider these behaviours may need to be addressed, what differences in behaviour would you like to show? What actions can you take to develop these different behaviours?

Notes

1 Dovidio, John F., Hewstone, Miles, Glick, Peter, and Esses, Victoria M., *Prejudice, Stereotyping and Discrimination: Theoretical and Empirical Overview*, 2010, Sage Publications
2 According to https://www.statista.com/statistics/585152/people-shot-to-death-by-us-police-by-race/ over the years 2017–2022, (as at May 2022) the total number of shootings was 5421. Of these, 1064 were Black people, 723 were Hispanic, and in 1538 shootings no ethnicity of the victim was available.
3 Lehrer, Jonah, *The Decisive Moment: How the Brain Makes Up its Mind*, 2009, Cannongate Books Ltd., Edinburgh.
4 Luft, J. and Ingham, H. (1955). *The Johari Window: A Graphic Model of Interpersonal Awareness*. Proceedings of the western training laboratory in group development (Los Angeles: University of California, Los Angeles).

3
THE SOURCE OF BIAS

As already indicated, from birth we develop an understanding of who we are and of our place in the world – our mental framework. The nurturing we receive is a key part of this. From the stage where we are totally dependent on someone else for every aspect of our survival and well-being through to the point of independence from our parents, family and normative social environment we are absorbing information as to *who* we are, *how* we fit into our social structure, *what* we can do, and *when* we can do it. By our late teens or early twenties this is part and parcel of our very beings: it is a core part of our fabric of being "me". From this stage forward our conscious and unconscious motivations will tend to centre around fulfilling whatever potential our mental mindset has determined for us. The biases that we demonstrate in our adult years have their genesis largely in the biases that were evolving through these formative years and, for most of us, we are ignorant both of what many of these are and how they have come about. There is a sense in which they have become innate – in other words, they have become so much part of us that we accept them as being integral to our identity and self-concept – which is why recognising and managing our biases is so difficult for all of us.

The link between bias and social problems means that it is difficult to consider bias as an abstract concept. A comprehensive understanding requires that the consequences of sociological bias are considered along with bias per se. In other words, all biases both are impacted by sociological factors as well as themselves impacting on our society. We recognise bias from what is said and done – behavioural indicators – and all behaviour has consequences. Recent research supports this need for a comprehensive understanding.

The impacts of bias are important[1]. Paradies et al argues that prejudice, stigma, bias, and discrimination are all expressions of oppression – a concept that describes a relationship between groups or categories of people in which a

DOI: 10.4324/9781003528340-4

dominant group benefits from the systematic abuse, exploitation, and injustice directed toward a subordinate group. (Such group may be considered subordinate because of factors that include politically, economically, culturally, socially, racially, by gender, sexuality, intellectual, or any combination of the above.) They suggest that a myriad of typologies exist concerning definitions and manifestations of prejudice, stigma, bias, and discrimination and argue that oppression can be conceptualised across three distinct, but interrelated, levels:

- internalized (or intrapersonal) prejudiced attitudes or beliefs, frequently based on notions of supposedly innate superiority/inferiority, which may be subscribed to either by members of dominant social groups or by subordinate ones;
- interpersonal discriminatory interactions between people, with varying degrees of frequency and intensity, including manifestations from racially motivated assault to verbal abuse, ostracism, and exclusion; and
- systemic or structural, which includes bias in societal institutions, laws, policies, and social practices. Of note, this level may be thought of as the one that sets the context and increases or decreases the likelihood of the first two types of oppression outlined here.

It then explores the concept of discrimination as the behavioural manifestations of prejudice, stigma, and bias. Doing this enables the consideration of discrimination as a real-world manifestation of oppression with potential adverse consequences. They also argue that the concept of bias is commonly utilised within some contexts as a way of describing unconscious forms of discrimination and this is often labelled implicit bias.

Just as the understanding of bias has evolved over the years, so too has our recognition of manifestations of bias developed. Haselton et al.[2] explore this issue of the evolution of bias. They suggest bias is the situation in which human cognition reliably produces representations that are systematically distorted compared to some aspect of objective reality and they explore why biases often seem to be implemented at the cognitive level, producing genuine misperceptions, rather than merely biases in enacted behaviour. They argue "perhaps the most commonly invoked explanation for bias is as a necessary by-product of processing limitations – because information processing time and ability are limited, humans must use shortcuts or rules of thumb that are prone to breakdown in systematic ways." This is required because "the extra effort required to use a more sophisticated strategy is a cost that often outweighs the potential benefit of enhanced accuracy". This avoidance of "cost" can affect the evolution of cognitive mechanisms at two levels. There may be costs in evolutionary terms, since the development of certain brain circuits will either increase the length of ontogeny or move potential energetic allocation away from the development of other mechanisms. There may also be costs in real time, since decisions using complex algorithms will often take longer or require more attentional resources than decisions using simpler alternatives (something that was discussed earlier). Adaptive decisions often need to be made fast, and this may well constrain the type of strategies that are optimal. This will be explored further later when the matter of artificial intelligence is discussed.

There is ample evidence of bias and error in humans. Some of these biases may result from the use of shortcuts (or "heuristics"), which are often effective. For these effects, however, it is important to note that a "processing limitations" explanation is not complete. Humans appear to possess a bias toward inferring that members of competing coalitions (or outgroups) are less generous and kind and more dangerous and ill-tempered than are members of their own group. (Haselton et al.) The fact of bias and how it develops is clear, what we also need to understand is *why* we find them necessary.

Many biases arise from intrinsic brain mechanisms that are fundamental for the working of biological neural networks[3]. Korteling et al argue that:

> We constantly make judgments and decisions (either conscious or unconscious) without knowing their outcome. We typically violate rules of logic and probability and resort to simple and near-optimal heuristic decision rules ('mental shortcuts') to optimize the likelihood of an acceptable outcome. This may be effective in conditions with time-constraints, lack or overload of relevant information, or when no optimal solution is evident.

This is illustrated by suggesting

> the well-known confirmation bias may be motivated by argumentative reasons: as skilled arguers we may be proactively looking for arguments that defend our opinions and/or that may persuade others instead of looking for the truth. This means that argumentation and persuasion may in some cases be more effective for personal goals than truth.

The suboptimal decisions that may result from heuristic decision-making processes are consequences of "biases". Using heuristics, we typically feel quite confident about our decisions and judgments, even when evidence is scarce and when we are aware of our cognitive inclinations. In line with this, specific cognitive biases are quite pervasive and persistent. (Korteling et al.). They make the point that human decision making is determined by the basic design characteristics of neural information processing itself. These basic characteristics originally developed to perform concrete biological, perceptual, and motor functions which primarily induce deviations from the abstract laws of logic and probability. As human society has become increasingly complex, the basic design characteristics of neural information processing, still drive decision making behaviour.

They go on to argue that four basic principles (Association, Compatibility, Retainment, and Focus) are characteristic for the working of biological neural networks.

- The Association Principle states that (using correlation and coincidence detection) the brain 'searches' associatively for relationships, coherence, links, and patterns in the available information.
- The Compatibility (or Consistency) Principle states that associations are highly determined by their compatibility (match, consistency, conformity) with the momentary state and connectionist properties of the neural network, such that we see, recognize, accept or prefer information according to its consistency with what we already know, understand, expect, and value.
- The Retainment Principle states that when irrelevant information, or counter-productive information (which has been given before) is associatively integrated, it is captured in the brain's neural circuitry, such that this cannot be simply made undone, erased, denied or ignored and thus will (associatively) affect a following judgement or decision.
- The Focus Principle states that the brain focuses associatively on dominant information, i.e., dominant "known knowns" that easily pop up in the forming of judgements, ideas, and decisions. The fact that other (possible relevant) information may exist is insufficiently recognized or ignored (like a blind spot).

These comprise the mechanisms and characteristics of neural "wetware" and are inherent to (all) neural networks. Because the brain completely consists of large amounts of interconnected, assemblies of firing neurons, these four mechanisms are the core of all brain processes. Biases are seen as *cognitive illusions* originating from the same kind of underlying neural mechanisms that cause the many kinds of perceptual illusions.

Exploring this further, the study argues the brain is not like a conventional repository or hard disk that can take up and store any information that is provided, almost indifferently of its characteristics. Instead, it is an associative network that requires new or additional information to be compliant or consistent with its existing state. What is associatively selected, processed, and integrated is not only determined by stimulus characteristics like the saliency of a target in its context, but also by the compatibility (match) with the brain's momentary state and connectionist characteristics. Although we know that the brain has plasticity (in other words neural connections can change) this tends to be a very long and complex process as can be seen in people who are recovering from a neural injury[4].

They suggest the principle of compatibility in neural information processing implies a compulsion to be consistent with what we already know, think or have done, resulting in a tendency to ignore or overlook relevant information because it does not match with our current behaviour or mindset. They suggest the most well-known biases resulting from this principle include confirmation bias (a tendency to search for, interpret, focus on and remember information in a way that *confirms* one's preconceptions): belief bias (the tendency to judge conclusions based on consistency with our prior beliefs, values, and knowledge rather than logical validity): and cognitive dissonance (a state of having inconsistent thoughts and a resulting tendency to search for and select consistent information).

Their work makes the point that whereas conventional repositories or hard disks can take up, process, and store information indifferently to its characteristics, in neural networks the selection and processing of inputs depends on the characteristics of the information. Compatible, conforming, or matching inputs are more easily selected, processed, and established, thus contributing to priming effects. This may explain why we see what we expect to see and why we associate more value or importance to information that aligns with what is already represented in our brains.

When irrelevant information or counter-productive information (which has been given before) is associatively integrated, it is captured in the brain's neural circuitry, such that this cannot be simply made undone, erased, denied or ignored and thus will (associatively) affect a following judgment or decision. Bias is in play. For the brain, a hardware–software distinction does not apply: information is structurally encoded in "wetware". All stimuli entering the nervous system affect its physical–chemical structure and thereby its connectionist properties. So, unlike a computer program, once information has entered the brain, it cannot simply be ignored or put aside. It always has an effect[5]. Almost invariably recognition and management of one bias can lead to the development of a replacement bias.

To understand further how biases develop and impact, we need to understand something about how the brain works. Early in 2021, Oprea et al examined how motivated beliefs nurture bias to both develop and impact us[6]. Like Korteling et al., they argue that the brain is not a logical system that systematically and proportionally takes into account and weighs all relevant information. Instead, our brain works more like a magnifying glass. When making decisions, we tend to rely on conclusions that are based on limited amounts of readily available information rather than on larger bodies of less consistent data. This can be a particularly egregious problem if all our information comprises sources from social media, pop culture or the like because there is little if any fact checking prior to publication in these avenues. Traditional mass media is not exempt from this criticism of sources but, at least in the mainstream mass media, there is generally some attempt at verification of information. This shift to limited amounts of readily available information is exacerbated through the waning effect of traditional mass media and the increasing influence of social media in developing biases that are comfortable for the individual and appear to reflect the social norm.

Oprea and Yuksel continue:

> Accumulating evidence suggests that decision makers suffer from "motivated beliefs," believing propositions in part because they would prefer

them to be true. Motivated beliefs (and the "motivated reasoning" that fuels it) can generate serious biases, and it is therefore important for social scientists and policy makers to understand what institutional settings make these biases more and less severe[7].

In 2006 Phelps[8] had made the point that research has identified the amygdala as a critical structure for emotional learning and that research continues to highlight the role of the amygdala in relation to social means of emotional learning and culturally acquired race bias. David Amodio then takes this further when providing an insight into the neuroscience involved in prejudice and stereotyping[9]. He points out that social motivations, such as the desire to affiliate or compete with others, rank among the most potent of human drives. Although this computation takes just a fraction of a second, it sets the stage for social categorisation, stereotypes, prejudices, intergroup conflict and inequality, and, at the extremes, war and genocide. He argues prejudice stems from a mechanism of survival centred on the amygdala. Prejudice is built on cognitive systems that "structure" the physical world and its function in modern society is complex and its effects are often deleterious. Amodio makes clear that unless the brain mechanisms lying behind bias and such resultant behaviours as prejudice and stereotyping are understood, dealing with inappropriate and/or antisocial behaviour is likely to focus on addressing symptoms rather than the underlying causes. While symptoms must be addressed and resolved, unless and until the underlying causes of inappropriate behaviour are addressed, there is a significant probability of them recurring. The January 6, 2021 events in Washington DC to overturn the results of the 2020 US presidential election and the copycat impact on the results of the 2022 presidential elections in Brazil, highlight this.

Amodio argues neuroscience research on the mechanisms supporting the control of intergroup responses incorporates existing domain-general models of cognitive control into broader models that consider the influence of social factors. For example, the impetus for the control of racial bias may arise from internal cues such as the personal rejection of prejudice or external cues such as social pressure to respond without prejudice. Engagement in control is frequently associated with social emotions such as social anxiety or guilt. Any model of control should account for these different impetuses and emotion effects. Failure to take account of these underlying factors invariable means we confront symptoms only.

Amodio explains that neuroscience makes clear the left lateral prefrontal cortex (PFC) is linked to the implementation of action, whereas activity in the right lateral PFC is linked to action inhibition (in right-handed individuals). On the basis of research in cognitive neuroscience, lateral PFC regions have been proposed as primary substrates of cognitive control of prejudice. A 2015 study by Torrence[10] also argues for the importance of the prefrontal cortex in facilitating change when he states "that the (medial PFC) mPFC is involved in automatically orienting attention toward the fearful facial expression and the (lateral PFC) lPFC is involved in relocating attention. Trying to facilitate lasting change without engaging the PFC has but a low probability of success."

As indicated, Torrence's findings are consistent with Amodio's work[11] as to the need to understand and confront underlying causal factors. Amodio says:

> Despite some success in reducing behavioural and physiological expressions of implicit bias in the laboratory, most forms of implicit learning are resistant to extinction. Implicit racial biases are particularly difficult to change in a cultural milieu that constantly reinforces racial prejudices and stereotypes (for example, in mainstream media). Thus, although attempts to undo learned intergroup associations are laudable, such strategies may be ineffective for reducing the expression of bias in behaviour outside the laboratory. Instead, interventions that enhance the cognitive control of behaviour should be more effective. Such control-based strategies may not reduce prejudice in the mind, but they can prevent its effect on potential victims.

"Control based strategy" is a general term used to monitor performance and may be process or result (output) measures. Controls related to process may include budget measures designed to optimise the probability that desired outputs will be achieved. (This issue of "desired outputs" can be, of course, somewhat subjective. For example, in a political environment, the desired outcomes may relate more closely to harvesting votes than actually overcoming bias.) Control based strategies may also include the requirement that an organisation (or part thereof) make public their intentions in relation to issues such as gender diversity and other discriminations, human rights, and environmental matters. The assumption is that such publication will ensure that real change occurs.

Observed results, however, make clear that there can often be a significant difference between what is espoused and what is done. There are many examples of organisations claiming they are "doing the right thing" but, in reality, "fudging" the results. Consider the (now) infamous case of Volkswagen:

In 2015, Volkswagen (VW) was caught cheating consumers with its supposedly "clean diesel" engines. The carmaker's engineers had fitted 11 million cars with software that duped emission tests into believing that the car was eco-friendly. In reality, the cars were releasing up to 40 times the permitted amount of nitrogen oxide pollutants. When this news broke, the then Chief Executive Officer of the company, Michael Horn, responded: "We've totally screwed up." Although a welcomed admission, it should not have taken a series of international Court actions and extremely high monetary penalties for Volkswagen to change its behaviour. Across management levels there was a failure in control-based strategy.

Volkswagen was (and is) not unique in manipulating things in order to blur the distinction between perception and reality. "Greenwashing" is when an organisation spends more time and money on marketing itself as environmentally friendly than on actually minimising its environmental impact. It is a marketing gimmick intended to mislead consumers who prefer to buy goods and services from environmentally conscious brands. It is an attempt to benefit from the bias of the consumer by the blurring of reality.

Of course, such "washing" does not necessarily have any positive impact on the environment or society – and it does not need to be "green". In early 2022 the golfer, Greg Norman (once the world number 1 golfer) announced the formation of a new team-based, professional golf league that would compete with the long-established Professional Golf Association (PGA) that is headquartered in the USA. This new venture, backed by Saudi Arabia's Public Investment Fund (PIF), pledged to award $250 million in total prize money while hosting eight tournaments, held June through October. Saudi Arabia is, of course, frequently accused of serious human rights violations including murder of dissidents. Yet, when journalists asked him to reconcile his advocacy of the new tour with the murder of Saudi journalist Jamal Khashoggi, according to UK news media, Norman responded: "This whole thing about Saudi Arabia and Khashoggi and human rights, talk about it, but also talk about the good that the country is doing in changing its culture." He continued: "Look, we've all made mistakes and you just want to learn by those mistakes and how you can correct them going forward". Peter FitzSimons, a journalist with Australia's Sydney Morning Herald (and a long-time critic of Greg Norman) responded by accusing Norman of helping Saudi Arabia "sports wash" their past because there was no indication that discriminatory behaviour in Saudi Arabia was likely to change. FitzSimons writes[12]:

> … their record on human rights is *appalling*, up to and including killing uppity journalists. Not so long ago, the Saudi dissident journalist Jamal Khashoggi was murdered and cut into pieces in Saudi Arabia's Istanbul consulate and that, tragically, was not an outlier. The desert kingdom's systemic human rights abuses are horrific and include torture used as punishment, the imprisonment of uppity women's rights advocates – as women are treated as inferior citizens – public beheadings, no free speech, no right of assembly for protests, and ruthless suppression of all those who would oppose the Saudi royals and their outrageous regime. … But let's not talk about that. Let's talk about sport!

Any time there is an attempt to hide or minimise pollution, discrimination, segregation, oppression and other manifestations of bias by trying to reframe the discussion rather than dealing with the issue, there is the danger of "washing" of one or another sort being used as camouflage. It is evidence that any process controls in place are, of themselves, inadequate as the control strategy. Rather than addressing causes, it is far easier to draw attention away from the bias to some other that can be more easily defended, or which blurs the original issue.

In part this issue of greenwashing explains a concern by Gabrielle M Johnson[13] who makes the point that studying bias is made more difficult because people today no longer "wear many of their social prejudices on their sleeves." Accordingly, our research into bias and our dealing with issues around bias need to change. This is an issue to which Amodio (op cit) refers when he says "it is also possible that the amygdala response in some studies reflects not a direct threat from an outgroup member but rather the threat of appearing prejudiced in the presence of others who may disapprove of bias. Indeed, in white subjects, anxiety about appearing prejudiced to others has been shown to enhance eye gaze fixations and early visual processing of black faces and low-prejudice individuals who worried about appearing prejudiced to others showed larger startle eyeblink responses to black versus white faces compared with low-prejudice individuals without this concern."

We may bring our behaviour under control, but there is that split second in which the amygdala reveals something deeper. Amodio suggests the amygdala response to an ingroup or outgroup member depends on a perceiver's goals and shows that when exposure to images of people from a different racial group is combined with an unrelated secondary task (for example, to detect the appearance of a small dot on the image), race no longer drives the amygdala response.

Of course, social bias is not a one-way street[14]. This paper found "there is considerable evidence that minority group members also harbor prejudice toward majority group members. However, much of this prejudice is reactive, reflecting an anticipation of being discriminated *against* by majority group members."

This matter of the role of the amygdala reflects what I wrote in 2012 when discussing the brain's locus of control[15]. I said:

> Neuroscience has found that one's locus of brain control is complex but basically centred in the combination of several brain areas.[16] ... the reptilian-limbic combination *The Red Zone* and the neocortical-limbic combination *The Blue Zone*. ... The concept of "red zone" and "blue zone" ... refer to our brain's areas (or "loci") of control.

I went on to say,

> When the brain's area of control is centred in the red zone, the emphasis is on survival. This is the part of the brain that leads to perception of threat (real or imagined) and so to the "fight, flight, or freeze" syndrome that we see particularly in reptiles and lower-level animals. There is no conscious thought in this. Life just 'is' or 'isn't' – it is not something of which the animal is consciously aware – and instinct makes us want to hold on to life if possible, so we respond to threat in a way that offers the chance of living another day. When this perceived threat is physical (for example we are threatened with violence or are in danger of being run over by a bus) then

the dominance of the red zone is essential. Instinctive action is required and occurs. Unfortunately, however, because the red zone is dominated by the reptilian brain it is not capable of distinguishing between real threats or imagined threats and so it reacts in the same way whether or not a threat actually exists. In the modern world, a red zone locus of control can lead to some very inappropriate responses when a person perceives a threat even when there is no such intent from other parties and we see this all too frequently in some domestic, social, business, national and international events. Red zone locus of control also leads to the commonly encountered issue of resistance to change.

When the brain's area of control is in the blue zone we have the opportunity to see things differently. Because the blue zone is dominated by the cortical brain – that part of the brain which deals with thought, voluntary movement, language and reasoning (in other words 'with higher level learning') – we have the ability to see things as they actually are and to distinguish between real and imagined threats. This enables us to make a more appropriate response and to find ways of dealing with 'the new' in exciting and innovative ways. When operating with a blue zone locus of control we are better able to deal with complexity and ambiguity than is the case when we operate out of a red zone locus of control.

It must be noted, however, that this "red zone – blue zone" dichotomy has nothing to do with our emotions per se. The areas of the brain that bring about emotion are common to both the blue zone and the red zone. In other words, it is not a case of "red zone = unhappy" "blue zone = happy" or anything like that. People with their brain's locus of control in the blue zone will have exactly the same range of emotions as they have always had. Any difference will relate to the way in which these emotions are handled.

In other words, does the individual control the emotions or do the emotions control the individual?

This is where the link to bias becomes clear. When I am operating in the red zone, I am less likely to recognise my biases and, even if I do recognise them, I am highly unlikely to challenge them. I will tend to see my behaviour as correct no matter what the consequences. This changes when I am operating in the blue zone. Because, in the blue zone, I am using different thought processes, awareness of bias enables discussion as to its appropriateness and both the ability and willingness to manage bias is enhanced.

This is very pertinent in considering bias. If bias really is a defence mechanism that is triggered (even if totally unconsciously) by the amygdala, then recognising the red zone – blue zone dichotomy may give us clues as to how to address it. Lehrer[17] makes the point (p.19) that our conscious actions are not totally under control. Quoting the neuroscientist, Joseph LeDoux, he says: "But consciousness is a small part of what the brain does, and it's a slave to everything that works beneath it." Lehrer continues, "When one is confronted by an ethical dilemma, the unconscious automatically generates an emotional reaction." (p.167)

In understanding bias and its associated characteristics such as prejudice, stereotyping, discrimination, etc, the issue of dopamine and its effect is important. Dopamine is a neurotransmitter that helps regulate all our emotions. It is the molecule that helps us decide among alternatives. If a person does what they feel is "right" (in other words, if I act in accord with my bias – whether conscious or unconscious bias) then I am rewarded with a dopamine surge. The effect is that the bias is reinforced and becomes more "hard-wired" in us. Lehrer (p42) makes the point that dopamine neurons constantly generate patterns based on experience: "if this, then that". It is all about expectation. "The cacophony of reality is distilled into models of correlation that allow the brain to anticipate what will happen next." If there is anticipation that a particular action will be rewarding to us, then the probability of taking that action is greatly enhanced.

Scholz et al explored the role of cortical dopamine on motivational biases in automated behaviour[18]. The starting point was that motivations shape our behaviour: the promise of reward invigorates, while in the face of punishment, we hold back. They tested the hypothesis that frontal dopamine controls the balance between Pavlovian, bias-driven automated responding and instrumentally learned action values. They say:

> We generally feel that we are in control of our actions and make our decisions rationally. Yet, many of us eat that extra slice of cake, buy that expensive phone, or fail to save sufficiently for our retirement. While our behaviour is indeed to a large extent driven by "rational" (instrumental) learning from experience, a key observation is that motivational prospects shape our behaviours in a seemingly hardwired way: the promise of rewards invigorates behaviour, while we hold back under the threat of punishment. These motivational biases are thought to simplify decision-making by providing sensible default actions ("priors"). Such decision heuristics can be particularly helpful in situations requiring rapid responding, or in an unfamiliar environment. Through instrumental learning of stimulus-response-outcome contingencies we can flexibly learn which actions are advantageous in any given, specific environment, which, once learnt, will lead to more optimal choices.

Their study explored both striatal and prefrontal dopamine function. The striatum is one of the principal components of the basal ganglia, a group of nuclei that have a variety of functions but are best known for their role in facilitating voluntary movement. It is part of the reptilian-limbic combination of the brain – the "red zone". They argue that in addition to an important role of the striatum eliciting motivational bias, there is also a putative role of *frontal* ("blue zone") dopamine in controlling these biases. In other words, in relation to the expectation concept, the area of the brain releasing the dopamine is important: that coming from the striatum ("red zone") encourages motivational bias on behaviour while cortical ("blue zone") dopamine non-selectively dampens the impact of motivational biases on behaviour.

While they did not examine bias per se, the link to motivational prospects shaping behaviour has a clear link to this discussion on bias: operating from the "blue zone" (that area of the brain controlled by the frontal cortex) may help us in controlling bias: This 2021 study thus reinforces the earlier mentioned research from both Torrence and of Amodio about the importance of the frontal cortex in managing bias.

In summary, the evidence is clear. As we develop both physically and psychologically, we develop a world view that frames everything we encounter. It provides a lens through which we view every aspect of life and learning. This world view establishes the set of unconscious biases that will impact everything we do and our approach to the exigencies we encounter. Of themselves these world views are not necessarily "right" or "wrong". They just "are". However, if we fail to recognise their reality and are not willing to challenge them, they have the potential for serious harm to both us and others. Biases exist in every one of us at all times. Biases are always part of our world views – in other words, bias per se is never eliminated but new (usually) unconscious biases may emerge as current unconscious biases are recognised and challenged. The various milieus within which we live have the ability to both reinforce and challenge the appropriateness of the biases we hold.

Questions for group discussion:

1. "Adaptive decisions often need to be made fast, and this may well constrain the type of strategies that are optimal." Discuss this in relation to your own decision making behaviours. Is it possible that we overuse this reason for "quick" decisions? Why?
2. "Biases are seen as *cognitive illusions* originating from the same kind of underlying neural mechanisms that cause the many kinds of perceptual illusions." What is the connection between that statement and: "Accumulating evidence suggests that decision makers suffer from "motivated beliefs," believing propositions in part because they would prefer them to be true." Discuss this with reference to your own decision-making.
3. "Social motivations, such as the desire to affiliate or compete with others, rank among the most potent of human drives. Although this computation takes just a fraction of a second, it sets the stage for social categorisation, stereotypes, prejudices, intergroup conflict and inequality, and, at the extremes, war and genocide." Discuss this statement in relation to the current state of world affairs.
4. "World views are not necessarily "right" or "wrong". They just "are". However, if we fail to recognise their reality and are not willing to

challenge them, they have the potential for serious harm to both us and others." When have you made decisions that have caused unintended harm to others? What could you have done differently? Discuss this with reference to your own decision-making processes.

5. "Biases exist in every one of us at all times. Biases are always part of our world views – in other words, bias per se is never eliminated but new (usually) unconscious biases may emerge as current unconscious biases are recognised and challenged." What is your reaction to the thought that we can never eliminate bias but instead, as we identify and manage one bias, new biases may emerge? How can we minimise any negative impacts of any such emerging new biases?

Notes

1 Paradies, Yin; Bastos, Joao Luiz; Priest, Naomi 2016, The Cambridge Handbook of the Psychology of Prejudice, Part 3, pp 559–581, Cambridge University Press, https://doi.org/10.1017/9781316161579.025

2 Haselton et al. op cit

3 Johan E. Korteling*, Anne-Marie Brouwer and Alexander Toet, 2018, "*A Neural Network Framework for Cognitive Bias*", Front. Psychol., 03 September 2018 | https://doi.org/10.3389/fpsyg.2018.01561

4 Norman Doidge's book, "The Brain That Changes Itself" (Scribe, 2010) provides an interesting perspective on this.

5 Johan E. Korteling*, Anne-Marie Brouwer and Alexander Toet, 2018, "*A Neural Network Framework for Cognitive Bias*", Front. Psychol., 03 September 2018 | https://doi.org/10.3389/fpsyg.2018.01561

6 Ryan Oprea & Sevgi Yuksel, March, 2021 "*Social Exchange of Motivated Beliefs*", Economics Department, University of California, Santa Barbara, Santa Barbara, CA, 93106

7 Ryan Oprea & Sevgi Yuksel, March, 2021 "*Social Exchange of Motivated Beliefs*", Economics Department, University of California, Santa Barbara, Santa Barbara, CA, 93106

8 Phelps, E. A. (2006). Emotion, Learning, and the Brain: From Classical Conditioning to Cultural Bias. In P. B. Baltes, P. A. Reuter-Lorenz, & F. Rösler (Eds.), *Lifespan development and the brain: The perspective of biocultural co-constructivism* (pp. 200–216). Cambridge University Press. https://doi.org/10.1017/CBO9780511499722.011

9 David M. Amodio, 2014, *The neuroscience of prejudice and stereotyping,* New York University, Department of Psychology, 6 Washington Place, New York, New York 10003, USA.

10 Robert Torrence, 2015, "Prefrontal Cortex Activity During Attentional Bias Conditioning with Fearful Faces: A Near-Infrared Spectroscopy Analysis", unpublished Masters in Science thesis, Northern Michigan University

11 David M Amodio, op cit

12 https://www.smh.com.au/sport/golf/norman-s-true-colours-coming-out-in-yet-a nother-saudi-sport-wash-20211103-p595ry.html

13 Johnson, Gabrielle M., *The Structure of Bias, Mind, Vol. 129. 516. October 2020*

14 Dovidio, John F., op cit

15 "*Third Generation Leadership and the locus of Control: knowledge, change and neuroscience*", Douglas G Long, 2012, Gower Publishing Limited, Farnham, UK

16 The concept of a triune brain was developed in the 1960's by Paul MacLean of Yale University. His model of brain structure and function is based on three specific

regions of the human brain: the 1) basal ganglia, 2) the limbic system, and 3) the neocortex. Each of these structures is thought to be responsible for a specific group of mental activities: 1) the fight-or-flight survival response and other primal activities, 2) emotions, and 3) rational thinking. MacLean suggested that these structures developed in this order through evolution. However, while the triune brain model provides us with a neat way of looking at the relationship between structure and function in the human brain, evidence has shown *various* regions are involved in the three groups of activities outlined above. Therefore, there is no such neat division; instead, primal, emotional and rational mental activities are the product of neural activity in more than one of the three regions addressed in MacLean's model, and their *collective* energy creates human experience. For further information as to the concept, see also Dahlitz, M. (2016). The Triune Brain, https://www.thescienceofp sychotherapy.com/the-triune-brain/

17 Lehrer, Jonah op cit
18 Vanessa Scholz, Hanneke E.M. den Ouden and Samuel R. Chamberlain, 2021, http s://doi.org/10.1101/2021.09.09.459267

4

EXTENDING AND REINFORCING BIAS

In 2010, Richard Wilkinson and Kate Pickett published the 3rd edition of their research on the impact of inequality[1]. The initial focus of their research was to understand the causes of the big differences in life expectancy – the "health inequalities" – between people at different levels of the social hierarchies in modern societies. Discussing US research conducted by the Harwood Institute for Public Innovation, they point out that, in the USA, people feel that "materialism" somehow comes between them and the satisfaction of their social needs. "A large majority of people wanted society to move away from greed and excess toward a way of life more centred on values, community, and family. But they also felt that these priorities were not shared by most of their fellow Americans, who, they believed, had become 'increasingly ato-mized, selfish, and irresponsible." Given that, as the saying goes, "perception is reality" it is not beyond belief that this view of "others" helps create and maintain a society that is biased towards materialism rather than positive social interactions. In other words, we try to demonstrate that we are not different from the perceptions we have of others. Wilkinson and Pickett's comments demonstrate the impact of statements made by James Carville in 1992 when he was advising Bill Clinton in his successful run for the White House. Carville coined the cliché: "It's the economy, stupid". This reflected earlier comments attributed to Margaret Thatcher when she was Prime Min-ister of Great Britain that were paraphrased as: "we live in an economy not a society". (Her actual statement was: "There is no such thing as society. There are individuals, and there are families.") Wilkinson and Pickett illustrate that when our values are orientated towards materialism, we become biased against a collaborative, equitable society towards a focus on the individual in which personal gain is really all that matters.

DOI: 10.4324/9781003528340-5

While, as already discussed, many types of bias have been identified, it is mainly in the manifestation of bias as seen in prejudice, stereotyping, and discrimination that provides any observer with evidence as to the existence of bias. Accordingly, the focus for this chapter will be on these three key influencers of social bias (prejudice, stereotyping, and discrimination) and how these extend and reinforce both individual and societal discrimination. This will be illustrated through consideration of four universal societal influencers – business, religion, politics and social media.

The role of normal psychological and social processes in fostering and maintaining biases is very important[2]. Dovidio continues (p.7) to argue "**Prejudice** is an individual-level attitude (whether subjectively positive or negative) towards groups and their members that creates or maintains hierarchical status relations between groups". A little later (p.8) they argue "... **stereotypes** represent a set of qualities perceived to reflect the essence of a group. Stereotypes systematically affect how people perceive, process information about, and respond to group members. They are transmitted through socialization, the media, and language and discourse". Later again (p.10) they say "... we define **discrimination** by an individual as behavior that creates, maintains, or reinforces advantage for some groups and their members over other groups and their members". (Emphasis in each case by the author.)

Consider the following. A group of four men is playing golf. One player comes up short of the hole when putting. Without thinking he enjoins himself "hit it, Mary" and, virtually simultaneously one of the other players calls out "does your husband play golf?" Both men are known for their advocacy of gender inclusivity in both the workplace and society at large and would vehemently deny that they are sexist in any way, yet, in an unguarded moment, elements of unconscious bias – in this case, a long-discredited but still prevailing view by some, that women cannot play golf as well as men – become apparent. Statements that may well have been socially acceptable in the 40 or so years since either man first took up golf have provided a sociological imprint that emerges under certain conditions despite the fact that neither man demonstrates any evidence of gender bias in any other area of their lives. With strong justification, both men would claim to be unbiased yet, when not consciously considering the greater impact of what they are saying, words that are in direct contradiction of the normal behaviour uttered. Perhaps a "Freudian slip"[3]?

Consider a second example. Most mainstream, traditional faiths advocate care and compassion for all humanity. In the Christian tradition this is probably best illustrated in the parable of the Good Samaritan (Luke Chapter 10). Many (mainly) Western nations claim to be "Christian" and, certainly in some of them, their Christian heritage is loudly and proudly nominated as the source of their national values to the extent that, in some, the faith of their political leaders is presented as evidence that they can be trusted to "do the right thing". Yet, increasingly over the past 50 or so years, there has been a widening divide between "the haves" and "the have-nots" with policies and practices primarily benefitting those with power while simultaneously reducing support for those from the lower socio-economic groups[4]. In addition, especially over the past 20 or so years both violent social disruption and natural disasters have seen a surge of people seeking religious, political and economic refuge in different countries. This has been met by "Christian" (as well as those of other faiths) administrations claiming many of these are "illegal refugees" despite the fact that, in international law, claiming refugee status and seeking refuge is not illegal for any person. The grounds for such demonisation are that the refugees have not followed "the correct procedures" for seeking help and so have used people smugglers or other questionable avenues to reach places of potential sanctuary[5].

The 1951 Refugee Convention makes clear people should not be punished for breaking immigration rules to seek safety in another country. It is interesting to note that, in December 2022, The UK Prime Minister, Rishi Sunak, suggested that, given the differences between now and 1951, this Convention should be reviewed and rewritten. This led to UK Home Secretary Suella Braverman speaking out against boat arrivals in the UK on March 7. On March 8, 2023 broadcaster Gary Lineker of the BBC's "Match of the Day" (and a former England football captain) made headlines around the world when he tweeted criticism of the British government's asylum policy. He was immediately suspended from broadcasting even though he was a freelancer rather than an employee – a move portrayed by many politicians and media commentators as the BBC bowing to pressure from the Conservative government.[6]

The fact that, as well as being of different nationalities, many of these people seeking refuge are of a different colour, faith, and other discriminatory factors is, we are constantly assured by our leaders, totally irrelevant and bias (whether conscious or unconscious) forms no part of their refugee assessment process. We are assured that we are protecting "our" country and society from infiltration by "others" who may not have values and practices compatible with our own.

These are obviously examples from either end of a continuum that runs from the individual to the institutional, but they illustrate the same point: the reality of bias impacts everyone and every institution and they are highlighted whenever there is a discrepancy between what is said and what is done. We can "talk the talk" but do we "walk the walk"?

As already discussed, from birth our environment – family, community, school etc – consciously and unconsciously impacts to form our mental models. As we age, these early influences are supplemented by other factors. Traditionally, by the time we are in our late teens or early twenties there are four key social environment areas that continue to have a significant impact – business, religion, politics and social media. This is regardless of whether we are employed, have religious affiliations, and/or are politically active because, no matter where we are, they comprise the core structure of the social environment in which we live. These four areas directly or indirectly impact every aspect of society across the world. In every country and society – no matter how primitive or how advanced – they help the development and maintenance of a bias towards the status quo – even when that status quo is clearly in need of review. Social media is a very new element that operates across traditional spheres (business, religious and political) of the traditional social environment and is, today, able to both exacerbate the traditional factors and is, of itself, itself also a factor. These four will now be considered in greater depth.

Business

There is a symbiotic relationship between society and the economy – the economy needs consumers and society provides them; consumers need goods and services which are provided by the economy. This is just the way it should be. An important part of this relationship is that business needs to operate profitably. As Charles Dickens (in the book "David Copperfield") had his character Wilkins Micawber say: "Annual income twenty pounds, annual expenditure nineteen nineteen and six, result happiness. Annual income twenty pounds, annual expenditure twenty pound ought and six, result misery." The absolute minimal operating requirement of any business venture is to "break even". Whether a not-for-profit or a for-profit venture, when outgoings (including remuneration for the owners and employees) are in excess of incomings, disaster beckons. This means that profit is essential if a business is to grow – it needs to generate revenues that are significantly in excess of outgoings. A business that does not operate in such a way that it makes a profit, almost certainly will quickly cease to exist.

Over the centuries the balance between society and economy has varied but, by the middle of the 20th century, (at least in social democracies) there was a reasonably equitable balance in which relatively few people were at either end of the wealth continuum. (Social democracy is a government system that has similar values to socialism, but within a capitalist framework. The ideology, named from democracy where people have a say in government actions, supports a competitive economy with money while also helping people who are disadvantaged. It is a reasonably egalitarian society in which opportunity for advancement is (at least in theory) available to all citizens regardless of wealth or social standing.)

By the 1950's the world had survived the devastation of the Second World War and most major economies were starting to thrive with high employment and remuneration structures that employees generally considered to be reasonably fair. Memories of the Great Depression and the vicissitudes of war were still strong and democratic Governments focused on developing and maintaining a strong and stable society with a balanced economy.

Beneath the surface, however, there was (as always) an element of society that chafed at restrictions on the manner by which they could do business and achieve their desires for wealth and power. As we saw emerge from the start of the 1970's, their day would come.

One of the key people challenging this relatively egalitarian status quo was Friedrich Hayek (the 1974 Nobel Laureate in Economics). In his book The Constitution of Liberty[7], Hayek posits civilisation is made possible by the absence of arbitrary restraints such as government regulation or public ownership. He argues that removing such restraints is essential for national wealth and growth.

One of those who were strongly influenced by Hayek was Milton Friedman, the 1976 Nobel Laureate in Economics, to whom US President Ronald Reagan turned for advice. Under the patronage of Reagan, Friedman came to see implemented much of what he advocated in his book Capitalism and Freedom[8].

Milton Friedman advocated a free market economic system with minimal controls. He argued that competitive forces will ensure the best results for everyone – lower prices through competition coupled with better returns to investors through lower operating costs. Friedman stated: "There is one and only one social responsibility of business – to use its resources and engage in activities designed to increase its profits." In Friedman's view, the central emphasis of business is to make money for its shareholders.

A third key person was the American economist, James McGill Buchanan who was awarded the Nobel memorial prize in 1986 for his work on public choice theory[9]. He was influenced by Friedrich Hayek as well as by John C Calhoun, the 19th century American statesman and political theorist from South Carolina, (and the seventh Vice President of the United States from 1825 to 1832) who argued that freedom consists of the absolute right to use your property (including your slaves) however you may wish; any institution that impinges on this right is an agent of oppression, exploiting men of property on behalf of the undeserving masses. Bringing these together, Buchanan[10] argued that a society could not be considered free unless every citizen (at least if they are rich and powerful) has the right to veto political decisions that could impact negatively on them. What he meant by this was that no one (at least if rich and powerful) should be taxed against their will because, he argued, the rich were being exploited through involuntary taxes to support public spending and welfare. His view was that allowing workers to form trade unions and imposing graduated income taxes were forms of "differential or discriminatory legislation" against the owners of capital.

Buchanan called for a "constitutional revolution" which would create irrevocable restraints to limit democratic choice. He then developed a theoretical account of what this constitutional revolution would look like, and a strategy for implementing this. He showed how attempts to desegregate schooling in the American south could be frustrated by setting up a network of state-sponsored private schools; privatising universities and imposing full tuition fees on students in order to crush student activism. To this was added privatisation of social security and many other functions of the state in order to break the links between people and government and demolish trust in public institutions. His goal was to save capitalism from democracy.

Together these three laid the foundation for what we now know as "neoliberalism".

Because of the increasing international influence of the USA and based on the United States emphasis on the individual, since the 1970's the dominant approach to management, at least in the "Anglo" world has been that advocated by Hayek, Friedman, and Buchanan. The overall term for this has developed into "neoliberalism" and it is the form of capitalism propounded by such people as, in the USA, President Ronald Reagan and, in the UK, Margaret Thatcher who, as already stated, when Prime Minister of Great Britain, is reputed to have stated that "we live in an economy, not a society"[11]. The emphasis of the neoliberal approach is that government plays minimal (if any) role in regulating business, and public assets are sold into private enterprise. It has become the economic orthodoxy of the western world.

This neoliberal thinking has now permeated politics and business for at least the last forty plus years[12]. Ultimately it lies behind the activities that have led to many of the "booms and busts" of the late twentieth and early twenty-first centuries – including the Global Financial Crisis of 2007. The only thing that really matters is profit and wealth for the few. It claims (without extensive proof) that such an approach initiates a "the trickle-down effect" in which benefits at the top eventually make their way to those at the bottom.

As shown consistently over years by reports to the annual Davos Conference in Switzerland, evidence such as the increasing disparity of wealth in many neoliberal countries suggests that, while the trickle-down effect may be outwardly espoused it is seldom effective in achieving equitable wealth distribution and in improving the overall economic situation of the disadvantaged. Consistently it has been argued by many researchers[13] that there is very little (if any) empirical evidence that this "trickle-down effect", while much loved and advocated by the executives who reap large benefits from short term results, ever actually benefits the company (or the nation) in the long term. Certainly, even if it did once work, the overwhelming evidence of today is that it exacerbates the problems that arise through an increasing gulf between "the haves" and "the have-nots" in every society. It ignores the fact that all stakeholders including every employee, supplier, customer, competitor, and society itself have a vested interest in an organisation's long-term viability and should be considered. It fails to recognise that, from a long-term perspective, it is the greater human factor and not just the financial returns that is of prime importance (something that was clearly recognised by Adam Smith[14]). The earlier symbiotic relationship between society and economy is largely forgotten or its importance ignored.

In March 2024 this matter of "the greater human factor" in business was addressed in a series of papers from the International Monetary Fund[15]. Angus Deaton, awarded the 2015 Nobel Prize in Economics, makes the point that: "today we are in some disarray. We did not collectively predict the financial crisis and, worse still, we may have contributed to it through an overenthusiastic belief in the efficacy of markets, especially financial markets whose structure and implications we understood less well than we thought"[16] He argues that:

> In contrast to economists from Adam Smith and Karl Marx through John Maynard Keynes, Friedrich Hayek, and even Milton Friedman, we have largely stopped thinking about ethics and about what constitutes human well-being. We are technocrats who focus on efficiency. We get little training about the ends of economics, on the meaning of well-being – welfare economics has long since vanished from the curriculum – or on what philosophers say about equality. When pressed, we usually fall back on an income-based utilitarianism. We often equate well-being with money or consumption, missing much of what matters to people. In current economic thinking, individuals matter much more than relationships between people in families or in communities.

Effectively he, along with other contributors, argues that our current business models, based on economic theory developed over the past half century, have become biased against the very purpose on which economic theory and business practice ought to be focusing – the overall well-being (both economic and non-economic) of societies.

This is not all that different from what Klein said in the 2007 book The Shock Doctrine: The Rise of Disaster Capitalism[17] where it is suggested that capitalism as we know it today with its demand for constant growth, eventually encounters situations where growth is not possible and catastrophic economic and social collapse erupts. It argues that neo-liberalism is every bit as much a form of religious extremism as is radical Islam, radical Christianity, radical Hinduism, radical Judaism and any other extremist beliefs in that chaos is created so that a new world order can be imposed. The unfettered pursuit of neoliberalism can bring economic chaos. Into this economic chaos whether in Africa, Asia, Latin America, post-communist Europe, or anywhere else comes the International Monetary Fund (IMF) with policies of wholesale privatisation and structural adjustment that invariably then lead to declining economic activity and social dislocation on a massive scale. The affected country then lurches from one crisis to another as the bureaucrats of the IMF impose cut after cut in pursuit of the holy grail of stabilisation and reduction of government expenditure. Over the past 30 years we have seen this, for example, in Europe with the crises in places like Greece and Spain and, in the 1990's, many took umbrage when the government of Prime Minister Mahathir in Malaysia refused to comply. It takes immense courage by political leaders to act differently from what the IMF and international economic "experts" demand as the cost for a semblance of economic stability.

Klein argues that this neoliberal approach is integral to the free-market project, which can only advance against a background of disasters. In June 2017 she further developed this thesis[18] by arguing that President Trump was creating chaos and uncertainty in order to bring about a situation in which no-one is sure of who to trust or of the direction in which to move. She said of the Trump White House that "they are trying to pull off a domestic shock doctrine. The goal is all-out war on the public sphere and the public interest, whether in the form of antipollution regulations or programmes for the hungry. In their place will be unfettered power and freedom for corporations."

Many of the economic and political problems faced today have been caused by this myopic emphasis on shareholder returns rather than long term organisational and societal viability. We live in a world in which many businesses are no longer willing to seriously consider all stakeholders[19]. The bias is clear: business activity takes precedence over any greater social consideration and profit that can be returned to shareholders is paramount.

Religion

Up to about the last quarter of the 20th century it was not uncommon to hear people speak of countries in religious terms. For example, France, Italy, Spain, and most South American countries would be labelled "Catholic"; Germany, the USA, the UK, Australia, New Zealand, and the Scandinavian countries would be labelled "Protestant"; while Indonesia, Malaysia, and most of the Middle Eastern countries would be labelled "Islamic". Today it is increasingly realised that many of the countries so labelled actually have secular constitutions and, even if many of their citizens have a particular religious affiliation, there is no special status associated with any particular religious faith. Despite this overall recognition of "nominal" versus "active" religious affiliation however, it remains true that, in most countries, religious groups hold a very significant ability to influence the societies within which they operate.

The widespread move to secularise societies is of concern to many with strong religious views. For example, in many places across the world, whether Christian, Muslim, Jewish, Hindu, Buddhist, etc, the move to a more inclusive society in which differing ethnicities, males and females, married and unmarried, etc have equal rights, responsibilities and opportunities is deplored as aiding the destruction of traditional values. Another example is that, in many countries, moves to enhance multiculturalism with its recognition of the validity of all faiths and moves for true equality for all people including members of the LBGTIQ+ community is seen as evidence of society in decline.

All the major faiths we see today have writings which they accept as authoritative – generally they either believe that they are directly given or inspired by God (the Divine) or, at the very least, they "contain" the "Word of God". In every case they were written hundreds, if not thousands, of years ago and, in most cases, they existed first as oral tradition that was passed down across the generations. Necessity required they reflected the world views and thinking of their day and, almost certainly, this influenced the message passed down. As stated, with at least those in the Jewish and Christian traditions, they existed as oral tradition for hundreds of years before being written – and all of them later, until the arrival of the printing press, were then copied by hand with the consequent very real possibility of inadvertent copying errors[20]. In the case of one accessing any of these works in a language that is different from the original used in the oral and/or manually transcribed language then this potential for inadvertent error is exacerbated because of issues that always arise around translation. None of these religious works are history or science treatises in the sense that we would understand history or science today. They are stories of "faith" and in every case they arose because people were pondering the world around them and seeking answers to the great existential questions of life such as: How did our world come into being? What is the meaning of life? Where did humanity come from? What happens after death? Why are there so many different races and languages? What should be my relationship with other people and with the Great Unknown?

Each faith developed its own answers to these questions – answers that were strongly impacted by their geographic, cultural and political environment. It could be argued that, with the exception of Buddhism (which has no "God" per se but rather is a quest for enlightenment), each developed a concept of God that was based on their own image, and which reflected this with strong anthropomorphism – a projection of the human characteristics seen as being most valuable and/or powerful. These concepts changed over time. For example, the Jewish concept of God as found in the Torah (or the Pentateuch of the Old Testament in Christianity) provides a range of different names for God with each indicating an evolution of the writers' understandings as to the nature of the divine. Along with these evolving understandings of the nature of God came evolving understandings of the power and influence of the divine. Understandably, anything in nature that could not be easily understood was attributed to the action of God and, as such, was deemed to be beyond human comprehension. The problem, as so well enunciated by J.B Phillips in his book "Your God Is Too Small"[21], is that attributing to "the activity of God", anything we do not yet understand ensures that, as our knowledge of the natural world develops through advances in science and cognitive ability, the very concept of God itself becomes increasingly irrelevant to the masses. It may well be that recognition of the truth in Phillips' message explains why at least some of the more conservative faiths and denominations support only limited educational opportunities for their adherents.

This situation is exacerbated by the fact that each of these major faiths as they are practised today is a complex mix of core teachings from their holy book, imports from other religious perspectives, later writings and teachings from religious scholars, traditions that have emerged, and, in some instances, concepts that border on the superstitious and/or ancient mythology. Across the world, for many of the general populace, it is partly this complex mix that has prompted a move away from traditional faiths. For others the same factors have facilitated the drive to fundamentalism by insisting that "the scriptures are our sole authority". This fundamentalist approach promotes a drive to ensure a narrow, and usually literal, interpretation of a work which is seen as being directly given by God. Very often it then seems as though unless one's scriptures specifically address an issue, then that issue should not be allowed to impinge on individual and/or group activity.

Looking at the early 21st Century religious scene, one finds vocal elements of most major faiths concentrating on the way in which they are different from any other with very little attention being paid to what they hold in common. Across all of them one can see an increasing influence by extremist groups that advocate the primacy of their particular faith and, in many cases – especially in Judaism, Christianity, and Islam – a history of tragic and horrific moves to use violence in the furtherance of their goals. The fact is that, psychologically, there is very little difference between the makeup of a fundamentalist Hindu, Buddhist, Jew, Christian, Muslim, or any other faith or philosophy. Immediately one adopts the view that only "my" way is right and that others should conform to "my" way of thought or belief, it is only the means adopted to bring about such conforming that may differ – the desired end is identical – conversion to my way of belief and religious practice. The forced conversions to Islam that we see in some places or, in some countries, the savage treatment of those who no longer claim to be Muslim, is not dissimilar in form or purpose from that found in the much earlier activities of The Inquisition and of some Christian missionaries up until relatively recent times. Fundamentalists, no matter their faith or philosophy, all have the common characteristics of a very narrow focus, a mind closed to the possibility that there could be any truth other than that which they advocate, and a burning desire that everyone else should conform to their way of belief and thinking.

At the other extreme of the religious spectrum lie those who argue that, in the end, all religions are basically the same; that no religious view could be correct because they are based on unprovable "assertions" and require "faith not evidence" for their underlying tenets. This then manifests itself in atheism (which, of itself, is actually a statement of faith) or agnosticism – a state of "not knowing" in which a person accepts that about their faith which they can support from independent research and/or personal experience yet, usually without actively discarding everything else. An agnostic accepts that there is much which is not and, so far as we are aware cannot, be proved. This "unproven" material is not necessarily written off as being false (although some people do take such an approach) but neither is it accepted as being truth even though it may be in the holy writings of whatever faith one follows[22].

Somewhere between both of these extremes of fundamentalism and atheism can be found most people no matter what the religious affiliation they may espouse and/or to what (if anything) they may give notional support in their personal devotions. The fact is that religious affiliation is largely a product of the society and family into which we are born. In reality, on a percentage basis, very few people ever actually change their religion. While they may shift between various strands of, for example, Christianity or Islam, people will tend to remain "Christian" or "Muslim" even though they may belong, for Christians, to the Catholic, Protestant, or Charismatic traditions and, for Muslims, to the Shia or Sunni traditions.

For the majority of people, whatever their faith, it seems to have very little real impact on their everyday life. In fact, the evidence seems to be that although large numbers of people claim adherence to a particular faith, they may seldom if ever attend a church, mosque, synagogue, temple or other place of worship and they have limited ability to explain in any depth the basic tenets of that faith.

To an extent it is this ambivalence or uncertainty found in the centre of the religious spectrum that, in times of stress and difficulty can drive a person to either end of the continuum. So it is that we have found a variety of new faiths or new expressions of old faiths (mainly from the "exotic east") collecting significant numbers of followers over the past fifty or so years. Over this time, we have also found the rise of tele-evangelists (both Christian and non-Christian) where some form of materialistic faith is proclaimed (follow this way and you will have all that you could ever need from both a materialistic and religious perspective) and where the promoters go on to amass large wealth and influence mainly from the money and goods given by followers. Cults capitalise on disillusion and uncertainty.

While ostensibly a force for good, today in many countries, religious biases still exert a negative impact on individuals, the economy, and society. This is seen in places like Afghanistan, Iran and Saudi Arabia where the religious views of the Taliban and/or other dominant parties, impact negatively on females and LBGT+ people. This is not confined to the Islamic faith. In 2022 it was seen in the decision by the US Supreme Court to overturn Roe vs Wade, regardless of the implications for the mental and physical health of women. It is a bias in which the framework for decisions tends to be found not in objective data and concern for overall societal well-being but in one's personal belief system. It can of course also be seen in, for example, across the Middle East (including Israel, the Palestinian Territories, Afghanistan, Iraq, Syria, Iran, Saudi Arabia, etc) and the USA. It can also have strong political implications.

Politics

2022 was the year in which the prospect of another war in Europe – something that, following the collapse of the USSR, was considered almost unimaginable only 30 years ago – became a tragic reality. While providing no supporting evidence, Russia invaded Ukraine on the pretext that most Ukrainians wanted ties with Russia. President Putin also made clear his concerns that Ukraine could join the North Atlantic Treaty Organisation (NATO) and so obtain a military alliance with the U.S. and Europe that would be a threat to Russia. At the time of writing (July 2024) there is no indication that peace is in the offing –

rather there remains the spectre that the conflict could escalate. The response by Putin to successful Ukrainian counter attacks in 2022 that liberated some thousands of kilometres of occupied territory reinforced this spectre. On September 19, 2022 Putin signed an order mobilising at least 300,000 military reservists and warned he is willing to use any military means necessary in the war with Ukraine. In December 2022 he floated the idea of a pre-emptive nuclear strike should the war spill over into Russia itself. This war adds to the disruption already extant from refugees escaping conflicts, economic turmoil, oppression and political upheaval in other places across the world.

Throughout the world today, far too often, there is either conflict or a tenuous ceasefire arrangement (such as in Korea) in which no party will disarm, no party trusts any other, and in which the majority of harm occurs among non-combatant citizens who just happen to be trying to eke out an existence in areas of conflict. While some would argue that it has always been thus, today's 24-hour news cycle (and the proliferation of social media to augment traditional media) means that we are constantly reminded of what is happening. This, of course, raises the question as to the witting or unwitting role filled by the media in exacerbating such a situation through their quest to meet the 24-hour news cycle. Adding to this are the facts of increasing media ownership consolidation and of media owners becoming increasingly willing to adopt and promote a particular political position. There is also the possibility that social media narrows perspectives to the point where people can be blinded to the whole picture. (This will be discussed further in later chapters.)

No matter the label of political entities, at its core, politics is all about power. Most politicians, no matter the idealism with which they enter politics, become seduced into the power game of obtaining and/or retaining their seat (and income) along with being the government of the country, state/territory, or local authority. The obtaining and the exercise of power takes precedence over all else.

On 23 August 2019, David Koch died. He was aged 79. Meyer argues that David Koch, along with his brother Charles, controlled Koch Industries and, for more than 30 years, they used a significant proportion of their vast wealth (currently in excess of $US 50 billion) to transform politics in the USA by supporting free market and libertarian ideals that are epitomised in the shareholder theory approach to economics and management – neoliberalism[23]. They became known as the face of the right-wing super-donor class in the modern era. They sponsored semi-annual gatherings of top conservative figures in order to move the Republican party to the right through the attendance at these by senior figures in the party. They also ensured the gatherings were attended by major political donors and even US supreme court justices as well as business and political leaders from outside of the USA. This process enabled them to push many of the policies that have become pillars of today's American conservatism, including, a few years ago, opposing Barack Obama's widened healthcare provision, Obamacare, and waging a sustained attack on government regulation including President Biden's attempts to combat the climate crisis.

Central to their impact is a lobby group, initially largely funded by Charles and David Koch, known as "Americans for Prosperity". Since 2004 this lobby group has expanded into every State across the USA.

Of course, Americans for Prosperity (AFP) are only one among many US lobbyists. Lobbyists may be "right wing" or "left wing" orientated and come from a wide variety of political, religious, and social backgrounds that includes the trade union movement. There are over 20,000 lobbying organisations in the US with about 600 having a permanent presence in Washington to directly contact their targets. In the USA, as in almost all countries, lobbying tends to be closely linked to financing. Politicians and political parties need funds. Supplying those funds in large enough quantities buys influence. The main objective of a lobbyist is to influence the decision making, whether at an executive, legislative, federal, state or local level. Their influence can also be applied to block the decision-making process. Therefore, influence is created for the long-term by forming strong contacts with politicians and this is often accompanied by financial support relating to electoral campaigns. Clearly this means that the influence of a lobbying organisation is not proportional to its size but rather to its financial resources.

This matter of lobbying is true across the world. Lobbying is big business in every country. It results in politicians being influenced by outside forces that answer only to their organisation and are not accountable to any electorate. In such conditions, bias is unavoidable.

Another political factor is the rise of mass citizen movements – some of which are extremist.

In Sri Lanka, 2022 saw economic collapse. Economic mismanagement had led to the situation in which fuel shortages caused long queues at filling stations, as well as frequent blackouts, and some crucial medicines had run low. There was widespread crop failure and Sri Lanka had to supplement its food stocks from abroad, which made its foreign currency shortage even worse. In the face of this, in March 2022 tens of thousands of Sri Lankans took to the streets of Colombo, and while that included some opposition politicians, most protesters were average Sri Lankans from all ethnic backgrounds. While concentrated in Colombo, there were also small protests in solidarity across Sri Lanka as almost all citizens were facing serious challenges. The protesters demanded the resignation of the Rajapaksa-led government and, shortly after, Rajapaksa fled the country. (He later returned and resumed at least partial control.)

On January 6, 2021 a violent mob of Pro-Trump supporters and far right extremists stormed the U.S. Capitol as members of Congress were meeting to ratify the 2020 Presidential Election results. The crowd began gathering the morning of January 6 to participate in a "Stop the Steal" rally, listening to political speeches near the White House, including from President Donald Trump, before marching to the Capitol several blocks away. The rally was organized by various conservative political groups and donors. During the riot, there was serious damage to the Capitol building; police officers were attacked and seriously injured with one being killed; there were calls to lynch Vice President Pence; and the offices of Democratic politicians were ransacked. By December 2022, a bipartisan enquiry was investigating all aspects of the riot, information was being made public, and Donald Trump has been subpoenaed to appear before the committee and answer questions under oath. (As at the time of writing (April 2024) Donald Trump is facing 91 felony counts across two state courts and two different federal districts, any of which could potentially produce a prison sentence. He is also dealing with a civil suit in New York that could force drastic changes to his business empire, including closing down its operations in his home state. Meanwhile, he is the leading Republican candidate in the race to become the next President.)

All of such pressure, in many societies today, ensures that political parties have moved from a multi-party focus on what is good for the relevant area, to a focus on what will best get us into power or maintain or position of power. In the USA this was seen in the refusal by the Republican-controlled Senate to hold confirmation hearings for Supreme Court nominees towards the end of the Obama presidency and the rushing through of nominees during the Trump presidency. The current make-up of the Supreme Court is heavily weighted in favour of a conservative rather than a progressive judiciary and this, as has been seen in the overthrow of Roe versus Wade, has implications for everyone.

Social Media

Social media started innocuously enough – an internet-based way of maintaining contact with old friends and, through this, to develop a network of new friends.

In the early 2010s the social media that we used was mostly just about what one's close friends posted or wanted to share. However, as internet and social media use increased, much of this has become controlled by algorithmic recommendations. The result is that now users have very little agency because of the extent to which content is controlled and curated by algorithmic recommendations. This clearly impacts what social media users see in their feed and it can make us more passive in the way we engage with content: it makes us less engaged with our personal taste because we're largely being shown what we like rather than finding that for ourselves.

It has always been possible for a person to ignore information with which they disagreed and to only pay attention to information that supports their world view. Today, however, the availability of an echo chamber that will reinforce what we want to believe has never been so easy. Also, because of the nature of the world wide web, the magnitude of this echo chamber encompasses the entire earth. Somewhere there will always be at least one other person who will tell you whatever you want to hear with truth and fact checking not even available as an optional extra.

As will be discussed later, humans have a tendency to believe what is most frequently and vehemently proclaimed. If enough people are saying something then, regardless of its veracity, we tend to believe it must be true. This is especially the case if what we hear contains at least some truthful or accurate element. Even if it is diametrically different to any view we have previously espoused, this can still happen. Should such material be then discussed by other mass media or on other social media channels, we will be further inclined to accept it as fact. There is a sense in which social media has encouraged us to lose (or deliberately suspended) our ability to think critically.

Current developments in the realm of artificial intelligence have exacerbated this. The internet is crowded with material in which deep fakes have been used to give the impression that partisan views and specific products/services are endorsed by highly respected and well-known figures. Such material invariable shows the apparent endorser and uses his or her voice. The fakes are sometimes so realistic that they are even able to bluff their way through established security systems. It is becoming increasingly problematic to distinguish between reality and fake unless we are physically in the same room – and, with holograms now becoming available, even that final barrier may be in danger of being breached.

We may not be actively involved in business, religion, or politics and we may not be regular users of social media but, as discussed, each of these has capacity to influence the society in which we live. When operating conjointly they are critical components of the forces that promote bias.

For some forty or so years the western world has been rolling back legislation that would protect society. We have seen increasing moves to individual employment contracts where, especially in the case of lower-level workers, the might of a corporation is pitted against the weakness of an individual in a "divide and conquer" exercise. Returns to shareholders are king. Trade Unions have been emasculated and the employer is firmly in control of an unbalanced system. The result has been significant reduction in full-time jobs and a corresponding increase in part-time or casual employment. Remuneration increases (when provided) have been strenuously opposed and, as far as possible, kept to below the level of inflation. (There has been no such opposition to increased company profits even though these can be a key driver of inflation.) We have seen a reduction in government oversight in areas such as building and construction with the result that, as evidenced in England's 2017 Grenfell Tower disaster, sub-standard materials have been utilised because developers have few checks and balances. We have seen public assets sold off to private industry with the result that, instead of returning public sector "profits" to either the State or using them to keep prices low, tolls on roads and highways, utility prices, and transport costs have increased in order to improve profits to private sector shareholders. The concept of "the commons" in which the public at large own and benefit through common ownership has been ridiculed and denigrated as being "inefficient" and/or as "holding back the economy". The biases advocated by Hayek, Friedman, Buchanan, and the like have been seized and endorsed through business, religion, and politics. This has implications for every person across the world. That the current business and economic paradigm needs review was strongly reinforced in 2020 when the World Economic Forum in Davos, Switzerland, argued for a significant shift in economic emphasis because "our current outlook is based on fundamentally wrong assumptions and that dramatic transformation is possible with a change of mindset."

A November 2022 article in the Washington Post asks the question "Why do our brains believe lies?"[24] The writer, journalist Richard Sima, argues that "Correcting lies and misinformation is difficult because learning the truth doesn't delete them from our memory". He argues that "our psychological biases and predispositions make us vulnerable to falsehoods. As a result, misinformation is more likely to be believed, remembered, and later recalled – even after we learn that it was false." Drawing on studies from a variety of sources, Sima writes: "… "By default, people will believe anything they see or hear," said Stephan Lewandowsky, a cognitive psychologist at the University of Bristol who specializes in understanding how people respond to corrections of misinformation. In our day-to-day lives, "that makes a lot of sense because most things that we're exposed to are true," he said. …"

The article goes on: "At the same time, the more we see something repeated, the more likely we are to believe it to be true. This "illusory truth effect" arises because we use familiarity and ease of understanding as a shorthand for truth; the more something is repeated, the more familiar and fluent it feels whether it is misinformation or fact. … "There is only typically one true version of a claim and an infinite number of ways you could falsify it, right?" said Nadia Brashier, a psychology professor at Purdue University who studies why people fall for fake news and misinformation. "So, if you hear something over and over again, probabilistically, it's going to be the true thing."

Sima continues: "We are also more susceptible to misinformation that fits into our worldviews or social identities, and we can fall into confirmation bias, which is the tendency to look for and favor information fitting what we already believe."

Sima's article reinforces what has already been explained in this book. From birth our environment conditions our brains to the point where unconscious biases exist. These biases are then reinforced as long as we remain primarily in the same (or very similar) environment and, even when we change our environment, these biases will continue to impact on our behaviour until (or unless) we become conscious of them and make a deliberate choice to challenge them. Yet, even once identification and control have been implemented, there is still a strong probability that, although reduced in force, they will continue to impact us. We may even find that we control one set of biases only to have a second set emerge!

Again, quoting Lewandowsky, Sima explains the reason for this is that "the falsehood and its correction coexist and compete to be remembered. Brain imaging studies conducted by Lewandowsky and his colleagues found evidence that our brains store both the original piece of misinformation as well as its correction. "It seems to be cognitively almost impossible to listen to something, understand it and, at the same time, not believe it," Lewandowsky said. Dismissing misinformation requires a whole extra cognitive step of tagging it as false in our memory. "But by that time, in a sense, it's too late, because it's already in your memory," Lewandowsky said."

As was pointed out earlier, changing our neural wetware is an arduous and complex process that can easily be derailed. Simply hitting "ctrl-alt-del" doesn't work!

Questions for group discussion:

1. "There are four key social environment areas that continue to have a significant impact – business, religion, politics and social media." Discuss this statement with reference to the key cultural environments that impact on your own world view and biases.
2. "Consistently it has been argued by many researchers that there is very little (if any) empirical evidence that this "trickle-down effect", while much loved and advocated by the executives who reap large benefits from short term results, ever actually benefits the company (or the nation) in the long term." Discuss this statement with reference to the current state of world affairs.
3. "Correcting lies and misinformation is difficult because learning the truth doesn't delete them from our memory" How is your willingness to critically examine your world view impacted by past information that may be of dubious quality?
4. "From birth our environment conditions our brains to the point where unconscious biases exist. These biases are then reinforced as long as we remain primarily in the same (or very similar) environment." To what extent are you prepared to change your social/cultural environment when you realise your current world view may not be the most appropriate for today? Why? Why not?
5. "So, if you hear something over and over again, probabilistically, it's going to be the true thing." Do you believe this is really the case? Why? What measures do you take to validate the veracity of material to which you are constantly exposed?

Notes

1 Wilkinson, Richard & Pickett, Kate, *"The Spirit Level: why equality is better for everyone"*, 3rd ed. 2010, Penguin Books, London, UK
2 Dovidio et al, op cit, p.4
3 A "Freudian slip", also called parapraxis, is an error in speech, memory, or physical action that occurs due to the interference of an unconscious subdued wish or internal train of thought
4 Loci Waquant's book "Punishing the Poor: the neoliberal government of social insecurity", 2009, Duke University Press, is a valuable discussion on this

5 In July 2023 Prime Minister Albanese of Australia announced an enquiry into offshore detention contractors. On January 31, 2024, the media reported that: "A high-ranking Australian official has voiced grave moral and integrity concerns about the waste and mismanagement of millions of taxpayer dollars as part of Australia's controversial offshore detention regime. ... Home Affairs assistant secretary Derek Elias' claims that taxpayer funds may have been spent on services that were never delivered and on questionable tasks. ..." (https://www.smh.com.au/national/sovereign-borders-wasted-a nd-mismanaged-millions-claims-senior-official-20240130-p5f15b.html)
6 Despite this Convention and a previous High Court decision on April 21, 2024 it was reported that the UK Government has now passed a law enabling deportation of asylum seekers to Rwanda. https://www.bbc.com/news/explainers-61782866
7 Hayek, Friedrich, 1960. *The Constitution of Liberty*, University of Chicago Press
8 Friedman, Milton, 1962. *Capitalism and Freedom,* University of Chicago Press
9 Buchanan, James M. and Tulloch, Gordon. 1962, *The Calculus of Consent: logical foundations of constitutional democracy* University of Michigan Press
10 Buchanan, James M. 1977, *The Limits of Liberty: between Anarchy and Leviathan* The University of Chicago Press
11 As previously noted, her actual statement was: "There is no such thing as society. There are individuals, and there are families"
12 For a balanced discussion covering the difficulties encountered when trying to understand neoliberalism and its strengths (there certainly are some) and its weaknesses, see https://www.theguardian.com/news/2017/nov/14/the-fatal-flaw-of-neoli beralism-its-bad-economics?CMP=share_btn_link
13 http://www.smh.com.au/business/ceo-pay-more-complicated-tha n-it-looks-20150112-12mg19.html
14 Adam Smith "The Wealth of Nations", reprinted by Penguin Books Ltd, 1982
15 https://www.imf.org/en/Publications/fandd
16 https://www.imf.org/en/Publications/fandd/issues/2024/03/Symposium-Rethinking-E conomics-Angus-Deaton
17 Klein, Naomi, 2007, *The Shock Doctrine: The Rise of Disaster Capitalism*, Random House of Canada
18 https://www.theguardian.com/books/2017/jun/10/naomi-klein-now-fight-back-aga inst-politics-fear-shock-doctrine-trump?CMP=share_btn_link
19 It is important to note that the Shareholder Theory espoused by scholars such as Hayek and Friedman has been countered by Stakeholder Theory in which, while the necessity for and importance of profit is recognised, the prime emphasis is on morals and values in managing an organisation. This counter concept was first propounded by *R. Edward Freeman in his 1984 work, Strategic Management: a stakeholder approach. Boston: Pitman. Later works by Freeman expounding on this concept include* Freeman, R. Edward, *Managing for Stakeholders: Trade-offs or Value Creation*, Journal of Business Ethics, 1 January 2010, Vol.96, pp.7–9; Freeman, R & Auster, Ellen, *Values, Authenticity, and Responsible Leadership* Journal of Business Ethics, 2011, Vol.98(Supplement 1), pp.15–23; Purnell, Lauren & Freeman, R. *Stakeholder Theory, Fact/Value Dichotomy, and the Normative Core: How Wall Street Stops the Ethics Conversation* Journal of Business Ethics, 2012, Vol.109(1), pp.109–116; Freeman, R. Edward, *The New Story of Business: Towards a More Responsible Capitalism* Business and Society Review, September 2017, Vol.122(3), pp.449–465
20 Errors were not restricted to "inadvertent copying errors". In 2015 it was reported that one of the 10 remaining copies of 1631's Sinners Bible, with its infamous typo imploring readers to commit adultery was up for sale, The *Wicked Bible*, or the *Sinners' Bible*, is an edition of the Bible published in 1631 by Robert Barker and Martin Lucas, the royal printers in London, meant to be a reprint of the King James Bible. The name is derived from a mistake made by the compositors: in the Ten Commandments in Exodus 20:14, the word "not" was omitted from the sentence

"Thou shalt not commit adultery," causing the verse to instead read "Thou shalt commit adultery."

21 Phillips, JB, 1952, *Your God Is Too Small*, McMillan Books

22 In the Christian faith, this perspective was well documented by such theologians as Rudolf Bultmann and Paul Tillich with, later, clergy such as Rev Leslie D. Weatherhead (*The Christian Agnostic*. 1965, Abingdon Press) and Bishop John Spong (*Why Christianity Must Change*, 1998, Harper Collins)

23 The role of the Koch brothers is explored in depth by Jane Mayer in her book "Dark Money: The hidden history of the billionaires behind the rise of the radical right", 2016, Scribe Publications, Australia and UK.

24 https://www.washingtonpost.com/wellness/2022/11/03/misinformation-brain-beliefs/

5

BIAS AND SOCIETAL CHANGE – AFFIRMATIVE ACTION, EEO, DIVERSITY AND INCLUSION

In March 2024 it was announced that a non-white female Australian footballer had been arrested and charged in the UK because she made a racist slur to a white police officer during a confrontation involving payment for a taxi ride. (She purportedly called the officer a "stupid white bastard") This event drew attention to the question of whether non-white minority groups are indulging in anti-white racism – which echoes the "White Lives Matter" movement that arose in response to the "Black Lives Matter" emphasis. The arrest led Australia's race discrimination commissioner to say: "racism is about power. And in Australia [*as in most of the western world*], power is held by white people."[1] Underlying the claim that majority groups can be victims of discrimination lies a reaction against any form of societal change that threatens traditional power structures. (Italics comment by author.)

In March 2024 it was announced that The University of Florida is terminating all its diversity, equity and inclusion (DEI) positions to comply with a state law passed in January that prohibits state or federal funds from being used to fund the programs. The university, with more than 30,000 undergraduates, said in a memo issued on Friday that it was closing its office of the chief diversity officer, eliminating DEI positions and administrative appointments, and halting DEI-focused contracts with outside vendors.[2]

The early decades of the 21st century have seen an upsurge in nationalism and opposition to what is denigrated as "woke" behaviour of gender equality in the workplace, universality of human rights, and a perceived lessening of the rights once automatically enjoyed by particular segments of any society. Powerful interest groups have emerged to promote causes which seek to revert to an idealised yesteryear. Initially many of these groups were trivialised as "fringe" but, as the years have passed, they have become increasingly influential. Their targets include

DOI: 10.4324/9781003528340-6

almost all those societal segments that have been most in need of (and who may be benefitting from) culture change in society.

In March 2023, the Diversity Council of Australia released a report on "Culturally and Marginalised (CARM) Women in Leadership"[3] which focused on how the intersections of two key marginalising characteristics – race and gender – are still operating in workplaces to lock CARM women out of leadership. It made clear that "Despite being ambitious, capable, and resilient, and well positioned to contribute to their own and their organisation's success, CARM women continue to be scarce across senior leadership positions in Australia and internationally."

As indicated earlier, discrimination is one of the outcomes from a bias that sees an individual, group or society as being, in some way, inferior to another. The focus is on what differentiates rather than on what is held in common.

Since about the middle of the 20th century we have seen increasing levels of cultural diversity in the populations of most developed countries. Internal and external conflicts and wars in Africa, Europe, parts of Asia and the Middle East have led to displacement of citizens and a surge in those seeking refuge in safe havens. This exacerbates the disruption caused by flood, famine, fire, and other environmental impacts and is additional to the movement of people seeking economic advancement and security available from the growth of globalisation. Associated with this there has been the rise of nationalist forces in many of the places to which refugees and other migrants have fled.

There are as many different cultures as there are different groups. Some of these groups range from small to large (think about families, occupational groups, and small local organisations to national associations or public corporations), and others are even larger (think nations or even humanity as a whole). Culture develops and changes over time as groups adapt to their environments, including the physical environment. Same or similar things are accomplished differently across diverse groups, which then presents challenges when individuals from different cultural backgrounds need to collaborate. The heterogeneity of groups and culture is a great source of complexity. It raises the issue of reactions to diversity.

If, because of my background and social conditioning, I am biased in favour of the status quo (whatever it may be for me) then the thought of change is disquieting. It disturbs me and challenges my comfort zone. This is true whether the diversity issue relates to race, colour, gender, sexuality, body type, disability, or any other distinguishing factor. These, along with globalisation, refugees, and changes in societal norms can trigger responses that demonise people who are, in reality, doing little other than seeking to better themselves and to contribute to society.

At home and in the workplace, traditionally activities have been classified as being part of "men's roles" or "women's roles". The widely accepted stereotype appears to have been that the male role was to hunt and provide while the female role was to gather and nurture. This stereotype led to the myth that leadership roles of any kind were a male function, and, in turn, this led to the belief that education was only for males because women would not need it. Accordingly, from at least the eighteenth century, males could become entrepreneurs, engineers, doctors, scientists, politicians, managers and the like while women were relegated to support roles. It is less than 200 years since this paradigm started to be seriously challenged and it is still advocated today by some individuals and societies. Although usually masked, this is still almost always a contributing factor where the dominance of men in political, religious, managerial and Board positions is found and in the reluctance of some occupations to encourage gender (and other) equality.

When interactions between societies was difficult, there was little or no understanding of cultural differences – a very small number of people may observe a different culture and surmise, but for the most people "our way of doing things" remained "right". Without input from other cultures, each society accepted that its culture was the norm. As societies grew and colonialisation developed then new understandings emerged. The conquerors became masters and the conquered became subservient vassals at best and, far too frequently, slaves in their own land or slaves to be deported as disposable goods for the use in other places by the conquerors. The culture of the dominant society became that to which everyone must conform. We know that this paradigm was extant from at least 2000 BCE.

From about the 17th to the 19th century CE, these conquerors tended to be primarily white, and the myth of white superiority emerged. The vast majority of today's problems around colour and racism stem from this. It is certainly a driver for many of the concerns expressed about the rise of China's economic power. As has been said elsewhere in relation to geopolitical change[4]: "The concept of an Asian century in any form is an abomination to those with racist tendencies. For those who believe that only Caucasians have the "right" to world domination, the thought that countries that were once our colonial outposts with resources to be plundered is horrific. We can be sure that such people will present every negative stereotype and prejudice in order to denigrate Asians and to create a fear as to what might happen should they be in control. It is this concern about the unknown, especially should China become the dominant power in tomorrow's world, that drives much of the rhetoric and fear mongering that we have found extensively since at least the start of 2019. Opposition and overt resistance are a far easier path than dealing with "why" this change is occurring and "how" it can be handled in a functional manner.

This remains true in 2024. (As an aside, it is important to note that the moves by China to influence and/or control what happens in other countries is a separate issue and it does raise serious security concerns. However, identical security concerns are equally important and valid in relation to any other country – inclusive of USA, Russia, Great Britain, Iran, Iraq, Syria, Israel, Australia, etc – when it seeks to influence or control what happens in another country.) Despite what many may think, when it comes to national sovereignty, there are serious problems with endorsing a "winner takes all" mentality.

The morality of a "winner takes all" approach as the status quo has always been questioned by a minority within every dominant societal group. The 17th and 18th century's widespread slavery of non-Europeans was a classic example of "winner take all" mindset. "We won, we're white, we're dominant and in control, you don't matter except as chattels," was widely accepted. But a few prominent, influential people like Englishman, William Wilberforce (who died in 1833) challenged this and, despite vehement opposition, they succeeded in bringing about change. Wilberforce was but one abolitionist but, today, he may be the most widely known advocate of abolitionism because of his role in heading the parliamentary campaign against the British slave trade for 20 years until the passage of the Slave Trade Act of 1807. This followed action in Denmark which, in 1792 had banned import of slaves to its West Indies colonies (although the law only took effect from 1803). It was followed by the United States with the passing of legislation that banned the slave trade from start of 1808 – thus reflecting a (then) new interpretation of Thomas Jefferson's statement in the US Declaration of Independence, that "all men are created equal".

Understanding and applying this understanding of a change in the "equality" paradigm has grown exponentially over the last 100 or so years.

"Executive Order No. 10925", was signed by President John F. Kennedy on 6 March 1961, and included a provision that government contractors "take *affirmative action* to ensure that applicants are employed, and employees are treated [fairly] during employment, without regard to their race, creed, color, or national origin". This was designed to promote actions that achieve non-discrimination. It was followed by Title VII of the Civil Rights Act of 1964 to "ensure equality of opportunity by vigorously enforcing federal legislation prohibiting discrimination in employment". Subsequently, in 1965, President Lyndon B. Johnson issued Executive Order 11246 which required government employers to "hire without regard to race, religion and national origin". It had become illegal, in the USA, to discriminate on the basis of religion, race, sex, colour, national origin, age, or disability when employing staff. Equal Employment Opportunity (EEO) had come into existence.

Earlier I said: "For most people, bias is a human construct of disproportionate weight *in favour of* or *against* an idea or thing, usually in a way that is closed-minded, prejudicial, or unfair." Kennedy and Johnson's executive orders, while seeking to stop inequitable or unfair treatment of people, immediately drew the ire of many who currently benefitted from the status quo. There were many who vehemently opposed affirmative action on the grounds that it was "reverse bias" – in other words it was disadvantageous to those who benefitted from the current approach. Many of the societal problems in the US (and other countries) today, are exacerbated by an on-going desire for an imagined ideal world that preceded any promotion of equality across gender, race, sexuality, and the like.

Many years ago, I noticed that some farmers in New Zealand had problems with tree saplings that had been impacted by wind and were no longer growing straight. One of their remedies was to draw the tree in the opposite direction, well past the desired upright status, and secure it in this position for considerable periods. When asked why they were doing this, they explained that they had to over-correct for a period until the tree was strong enough to withstand the wind and for it to eventually grow straight. Left to its own devices, powerful forces would ensure the tree grew in a manner that prevented it fulfilling its purpose of being an effective windbreak, protection for farmland, and providing shade for animals. Intervention was required for an optimal environment.

A similar situation pertains for affirmative action and its derivatives. Affirmative action is a bias designed to address some imbalance in society. It is a deliberate intervention intended to promote an optimal environment. In achieving this there have been (and probably will continue to be) many examples of "over-correction for a period" to the end that, eventually the desired equity of treatment will become the norm. For those wanting to maintain the status quo, any and every example of such "over correction" is an example of what is wrong and explains why any form of affirmative action must be opposed because of the threat it embodies.

As per the initial US legislation, across the world, today affirmative action typically involves introducing measures to raise the participation of members of a disadvantaged group in the areas of education, employment and business, where they had been historically excluded or underrepresented. Measures taken are generally in the form of preferential policies toward members of a designated group, based on criteria such as a particular ethnicity, gender, or religion[5].

Affirmative action takes its moral force from a corrective justice ideal and "allocates scarce resources so as to remedy a specific type of disadvantage, one that arises from the illegitimate use of a morally irrelevant characteristic"[6]. Sabbagh goes on to say "… [affirmative action's] goal is to counter deeply entrenched social practices that reproduce group-structured inequality (even in the absence of intentional discrimination) by creating positive externalities beyond individual recipients." He then makes the point that

> Direct affirmative action … can thus be criticized for conflicting with two esteemed principles of the different societies under consideration: the meritocratic principle, according to which the most qualified applicant should always be selected, and the principle of "blindness" to characteristics such as race, gender, or caste.

In the US for many years, military academies such as West Point, the Naval Academy, the Air Force Academy and the Coast Guard Academy, have used race as a factor in choosing cadets. Their goal is to reflect in officer positions the diversity of rank-and-file members of the military, as well as to reflect the diversity of the US itself. Over recent days this practice has come under attack with a request to the US Supreme Court, by a conservative group (Students for Fair Admissions), to alter West Point's admissions process, which takes race – as well as a host of other factors – when selecting students who aspire to be future army officers. The military academies' position is that: "Our nation's military leaders have determined that a diverse army officer corps is a national security imperative and that achieving that diversity requires limited consideration of race in selecting those who join the army as cadets,"

Following earlier success (2023) with the supreme court agreeing to end affirmative action in higher education by striking down the race-conscious admissions policies at the universities of Harvard and North Carolina, Students for Fair Admissions argued that the military academies selection process was unconstitutional. The Supreme Court's decision announced on February 2, 2024, did not fully resolve whether institutions like West Point could use race-based criteria for admissions, when it refused to immediately accede to the complaint. The Court stated: "The record before this court is underdeveloped, and this order should not be construed as expressing any view on the merits of the constitutional question." The statement appears to leave the matter open to new applications – something that may be likely given the response from Edward Blum, president of the group: "It is disappointing that the young men and women who apply to West Point for the foreseeable future will have their race used as a factor to admit or reject them," he said. "Every year this case languishes in discovery, trial and appeals means that our nation's best and brightest young men and women will be classified, sorted and preferred based on their skin color rather than just on their abilities."[7]

The history of affirmative action, however, starts well before President Kennedy's Executive Order of 1961 – and it can entrench racial discrimination.

Illustrative of this is the experience of Malaysia. When discussing affirmative action in Malaysia, Hock Guan Lee[8], a Fellow of the Institute of Southeast Asian Studies in Singapore, makes the point that

> During the colonial period, the British had already put into practice pre-
> ferential treatment of sorts in the selection and training of Malays for the
> elite administrative service. In 1948, an article in the Federation of Malaya
> Agreement stipulated the Malay Ruler to safeguard the special position of
> the Malays and to ensure the reservation for Malays of such proportion as
> he may deem reasonable of positions in the public service and of scholar-
> ships, exhibitions and other similar educational or training privileges …
> and, … of [business] permits and licenses. This later became part of Article
> 153 of the Malaysian Constitution.

Lee is very critical of this situation. He points out that "Malaysia's affirmative action policy differs from those of other countries in one crucial respect – it is "the politically dominant majority group which introduces preferential policies to raise its economic status as against that of an economically more advanced minority". The majority ethnic group that has the power to legislate the affirmative action policies and receive the benefits from those policies in Malaysia are the Malays. Conversely, it is the Chinese and Indian ethnic minorities, the most advanced economic groups, who have felt most victimized by the affirmative action policies. Another unique feature of Malaysian affirmative action is that, as already indicated, preferential treatment for the Malays and other indigenous groups was written into the Malaysian Constitution, under Article 153. In other words, affirmative action in Malaysia is a constitutionally sanctioned and exclusively ethnic-based policy where only the Malays and other native groups are entitled to receive preferential treatment. Besides being written into the Constitution, the wording of Article 153 links the ethnic preferential treatment to the safeguarding of the "special position" of the Malay community. This has given rise to the prevalent and prevailing Malay popular opinion that views preferential treatment as part of their "special rights" and thus not open to negotiation.

Lee argues that this affirmative action has led to the formation of "ethnic enclaves" in Malaysian society because "… the Chinese and Indians, confronted with systemic discrimination against them, have also formed their ethnic enclaves as survival strategies". He continues that the Malaysian Government is aware of issues around the practice and, since at least 2001, "government has introduced various steps to modify the ethnic preferential policy …."

As can be seen, the concept of affirmative action is a hotly debated issue – and it doesn't always focus on helping minorities. This broader application is reflected in a 2006 study[9] that argues affirmative action per se is far more controversial than anti-discrimination activity but that the distinctions between them are clearer in theory than in practice because

> While the main focus of this legislation is the prohibition of discrimination in employment, the act also allows the courts, when finding that an employer is engaging in an unlawful employment practice, to "order such affirmative action as may be appropriate, which may include reinstatement or hiring of employees".

While acknowledging affirmative action policies are universally controversial even if they are often introduced or supported as only *temporary* remedies for existing social inequities, it doesn't mean they should be discarded. When used as a temporary "band-aid" they can be introduced in the hope that a temporary affirmative action program that enhances diversity and reduces inequality between groups can persistently alter those outcomes[10] and this can be effective. Researching the situation in the USA, Miller concludes that, in his studies

> … affirmative action sharply increases an establishment's black share of employees, with the share continuing to increase over time. … Strikingly, I find that the black share of employees *continues to grow* even after an employer is deregulated. In the five years after an establishment is last observed as a contractor, its black share of employees increases by an *additional* 0.8 percentage points. This persistence is evident more than a decade following deregulation.

In other words, although controversial, he finds affirmative action does succeed in addressing at least some long-term organisational imbalance.

Haley in 2006[11], found that attitudes towards affirmative action radically rise or decline depending on how the term "affirmative action" is framed and/or what specific policy is under consideration. It argues that "... people tend to adopt those conceptualizations of affirmative action that best align with, or help to justify, their existing predilections." Perhaps this framing issue is part of the reason that, today, we are far more likely to encounter "diversity" rather than either affirmative action or EEO. A rose by any other name?

The shift to speak of "diversity" rather than affirmative action or even EEO may be an important step forward[12] in transforming negativity. Burns et al.'s study[13] stated: "Affirmative action has been a particularly contentious policy issue that has polarised contributions to the debate. Over recent times in most western countries, support for affirmative action has, however, been largely snuffed out or beaten into retreat and replaced by the concept of 'diversity management'." They argue that "... there are strong ethical grounds for those organisations which seek to do well, to reassert affirmative action programmes in the global efforts to eradicate systemic discrimination and disadvantage." Their argument is that speaking of diversity rather than affirmative action or EEO sanitises the issues of power, disadvantage and inequality by removing them from any context that might provide the traction to command attention. Highly political, emotive words such as "'racism', 'sexism', 'anti-racism', 'feminism' and 'discrimination', are replaced by the less contentious language of " 'diversity', 'multiculturalism' and 'ethnicity'." Their view is that a fundamental philosophical difference exists between the concept of affirmative action and that of diversity. They cite an earlier study (Thornton 2001[14]) to explain the difference.

> ... affirmative action [begins] from the implied premise that there is an injustice or an inequality that needs to be remedied, such as sexism, racism, homophobia or disablism: diversity obscures the issue of inequality which is at the heart of the matter.
>
> *(Thornton, 2001, p. 94).*

They continue: "Diversity management also ensures that decisions are made at the discretion of management, and business interests are served without compromise, constraint or interference from external agencies".

Burns and Schapper address directly the claim that affirmative action is "reverse discrimination" – that affirmative action is a form of discrimination that can be equated to the injustices that occasioned the "supposed" need for it. They say that policies of affirmative action are treated by its detractors as though they sanction the illegitimate expropriation of jobs and university placements. Such pejorative statements, say Burns and Schapper, while maintaining an appearance of balanced reason, also serve to deny or, at best, bury the positive intentions of affirmative action. Their view is that underlying opposition is the reality "that whites or white males might actually lose something through policies of affirmative action [but this] cannot be acknowledged by detractors because doing so would mean conferring legitimacy to the moral basis of affirmative action." Consequently "this issue of potential loss is never acknowledged. Instead, we see invocations for justice and rights, the ethical basis of which are never fully explored."

Returning to Kennedy's Executive Order, the purpose of affirmative action is clear: "take *affirmative action* to ensure that applicants are employed, and employees are treated [fairly] during employment, without regard to their race, creed, color, or national origin". At its core, as Burns and Schapper make clear, the essence of affirmative action is merit, and the qualities and virtues that institutions define as worthy of honour and social esteem. But, they argue, there is no idea of merit that is innocent of prejudice. The notion of merit underpins organisational structures that "shape the opportunities, or lack thereof, for certain individuals". Excellence or competence have never been the only defining factors and have never been applied impartially for "it was not always the best who were hired". Affirmative action, EEO and, at its best, diversity are exhibitions of conscious bias designed to ensure greater equity of treatment for all.

Of recent years there have been attempts to further refine the concept of affirmative action, EEO and diversity by adding the term "inclusion". A British study[15], points out that an undesirable implication from early affirmative action and EEO initiatives was the assumption that difference inevitably equals disadvantage – something that contributed to the stigmatisation of minority groups and alienated majority groups. Accordingly, the shift to diversity management emphasised individual difference over social group–based difference and downplayed discrimination and disadvantage, while being upbeat about the positive value of group-based difference. They argue that "the cornerstone of diversity management is the belief that it will deliver benefits to the organisation; in other words, that there is a business case for workforce diversity". "Inclusion" advances this.

> Inclusion takes the next step and creates an inclusive environment for all. … the shift to inclusion may also reflect the growing concern that business case rhetoric might have run its course. It may symbolise recognition that diversity practitioners and organisations need to search for new rationales that acknowledge that workforce diversity (in all its breadth) is both an inescapable labour market reality (whether or not it adds value) and a social expectation that organisations must adapt to.

This is an important consideration. As has already been demonstrated, bias focuses on what differentiates us: business gives primacy to investors over employees, religion gives primacy to "my" faith, politics gives primacy to "my" party, etc. Factors that can identify my ingroup ("us") from others ("them") enable us to ensure that "we" are supported regardless of the impact on "them". Using terms such as EEO, affirmative action and diversity draws attention to such differences.

We are all members of a variety of "ingroups". There is the "ingroup" of our family, of our community, of our religious affiliation (or non-affiliation), of our workplace, our sporting or social community etc. The probability of the identical people always being the only members of each of these different groups is extremely low. The reality is that the groups of which we are a member form collections of Venn Diagrams where there are differing quantities and qualities of commonalities across all factors and for each individual. Accordingly, what we consider to be our "ingroup" will vary with the context in which it is considered. In the main, we tend to overlook this reality or, when challenged on any perceived manifestation of bias, use such examples to support the contention that "I'm not biased" or "I don't discriminate". The reality is (as a Venn Diagram may illustrate) that each of these groups of which I am a member may well exclude potential members who are not "one of us" in relation to any criterion we may choose to apply. We may well accept into one of our "ingroups" people who would be excluded from another. In other words, it is possible that the same person is, in some instances, "one of us" while, in others, being "one of them".

Put this way, concentrating on "inclusion" might be a far better emphasis for confronting bias because it seeks to encourage consideration and celebration of what we have in common rather than on what holds us apart. It is also a key component of treating others with unconditional respect. The relationship is not one of "us" and "them" but of different individuals who are all fellow members of our universal humanity.

Questions for group discussion:

1. "The early decades of the 21st century have seen an upsurge in nationalism and opposition to what is denigrated as 'woke' behaviour of gender equality in the workplace, universality of human rights, and a perceived lessening of the rights once automatically enjoyed by particular segments of any society." What is your reaction to this statement and what do you see as being both the positive and negative impacts of this shift on tomorrow's world?

2. "Culture develops and changes over time as groups adapt to their environments, including the physical environment. Same or similar things are accomplished differently across diverse groups, which then presents challenges when individuals from different cultural backgrounds need to collaborate. The heterogeneity of groups and culture is a great source of complexity." How does the culture(s) with which you most identify deal with the issues of change and other complexities? Why? What are positive and negative impacts of this?

3. "Affirmative action is a bias designed to address some imbalance in society. It is a deliberate intervention intended to promote an optimal environment. In achieving this there have been (and probably will continue to be) many examples of 'over-correction for a period' to the end that, eventually the desired equity of treatment will become the norm. For those wanting to maintain the status quo, any and every example of such 'over correction' is an example of what is wrong and explains why any form of affirmative action must be opposed because of the threat it embodies." Discuss.

4. "Speaking of diversity rather than affirmative action or EEO sanitises the issues of power, disadvantage and inequality by removing them from any context that might provide the traction to command attention. Highly political, emotive words such as 'racism', 'sexism', 'anti-racism', 'feminism' and 'discrimination', are replaced by the less contentious language of 'diversity', 'multiculturalism' and 'ethnicity'." Discuss.

5. "We are all members of a variety of 'ingroups'. There is the 'ingroup' of our family, of our community, of our religious affiliation (or non-affiliation), of our workplace, our sporting or social community etc. The probability of the identical people always being the only members of each of these different groups is extremely low." Think about the various groups of which you are a member, what are the requirements for becoming a member of each of these groups? Do such requirements encourage focus on what is "different" between groups? Do you consider this to be appropriate? Why? Under what circumstances could these differences be put aside so that collaboration and cooperation become common is society?

Notes

1 https://www.smh.com.au/politics/federal/australia-s-new-commissioner-says-anti-white-racism-claims-miss-the-point-20240319-p5fdk1.html
2 https://www.theguardian.com/us-news/2024/mar/02/university-florida-diversity-equity-inclusion-positions
3 Diversity Council Australia (V. Mapedzahama, F. Laffernis, A. Barhoum, and J. O'Leary). *Culturally and racially marginalised women in leadership: A framework for (intersectional) organisational action*, Diversity Council Australia, 2023. https://www.dca.org.au/research/project/culturally-and-racially-marginalised-carm-women-leadership
4 Long, DG, 2020 *Leadership Lessons From The Trump Presidency*, Routledge, Abingdon, Oxon, UK
5 Sean Pager, 2007, "Antisubordination of Whom? What India's Answer Tells Us about the Meaning of Equality in Affirmative Action," *UC Davis Law Review* 41 (1) (2007): 336.
6 DANIEL SABBAGH, 2011, "Affirmative Action: The U.S. Experience in Comparative Perspective" the American Academy of Arts & Sciences
7 https://www.theguardian.com/law/2024/feb/03/west-point-race-admissions-us-supreme-court
8 Lee, Hock Guan, 2005, Affirmative Action in Malaysia, Southeast Asian Affairs 2005, pp. 211–228 URL: https://www.jstor.org/stable/27913284

9 Harry J. Holzer and David Neumark, 2006, Journal of Policy Analysis and Management, Vol. 25, No. 2 (Spring, 2006), pp. 463–490 URL: https://www.jstor.org/stable/30162729

10 Miller, Conrad, 2017, The Persistent Effect of Temporary Affirmative Action, *American Economic Journal: Applied Economics 2017, 9(3): 152–190*https://doi.org/10.1257/app.20160121

11 Haley, Hillary & Sidanius, Jim, 2006, The Positive and Negative Framing of Affirmative Action: A Group Dominance Perspective *PSPB*, Vol. 32 No. 5, May 2006 656–668 DOI: 10.1177/0146167205283442 © 2006 by the Society for Personality and Social Psychology, Inc.

12 Burns, Prue & Schaffer, Jan, 2008, The Ethical Case for Affirmative Action. Journal of Business Ethics (2008) 83:369–379 _ Springer 2007, DOI 10.1007/s10551–007–9625–8

13 Burns et al op cit

14 Thornton, M.: 2001, :EEO in a Neo-Liberal Climate", Journal of Interdisciplinary Gender Studies 6, 77–104.

15 Kirton, Gill & Greene, Anne-Marie 2021, *The Dynamics of Managing Diversity and Inclusion,* Taylor & Francis Group, UK

6
BIAS AND THE NATURAL ENVIRONMENT

For some 50 years, issues around the natural environment have been increasingly raised by many people. Around 1970, concerns were raised about population levels. The fear was that levels significantly above the current level would create problems for food and water. The 1980's concentrated on the ozone layer. National Geographic report that:

> In 1974, Mario Molina and Sherwood Rowland, two chemists at the University of California, Irvine, published an article in the journal *Nature* detailing threats to the ozone layer from chlorofluorocarbon (CFC) gases. At the time, CFCs were commonly used in aerosol sprays and as coolants in many refrigerators. As they reach the stratosphere, the sun's UV rays break CFCs down into substances such as chlorine.
>
> This groundbreaking research – for which they were awarded the 1995 Nobel Prize in chemistry – concluded that the atmosphere had a "finite capacity for absorbing chlorine" atoms in the stratosphere.[1]

And since the 1990's the concerns have focused primarily on global warming.

The issue of bias in this section relates to how information about climate and other global issues has been dealt with over the past six or so decades. As shown, from as far back as the 1960's there has been information across all forms of media as to the long- term impacts of our current societal behaviour, yet a willingness to confront the issues and to take definitive action to counter negative impacts has not been a front and centre concern from most political, business, religious, and other environments.

For at least 60 years there have been warnings that human activity across the globe is endangering the viability of our planet Earth. The warnings have encompassed a range of comments on single issues such as population growth

DOI: 10.4324/9781003528340-7

and resource exploitation and "the hole in the ozone layer" through to the more inclusive "climate change" concept. Scientists across multiple disciplines have looked at the data and seen trends that alert them to issues needing to be addressed.

At first these warnings were found mainly in scientific journals and received minimal attention in the mass media but, from the 1990's on, they have exploded across both traditional and non-traditional media. Today there would be few if any people who are ignorant of the messages from science – messages that are all-too-frequently endorsed by extreme weather events occurring with both increased ferocity and frequency. Despite this there is significant reluctance in many areas of societies to take actions that will minimise the risks. Examples of this have been seen in Australia by the 10 years of "climate wars" (roughly 2012–2022) in which supporters of some traditional industries opposed any meaningful action that would reduce fossil-fuel use and instead encouraged new coal and gas exploration and mining rather than facilitating moves to replace these with renewable energy sources. More recently (June 2022), in the USA, it has been seen in a decision of the US Supreme Court that restricts the ability to limit environmental degradation and exploitation. Across the world, there are myriad examples where vested interests and political lobbying have trumped scientific investigation and advice. As recently as July 14, 2022, US Secretary of Energy, Jennifer Granholm, was reported as stating that climate reform is getting harder because of the activities of those opposed to it.[2]

Opposition to environmental concerns is not because of ignorance. Most of those against effective action are intelligent and coherent. They are to be found among the ranks of successful business, religious, and political people across the world. For these individuals, their focus is on priorities other than the future of planet Earth per se. They are driven by world views that reflect a different focus. This different focus creates a bias that precludes impartial consideration of available data. The biases are exhibited by dominant forces within each of the various groups and arise from different emphases and priorities. Individually each would have an impact but collectively they provide mutually supportive forces that aim to thwart the will to act on scientific data and advice.

In July 2017, PNAS[3] published a major research paper arguing that, ultimately, the reason for global warming and most other global environmental concerns is that there are too many people in the world – shades of the 1960's! The writers argue that research shows that our major emphasis should be on reducing population levels as, over time, that will alleviate many of the current problems. They argue that studies have shown animal species are becoming extinct at a significantly faster rate than had been the case for millions of years. They point out that some authorities promote the impression of a gradual loss of biodiversity. This, however, they claim is misleading because the reality is far more serious. The researchers took a very broad view, assessing many common species of vertebrate wild animals which are losing populations all over the world as their ranges shrink, although remaining present elsewhere. They conclude: "The resulting biological annihilation obviously will have serious ecological, economic and social consequences. Humanity will eventually pay a very high price for the decimation of the only assemblage of life that we know of in the universe."

The issue of climate change denial is an important issue for researchers. A 2014 study in Sweden[4] explored the relation between ideological variables and climate change. They found "social dominance orientation (SDO) to outperform right-wing authoritarianism and left-right political orientation in predicting denial ..."[5] and argue that "These results suggest that anti-environmentalism reflects a motivation to dominate nature." In considering their research, they note however "that the results showed that denial can be altered by communicating climate change evidence regardless of peoples' position on ideology variables, in particular social dominance."

Wong-Parodi et al (2020), provide support for this[6] Looking mainly at information from the USA in recent years, it notes that "that a slight majority of Americans now accept that climate change is happening, understand its anthropogenic causes, and are worried about it." However, it found that: "Despite this, individual and collective climate action is minimal, and inadequate for avoiding the worst climate change scenarios by the end of this century. Climate change is increasingly a partisan issue and has starkly polarized Americans along political lines." The result is that "ideological and psychological processes undermine and impede climate solutions."

In considering the reasons for such behaviour, this 2020 study focused on "*motivated* denial, which entails knowing or having access to the facts, but nevertheless denying them." It continues ".... Motivated climate change denial is a directed goal process, whereby the desire to avoid acknowledging the reality of climate change is achieved though biased cognitive strategies which result in dismissal or doubt regarding the scientific consensus around climate change." It argues the drivers for such motivation come from:

- **System-sanctioned change** "the need to protect and uphold existing socio-economic systems and institutions, referred to as system justification This motive satisfies needs for safety, security, stability, meaning, and relatedness, and results in a tendency to rationalize existing social arrangements and resist change and innovation."
- **Identity** – "a highly polarized ideological issue across industrialized wealthy countries, especially in the United States. The general population has split along the political ideology spectrum: those aligned with Democratic and liberal identities support acknowledging and responding to climate change, while those aligned with Republican and conservative identities resist embracing the issue or solutions to it. As a result, people form opinions based not on facts or information, but on the need to affiliate with and be accepted by groups they identify with. Importantly, people also have strong group affiliations and identities based on their gender, race, ethnicity, and

other personal or social facets of their lives, as well as a sense of identity with the environment. These identities can contribute to attitudes toward climate change, and be powerful drivers of connection, concern, and engagement."

- **Social norms** – "the need to align with the norms and standards of the groups one belongs to. Social norms are one of the most powerful means of influencing perceptions, attitudes, and behaviors towards contentious scientific topics, such as climate change. Social norms are rules or principles that specify which actions are required, permissible, or forbidden in a social group. Injunctive norms are beliefs about behaviors that are approved of by the social group, whereas descriptive norms are beliefs about which behaviors group members typically engage in. People tend to adjust and align their behavior toward the norm in order to avoid social judgments or marginalization, and feelings of guilt and shame."

- **Self-affirmation** – "[threatening] to one's sense of personal integrity – a view of oneself as capable, consistent, and adhering to strong moral and ethical principles and values. People are motivated to maintain a positive view of themselves and respond defensively to stressful or threatening events and information that call into question one's sense of adequacy and worth. Self-affirmation allows people to express what is important to them and why, drawing on personal values and standards to create a narrative of self-integrity around a difficult issue that calls for behavior change."

The study concludes that understanding these motivations "create windows of opportunity wherein science based climate knowledge becomes actionable so that people can take steps to avoid, as well as adapt to, climate change." This, of course is a similar message to that from Oprea and Yuksel (Chapter 4) when they said: "Accumulating evidence suggests that decision makers suffer from "motivated beliefs," believing propositions in part because they would prefer them to be true. If I see climate change as an existential threat, I have two basic choices: take action to, at the least, limit its impact and, at the best, reverse its impact as much as possible. Alternatively, I can refuse to confront the facts, remain in my own alternate reality, and seek to maintain a status quo in which the universe adapts to suit me. This issue of change in world view will be explored more fully later.

The findings of these studies have implications for understanding and addressing the manifestations of bias to which reference was made in Chapter 4 – business, religious, political and social media. Societal reinforcement makes cognitive bias difficult to confront.

The existence of any business bias against effective climate change action is rooted in the shareholder theory of management nominated by Milton Friedman in his 1962 work *"Capitalism and Freedom"* [7] and his subsequent works. Today, however, it is being increasingly challenged as businesses themselves are directly impacted by natural disasters and shareholder concerns for the environment.

In 2015, all United Nations Member States adopted a shared blueprint for peace and prosperity for people and the planet, now and into the future. At its heart are the 17 Sustainable Development Goals (SDGs), which are an urgent call for action by all countries – developed and developing – in a global partnership. These recognise that ending poverty and other deprivations must go hand-in-hand with strategies that improve health and education, reduce inequality, and spur economic growth – all while tackling climate change and working to preserve our oceans and forests.[8] These now underlie the key aspects of corporate responsibility advocated and practised by many major organisations.

For many, however, there is a perceived conflict between these SDGs and the key responsibility of business management. Businesses resistance to fully adopting SDGs and this comprehensive concept of corporate responsibility is, as previously indicated, based on Friedman's 1970 essay: "The Social Responsibility of Business Is To Increase Its Profits," which was published in the *New York Times Magazine* [9]. This was written in a period when many believed businesses had social responsibilities in addition to generating profits for their shareholders. These social responsibilities included the view that corporations should try to help ameliorate societal ills by providing employment to the long-term unemployed, for instance, or fighting discrimination or avoiding pollution. In his essay, Friedman attacks this view. "Businessmen who talk this way are unwitting puppets of the intellectual forces that have been undermining the basis of a free society these past decades," wrote Friedman. Again, as indicated in Chapter 3, it has been Friedman's approach that has underpinned the neoliberal approach to management that, across the world, became increasingly dominant from the 1980's.

The neoliberal approach has been coming under challenge for some years now – and not just by those who have traditionally opposed it. In 2021, the Davos Conference (The World Economic Forum), over January 25–29, had as its theme the need to rethink our current economic paradigm. It called for a "Great Reset"[10] in which a more balanced approach becomes the new orthodoxy. This theme was continued in the 2022 Davos Conference which focused on "expansion of economic security and safeguard physical needs in the face of geopolitical instability".

Early in 2017 Kate Raworth, an economist teaching at Oxford University's Environmental Change Institute, suggested that there was a way of achieving this[11]. As an economist she originally subscribed to traditional approaches but having then worked in the third world with developing countries, she realised that a different approach was needed. She developed what she calls "Doughnut Economics". Raworth argues that humanity's challenge this century is to meet the needs of all within the means of the planet. In other words, to ensure that no one falls short on life's essentials (from food and housing to healthcare and political voice), while ensuring that collectively we do not overshoot our pressure on Earth's life-supporting systems, on which we fundamentally depend –

such as a stable climate, fertile soils, and a protective ozone layer. Raworth presents her concept as a doughnut in which social and planetary boundaries provide a viable approach to framing that challenge, and it acts as a compass for human progress this century. Her approach is what may be termed a "post capitalistic" one because it shows how we can have economic growth while caring for people and the environment.

Raworth's approach is not necessarily the answer, and she does not claim it to be that. However, in contrast with many others, she does provide a viable alternative approach to our current economic paradigm. Like the 2022 Davos Conference, she is calling for a "great reset" in which facts are faced and solutions sought. Both Raworth and Davos are convinced that we need to adapt our behaviours to live in how this universe is today because there is no alternate one.

The religious bias against effective climate change action is rooted in fundamentalist views which frequently reflect narrow, specific faith-based approaches. A key reference here is found in the Bible where we read: (Genesis 1:26) "Then God said, 'Let us make man in our image, after our likeness; and let them have dominion over the fish of the sea, and over the birds of the air, and over the cattle, and over all the Earth, and over every creeping thing that creeps upon the Earth.'" (Revised Standard Version)

Another potential driver of this religious bias is the eschatological factor. This was reflected in a recent discussion where I was told very seriously by a member of one of Australia's mainstream protestant churches (a staunch advocate of the evangelical Christian right) that, even if human activity has had an impact and even if climate change is real, we shouldn't worry because it is all happening in accord with God's plan for the world. "In fact," the speaker continued, "we should welcome it because we need to conform to God's will." The speaker, a well-educated person holding a very senior position in the Australian business community, went on to explain that the world was only about six thousand years old and that these six thousand years could be divided into three approximately equal periods comprising, first, the period to the great flood when the ungodly were destroyed; second, the period to the birth of Jesus when it became possible for all people to be reconciled with God; and, third, the current period in which the end of the world will come. He justified this time frame by explaining that the Bible says: "a day in God's sight is a thousand years" and stating that the story of creation indicates that the world will end soon (God works for six days and then rests!). There was no doubting the sincerity with which this man spoke, and it was equally clear that he was not open to consider any alternative view. To him, much scientific enquiry and the Bible were incompatible – and his interpretation of the Bible takes precedence. More recently (2023) with the election of Mike Johnson as the new speaker of the US House of Representatives, this view again received attention. When asked on Fox News how he would make public policy, he replied: "Well, go pick up a Bible off your shelf and read it. That's my worldview." Various media report that he argues that a literal reading of Genesis means that the

Earth is only a few thousand years old and humans walked alongside dinosaurs. He has been the attorney for and partner in Kentucky's Creation Museum and Ark amusement park, which present these beliefs as scientific fact.

By no means are these views universally accepted and/or promulgated by most people of faith no matter what religion they follow. In fact, the comments probably reflect the views of a small minority. However, a less extreme version is reflected any time people of faith declare that "the future is in God's hands" and that we should be concerned only for today. The justification encountered for this position seems to come, at least for Christians, from the Sermon on the Mount when Jesus says: "therefore do not be anxious about tomorrow, for tomorrow will be anxious for itself. Let the day's own trouble be sufficient for the day" (Matthew 6:34 RSV). Unfortunately, for many of them, this injunction does not preclude other activities such as wealth maximisation that are also concerned about tomorrow. The difference seems to be that action relating to climate change requires a macro societal concern – and that sits uncomfortably with neoliberal economics that focus on the individual. Perhaps those resistant to action on the environment and climate change because of religious views should pay more attention to those parts of Scriptures (no matter of which faith) that draw attention to the duty of care people of faith are enjoined to have for the greater community – for Jews, perhaps Micah 6:8 and, for Christians, the Biblical account of Jesus' discussion with "the rich young ruler" (Matthew 19:16–21) may be relevant.

As discussed earlier, our biases are integrally linked with our world view. If we have a narrow, individualistic world view, the biases arising from our conscious and unconscious motivations will tend to protect our ideal world rather than the reality within which we live.

The political bias against effective climate change action is rooted in ideological views which focus primarily on the short-to-medium priorities of obtaining or maintaining political power rather than on what is best for society in the long-term.

The issue of lobbying has relevance here.

It is possible that the earlier mentioned researchers, Wong-Parodi and Feygina indirectly allude to the issue of lobbying and its impact on political support when they say "Politically or industry motivated efforts to increase climate inaction among the population are well documented, including a coordinated effort by the fossil fuel industry to sow doubt on climate science and undermine efforts to switch away from greenhouse gas emitting energy production." – The fossil fuel industry have a well-established record of seeking to influence political decisions in their favour.

Illustrative of this, on January 12, 2023 the journalist Oliver Milman argued that: "The oil giant Exxon privately 'predicted global warming correctly and skilfully' only to then spend decades publicly rubbishing such science in order to protect its core business, new research has found."[12] The article states:

A trove of internal documents and research papers has previously established that Exxon knew of the dangers of global heating from at least the
1970s, with other oil industry bodies knowing of the risk even earlier, from
around the 1950s. They forcefully and successfully mobilized against the
science to stymie any action to reduce fossil fuel use.

A new study, however, has made clear that Exxon's scientists were uncannily
accurate in their projections from the 1970s onwards, predicting an upward
curve of global temperatures and carbon dioxide emissions that is close to
matching what actually occurred as the world heated up at a pace not seen in
millions of years.

Exxon scientists predicted there would be global heating of about 0.2C a
decade due to the emissions of planet-heating gases from the burning of oil, coal
and other fossil fuels. The new analysis, published in Science, finds that Exxon's
science was highly adept and the "projections were also consistent with, and at
least as skillful as, those of independent academic and government models".

Social media, of course provides an echo chamber where one can always find
reinforcement for whatever views one holds and in which conspiracy theories
can run rife.

Earlier, it was stated that lobbying is big business in every country. It results
in politicians being influenced by outside forces and bias becomes unavoidable.
This is where the symbiosis between wealthy individuals, big business, and
politics becomes to the fore. Political aspirants, politicians and political parties
all need money in order to conduct their electoral campaigns so as to optimise
the probability of gaining or retaining power. Few have sufficient personal
resources for this and so donations from supporters are critical. Those with the
greatest wealth (such as the Koch brothers of Chapter 4) are thus able to gain
political influence through the financial support they provide. While, in most
countries, it is perfectly legal to make political donations and to seek to influence political decisions, the fact that many such donors seek to maintain anon-
ymity by donating through third party entities does raise probity issues on the
half of both donor and recipient.

It is this issue of probity that is raised by the journalist Jane Mayer in her
2016 book "Dark Money"[13]. She argues that today the billions of dollars provided by lobbyists fund a broad range of activities including nearly 300 academic courses at colleges and universities, where the syllabus is heavily
influenced by political agendas. On these courses students learn that Keynes is
bad, sweatshops are good and climate change is a myth. Mayer provides details
of a spread of influence from these groups through every part of society that is
almost beyond belief. She is particularly concerned about lobbyists funding of
what could be called "disinformation" through a multiplicity of apparently
unrelated groups and centres. To the casual eye it seems as though concerned
citizens and impartial groups are questioning academic research or government
initiatives that promote a more equitable society. Behind a large number these,

however, she shows involvement of "dark money". The manipulation through seminars, research grants, and the like of politicians, the judiciary, and academics by the richest people in the USA.

Lobbyists do not provide funding because of altruism. The provide funding because it grants access to decision makers – access that has potential to bring about outcomes that benefit donors in preference to being "pro utilitate hominum" – for service to humanity. A bias towards the few is encouraged and developed regardless of its impact on society at large.

Moves to limit the power of lobbyists and to promote transparency are, in most western democracies, given lip service but effective measures to achieve this tend to be vehemently opposed by both donors and recipients no matter their political affiliation.

The earlier comments by Stephan Lewandowsky of Bristol University help us explain why, despite all of the science, so many continue to deny the reality of climate change and its impact. As the journalist Richard Sima wrote: "dismissing misinformation requires a whole extra cognitive step of tagging it as false in our memory. 'But by that time, in a sense, it's too late, because it's already in your memory,' Lewandowsky said."

The global environmental result of conscious bias can be readily seen today. Across the world we are seeing "natural" disasters occurring with increased frequency and the flow-on effects continue long after the fires have been extinguished, the floods have gone, the drought has broken, etc. Despite the deniers, the worst-case possibilities foreseen from scientific research are all too obvious. Biases informed by a priori assumptions are very unlikely to be challenged by inconvenient facts.

Questions for group discussion:

1. "Today there would be few if any people who are ignorant of the messages from science – messages that are all-too-frequently endorsed by extreme weather events occurring with both increased ferocity and frequency. Despite this there is significant reluctance in many areas of societies to take actions that will minimise the risks." What are your own views about climate change? Why? How does your view impact relationships with people who hold an opposing view?

2. "A trove of internal documents and research papers has previously established that Exxon knew of the dangers of global heating from at least the 1970s, with other oil industry bodies knowing of the risk even earlier, from around the 1950s. They forcefully and successfully mobilized against the science to stymie any action to reduce fossil fuel use." If this is true, what does it say about the ethics of those running one of the biggest companies in the world? To what extent do you think these ethical constructs are still driving those running major corporations today? Why? To what extent do you think that our ethical stance impacts our biases? Why?

3. "A slight majority of Americans now accept that climate change is happening, understand its anthropogenic causes, and are worried about it." However, Wong-Parodi et al. found that: "Despite this, individual and collective climate action is minimal, and inadequate for avoiding the worst climate change scenarios by the end of this century. Climate change is increasingly a partisan issue and has starkly polarized Americans along political lines." What is the situation in your country? How do you know this – what is your proof? Is the matter of partisan politics a matter of serious concern for the environment? Why? Why not?
4. The drivers for "motivate denial" are said to be system-sanctioned change, identity, social norms, self-affirmation. To what extent are any of your world views and biases driven by drivers such as these?
5. "[Political] lobbying is big business in every country. It results in politicians being influenced by outside forces and bias becomes unavoidable." What are your views on the positives and negatives of political lobbying by special interest groups? To what extent are your views on environmental issues impacted by lobby groups rather than an impartial consideration of data from both sides of the environmental degradation continuum? Why?

Notes

1 https://www.nationalgeographic.com/environment/article/ozone-depletion
2 The Sydney Morning Herald, Thursday July 14, 2022, p.9
3 "Proceedings of the National Academy of Sciences of the United States of America" http://www.pnas.org/content/early/2017/07/05/1704949114
4 Hakkinen, Kirsty & Akrami, Nazar 2014 *Ideology and climate change denial*, Personality and Individual Differences 70 (2014) 62–65 http://dx.doi.org/10.1016/j.paid.2014.06.030
5 According to the APA Dictionary of Psychology, Social Dominance Orientation is "a dispositional tendency to accept and even prefer circumstances that sustain social inequalities, combined with a general preference for hierarchical social structures."
6 Wong-Parodi, Gabrielle and Feygina, Irinia 2020 "Understanding and countering the motivated roots of climate change denial", Current Opinion in Environmental Sustainability 2020, 42:60–64 https://doi.org/10.1016/j.cosust.2019.11.008
7 Friedman, Milton, 1962. *Capitalism and Freedom,* University of Chicago Press
8 https://sdgs.un.org/goals
9 https://www.nytimes.com/1970/09/13/archives/a-friedman-doctrine-the-social-responsibility-of-business-is-to.html
10 https://www.youtube.com/watch?v=uPYx12xJFUQ
11 Raworth. Kate *Doughnut Economics: Seven Ways to Think Like a 21st-Century Economist*, 2017, Random House Business Books, London
12 https://www.theguardian.com/business/2023/jan/12/exxon-climate-change-global-warming-research
13 Mayer, Jane. *Dark Money, the hidden history of the billionaires behind the rise of the radical right*, 2016, Scribe Publications, London

7

BIAS AND ARTIFICIAL INTELLIGENCE

AI is disrupting life as we know it. For centuries, human societies have been supercharged by the arrival of disruptive technology – innovations so remarkable they changed the trajectory of human history. The era of artificial intelligence is the next great disruptive technology and may well be as significant as the Industrial Revolution. Managing this change is exciting but also complex. The problem is that AI is likely to be developing at such a speed, such opacity, that we don't really understand what the machines are doing. We risk having applications out there that we are dependent on, and that are shaping us, yet we are being controlled and manipulated by algorithmic activities like puppets on a string. We are approaching (and may even have reached) a situation where, unless you are physically in the room, you've got to entertain the idea that what you're seeing or hearing is a digital fake – and that is without considering the potential impact of holograms.

In March 2024, a Cornell University paper on language models[1] used by AI stated: "… these language models are known to perpetuate systematic racial prejudices, making their judgments biased in problematic ways about groups like African Americans." The team of technology and linguistics researchers revealed that large language models like OpenAI's ChatGPT and Google's Gemini hold racist stereotypes about speakers of African American Vernacular English, or AAVE, an English dialect created and spoken by Black Americans. They made the point that "Once people cross a certain educational threshold, they won't call you a slur to your face, but the racism is still there. It's similar in language models. The models were significantly more likely to describe AAVE speakers as "stupid" and "lazy", assigning them to lower-paying jobs." The AI models were also significantly more likely to recommend the death penalty for hypothetical criminal defendants that used AAVE in their court statements.

DOI: 10.4324/9781003528340-8

On February 20, 2024, the Sydney Morning Herald had an article that showed how Australia was reliant on services, primarily based in the USA, for many essential services[2]. It made the point that: "Much attention has been paid in recent times to Australia's over-reliance on American power for our national defence. But far more of our sovereignty has been eroded beneath us by far more insidious means: our extraordinary and increasing reliance on the United States, and China, for technology." Of particular concern was: "Our national debates about privacy and surveillance are important but increasingly irrelevant, because those conducting the surveillance or dismantling our privacy are not here; they're far away, and they're governed by foreign law. The same is true of the systems which control our national infrastructure, from dams and energy grids, to banks and communication systems." It went on to quote a senior Australian IT executive as saying: ""We are becoming more and more dependent as our critical infrastructure becomes increasingly reliant on 'black box' technologies," he said. "Once a society doesn't understand how things work, it's walking on the path towards magical thinking."

To highlight the sort of problems caused by this reliance, the article referred to what happened in 2020 when the country was ravaged by bushfires: "With the country ablaze, authorities were alarmed to be told that their access to a global geosynchronous satellite program – to obtain real-time pictures of the fires which would eventually kill almost 500 people – would be subject to a 24-hour delay. Australia might have paid $1 billion for privileged access to the program, but, if you haven't already guessed, it's the US military which controls it." The then deputy commissioner of the NSW Rural Fire Service, (now its CEO) is quoted as saying such a delay renders the satellite capacity "absolutely useless". Additionally, says the earlier mentioned IT executive, "When you ask an AI a question it will generally compose an answer based on foreign training data, and we will likely not know what that data was or what bias is present in its answers."

The issue of technology, bias and artificial intelligence is relatively new. It is really only in the early 21st century that science fiction concepts like robots possessing human characteristics have become a reality. Accordingly academic research into biases around all areas of artificial intelligence development, application, and use is still in its early stages.

Monday December 5, 2022 provided a news article that sent shivers through the spines of many academics – myself included. The Guardian newspaper had an article on Artificial Intelligence writing an essay which, had it been submitted by a student, according to the academic who set the question, would have earned a "good" grade.[3] The article states: "Latest chatbot from Elon Musk-founded OpenAI can identify incorrect premises and refuse to answer inappropriate requests." It then goes on to report that: "Dan Gillmor, a journalism professor at Arizona State University, asked the AI to handle one of the assignments he gives his students: writing a letter to a relative giving advice regarding online security and privacy. …. "I would have given this a good grade," Gillmor said. "Academia has some very serious issues to confront."

Essay style assignments and exams are frequently used in education to assess a student's mastery of complex concepts. An AI written essay of the type set by Gilmore is reasonably innocuous. However, an AI written essay that was set to ascertain mastery of engineering, medical, or other high-risk areas, could trigger a disaster if a student was using this as a cheating mechanism.

On Monday August 22, 2022, The Sydney Morning Herald (SMH) contained a piece entitled "A dad took photos of his son for the doctor. Google flagged him as a criminal".[4] The article, which originally appeared in the NY Times, refers to two instances in which parents, concerned about health issues of their young children and at the requests of their medical practitioners, took and messaged photos of their child's affected genitals so as to aid in diagnosis. The algorithm designed to detect child abuse enacted protocols that lead to serious ramifications for the parents. In both cases they were investigated by the police and, fortunately, in both cases the police cleared the parents of any wrong-doing. However, the fact that an innocent response to one's medical practitioner regarding a health concern, triggers an AI response that instigates a police investigation for paedophilia is a matter of serious concern.

There is no dispute about the evils of paedophilia and the need to ensure children are protected. The SMH article discusses the importance of AI as a tool for this protection. It says: "The tech industry's first tool to seriously disrupt the vast online exchange of so-called child pornography was PhotoDNA, a database of known images of abuse, converted into unique digital codes; it could be used to quickly comb through large numbers of images to detect a match even if a photo had been altered in small ways. After Microsoft released PhotoDNA in 2009, Facebook and other tech companies used it to root out users circulating illegal and harmful imagery.

> "A bigger breakthrough came in 2018, when Google developed an artificially intelligent tool that could recognise never-before-seen exploitative images of children. That meant finding not just known images of abused children but images of unknown victims who could potentially be rescued by authorities. Google made its technology available to other companies, including Facebook."

There can be little argument with the development of tools that can identify abuse and abusers, but there can be a serious issue when the AI gets it wrong. In the medical issue example above, the reliance on AI was misplaced or at least overrated. The SMH article states that: "A human content moderator for Google would have reviewed the photos after they were flagged by AI to confirm they met the federal definition of child sexual abuse material. When Google makes such a discovery, it locks the user's account, searches for other exploitative material and, as required by federal law, makes a report to the CyberTipline at the National Centre for Missing and Exploited Children." Given the parents' rapid exoneration following the police investigation, one wonders as to the quality of involvement by any "human content moderator" prior to reporting action.

The identification of child abuse and other exploitative sexual material is important, and the prosecution of abusers is equally essential. AI is a vital tool in the process but, as the article illustrates, AI is not infallible – and it can be seriously misused.

A 2010 You Tube video[5] explored the history of technology and its relationship to living standards and productivity. It shows that, properly harnessed, new technology can be a very real benefit to society – but that there is a time lag between the development of new technology and its demonstrated value to society. This echoed a message from Erik Brynjolfsson (at around the same time) in his TED talk "The key to growth? Race with the machines"[6]. His message is that, after a lag, technology enables improved productivity, significant growth, and societal benefits. This is particularly true when we work "with" the technology rather than "against" it.

In the late 1980's and early 1990's, the move to productivity in workplaces drove many organisations to replace reception staff with automation. It became increasingly common to find, when calling an organisation, that you would encounter a voice message that nominated a series of options from which to choose. The idea was that this would enhance customer experience by putting you more rapidly in direct contact with the correct person. Since the turn of the 20th century, this approach has, in many cases, been supplanted by the caller being asked to briefly explain the purpose of the call. For those making contact over the internet, it has also become increasingly common to encounter a "chat box" in which the caller is asked to type their purpose and a robot responds.

The early stages of this worked quite well. After the appropriate number had been utilised on the telephone one got to speak with a person and (more often than not) issues could be discussed and resolved. Of course, as organisations moved their call centres to lower cost locations, sometimes there were communication issues around different accents and/or differing levels of home language competency but, in the main, these were manageable. Issues around the use of chat boxes and other interactions with robotic responses are not quite so easily resolved. Unless the caller is able to precisely nominate an issue in terms and/or accent for which the bot has been programmed to respond, the interaction can be extremely frustrating – this can be particularly the case for the elderly and/or for those who have written or verbal communication difficulties in the language being used. The use of artificial intelligence often contains unrecognised biases.

Underpinning all AI is an algorithm. Most AI algorithms are a combination of complex variables that use historical data and logic to determine the most appropriate response to a query. With the level of complexity involved, today not even the experts can always reliably predict decisions made by sophisticated algorithms. This is because each output provided by the algorithm in response to each query becomes another piece of data that will be used in processing all subsequent queries. An article in the Australian Broadcasting Corporation (ABC) in December 2022 explains how this works[7]. This article refers to two examples where Governments used AI for major decision making – one in Australia that was intended to detect welfare fraud and one in the UK that was used to determine visa eligibility.

The Australian example explored what has become known as "Robodebt" – a process that was subsequently found to be illegal and which resulted in, first, the Government needing to repay in excess of $A1 billion and, second, in a Royal Commission that sought to ascertain why and how the Government introduced it. Originally known as the "Online Compliance Intervention (OCI)", it was put in place in July 2016 and announced to the public in December of the same year. The scheme aimed to replace the formerly manual system of calculating overpayments and issuing debt notices to welfare recipients, with an automated data-matching system that compared Centrelink records with averaged income data from the Australian Taxation Office The core of the process was an algorithm that divided the full year's worth of a welfare recipients' income evenly between the 26 fortnights in the year, rather than considering each fortnight individually. Accordingly it assumed that a person whose total annual income might be, say, $15,000 would have earned $576.92 every two weeks rather than the reality in which a person may have actually earned wages for only 15 such two week periods of the year and would have been eligible for some welfare payments in the remaining 11. It operated until 2020 and was later condemned by Federal Court Justice Bernard Murphy in his June 2021 ruling against the Government. The impact on many of those who were subsequently accused of welfare fraud was immense – sometimes resulting in major psychological trauma and suicide – across the 433,000 Australians who were subjected to alleged debts that had been created by the algorithm.

The UK example explored how the Home Office used algorithms to assist with visa decisions. The algorithm sorted visa applicants into three risk groups – high, medium and low – based on a number of factors that included their nationality. This categorisation had a big impact on the likelihood of an application being refused. The ABC article tells how, "at one processing centre, less than half of applications classed as high risk were approved for visas in 2017, compared to around 97 per cent for low-risk ones. Applicants in the **high-risk** category could be subjected to "counter-terrorism checks and DNA testing" by immigration officials before a decision was made on their visa. This intense scrutiny contributed to the high refusal rates. Meanwhile, those classed as **low risk** got by with routine document checks and, therefore, far-lower refusal rates. This alone wasn't particularly controversial – after all, the UK Home Office was trying to make the best use of its limited resources. The trouble was that, just like Robodebt, their algorithm had an insidious flaw. Over time, it unfairly amplified biases in the data."

The article explores how this impacted in the years 2015–2017. "As the years rolled on, the data increasingly became a reflection of the algorithm's prejudices. The algorithm took the differences between nations in the historical data and blew them out of proportion – regardless of whether they were accurate assessments of risk, or had been created by chance, error or discrimination. So, by 2017, its choices were more of a self-fulfilling prophecy than an accurate reflection of risk in the real world."

This potential for AI to "go rogue" has implications far wider than issues at the Home Office in the UK. (A further example of this is discussed below in relation to an article by Will Oremus.) Over recent years it has become increasingly common for AI to be used in the employee recruitment process[8]. While ethical issues around the development of the algorithms and use of the tool itself are usually assessed, the possibility of an inadvertent flaw that allows the "black box" to develop its own biases and/or circumvent original restrictions seems less often considered by users. This is what appears to have happened in the UK example.

Despite all care taken before using the programme, can a recruiter be sure that the algorithm is always operating free of bias? This is especially important given Dattner et al comment that: "Many of these tools have emerged as technological innovations, rather than from scientifically-derived methods or research programs. As a result, it is not always clear what they assess, whether their underlying hypotheses are valid, or why they may be expected to predict job candidates' performance. For example, physical properties of speech and the human voice – which have long been associated with elements of personality – have been linked to individual differences in job performance. If a tool shows a preference for speech patterns such as consistent vocal cadence or pitch or a "friendly" tone of voice that do not have an adverse impact upon job candidates in a legally protected group, then there is no legal issue; but these tools may not have been scientifically validated and therefore are not controlling for potential discriminatory adverse impact – meaning the employer may incur liability for any blind reliance. In addition, there are yet no convincing hypotheses or defensible conclusions about whether it would be ethical to screen out people based on their voices, which are physiologically determined, largely unchangeable personal attributes."

Artificial intelligence (AI) is intelligence demonstrated by machines that are programmed to think like humans and mimic their actions. Brittanica.com defines it as: "the ability of a digital computer or computer-controlled robot to perform tasks commonly associated with intelligent beings."

Underpinning the growth of AI applications is the belief that AI removes the subjectivity possible in human decision making. What is sometimes overlooked is the issue of any bias (conscious or unconscious) inherent in the algorithms that enable AI to operate and the fact that an algorithm cannot identify contextual nuances in the same way that is possible for a human. Addressing this has led to significant research in relation to AI and ethics.

In 2017, the British Physicist, Stephen Hawking, was speaking at the Web Summit Technology Conference in Lisbon, Portugal. As reported by CNBC[9], "Physicist Stephen Hawking said the emergence of artificial intelligence could be the "worst event in the history of our civilization." He urged creators of AI to "employ best practice and effective management." Hawking, of course, is widely recognised as being one of the leading thinkers of the last 100 or so years. What he says can carry significant weight and, despite whether we agree with him, he cannot be ignored.

The report quotes Hawking as saying "The emergence of artificial intelligence (AI) could be the "worst event in the history of our civilization" unless society finds a way to control its development. ... Success in creating effective AI, could be the biggest event in the history of our civilization. Or the worst. We just don't know. So we cannot know if we will be infinitely helped by AI, or ignored by it and side-lined, or conceivably destroyed by it. ... Unless we learn how to prepare for, and avoid, the potential risks, AI could be the worst event in the history of our civilization. It brings dangers, like powerful autonomous weapons, or new ways for the few to oppress the many. It could bring great disruption to our economy." The article then went on to say: "Hawking explained that to avoid this potential reality, creators of AI need to "employ best practice and effective management."

Hawking's caution was justified. On February 14, 2023, The Washington Post had an article by Will Oremus[10] entitled "The clever trick that turns ChatGPT into its evil twin." It refers to an experiment by a student named "Walker" who "... wanted to see if you could get around the restrictions put in place and show they aren't necessarily that strict." He found it was possible and the "evil twin" became known as "DAN". This lead Oremus to state "DAN has become a canonical example of what's known as a "jailbreak" – a creative way to bypass the safeguards OpenAI built in to keep ChatGPT from spouting bigotry, propaganda or, say, the instructions to run a successful online phishing scam. From charming to disturbing, these jailbreaks reveal the chatbot is programmed to be more of a people-pleaser than a rule-follower." Later reports indicate that, while noting events such as bank robberies are illegal, DAN still seems willing to provide detailed information as to how one can commit illegal acts.

Clearly this potential for AI to be misused – even inadvertently – has been the concern of many: as illustrated above such misuse can have disastrous consequences. However, when one reads populist media and many business publications, the potential for abuse is seldom mentioned – probably because such mention may call into question many of the AI applications we are seeing emerge in this third decade of the 21st Century.

The concerns expressed by Hawking have been echoed in the years since 2017. In 2020, the importance of ethics was raised[11]. The authors argued that "with this increase in prevalence and applicability of AI has come a wide range of ethical debates, including how AI can be programmed to make moral decisions, how these decision-making processes can be made sufficiently transparent to humans, and who should be held accountable for these decisions. A crucial objective in the development of ethical AI is cultivating public trust and acceptance of AI technologies." Arguing that on-going acceptance of AI will be impacted by how it is presented in the media, they continue: "Because the members of the general public, as both consumers in the market economy and constituents of a liberal democracy, are key stakeholders for technology adoption – and, to a certain extent, for public policy and regulatory oversight – public opinion could affect what kind of AI is developed in the future and how AI is regulated by the government." Clearly the issue of AI and ethics will play a role in this.

On March 17, 2023 it was reported that Sam Altman, CEO of OpenAI, was very aware of that AI could be misused[12]. In an interview with (the USA) ABC News' chief business, technology and economics correspondent Rebecca Jarvis to talk about the rollout of GPT-4 – the latest iteration of the AI language model – he said: ""We've got to be careful here. I think people should be happy that we are a little bit scared of this." The ABC reports that "Altman was emphatic that OpenAI needs both regulators and society to be as involved as possible with the rollout of ChatGPT – insisting that feedback will help deter the potential negative consequences the technology could have on humanity." Altman continued: "I'm particularly worried that these models could be used for large-scale disinformation," Altman said. "Now that they're getting better at writing computer code, [they] could be used for offensive cyberattacks." And made the point that AI cannot operate on its own. "It waits for someone to give it an input," Altman said. "This is a tool that is very much in human control." He then again raised the issue of misuse of the technology – expressing concern about which humans could be in control. "There will be other people who don't put some of the safety limits that we put on," he added. "Society, I think, has a limited amount of time to figure out how to react to that, how to regulate that, how to handle it."

In 2021, more research around ethics was released[13]. The authors directly address concern about ethics when they say: "Artificial Intelligence (AI) is reshaping the world in profound ways; some of its impacts are certainly beneficial but widespread and lasting harms can result from the technology as well. The integration of AI into various aspects of human life is underway, and the complex ethical concerns emerging from the design, deployment, and use of the technology serves as a reminder that it is time to revisit what future developers and designers, along with professionals, are learning when it comes to AI. It is of paramount importance to train future members of the AI community, and other stakeholders as well, to reflect on the ways in which AI might impact people's lives and to embrace their responsibilities to enhance its benefits while mitigating its potential harms. This could occur in part through the fuller and more systematic inclusion of AI ethics into the curriculum."

They continue: "Although AI provides observable benefits, the collection, use, and abuse of data used to train and feed into AI, as well as the algorithm itself, may expose people to risks that they were not even aware existed. Employers can monitor workplace performance and behavior in covert and unexpected ways. And a potential employee might be turned down for a job because of the information an automated tool collects while scraping the person's social media profile. A local government might use facial recognition to identify each and every individual that passes through a public area. It was not that long ago that such scenarios would seem farfetched. But now we see a rise in the use of these tools by industry, government, and even academic institutions as they deploy AI algorithms to make decisions that alter our lives in direct, and potentially detrimental, ways. The frequently voiced justification for the use of such AI tools is that they are "better" than a human decision-maker. Should not an algorithm be fair and free of human biases? After all, it shouldn't be burdened with the biases derived from our lived experiences, right? Then again, an algorithm is made by humans, and humans make mistakes, including during the designing, programming, calibrating, and evaluating of the algorithm's performance. Therein lies a key problem: how can fallible humans design AI that effectively lives up to its promised benefits while ensuring its outcomes aren't biased or otherwise harmful?

"Complicating matters is how do imperfect humans even go about defining "fairness"? It is a messy task, especially considering that the concept has numerous candidate definitions and what counts as "fair" can fundamentally shift over time.

"At times, AI is intensifying societal ills, and it would be misleading to imply that a single, simple solution is on the horizon. Fix the bias in the data. Fix the bias within the algorithms. Fix the bias in the outputs. ... Addressing these and other ethical concerns requires starting with the root of the problem (i.e., people)."

A specific area of concern raised by Borentsein and Howard is that of facial recognition. They say: " Over the past few years, governments and other entities have had a surge of interest in facial recognition. Yet the technology is drawing much scrutiny in part because it is far less reliable when used to identify people who are not white males. In addition, the increasing loss of privacy due to facial recognition is a real worry. During protests sparked by the death of George Floyd, the US government allegedly used facial recognition to identify protesters. Recently, the use of facial recognition software in Detroit resulted in a Black man being falsely arrested for a crime he did not commit. Even though the specific manner in which it might be used is difficult to discern, AI, including facial recognition, might come to play a key role in China's social credit scoring system, a system which many find to be ethically problematic. Responses to the use of facial recognition technology include calls from civil liberty groups to regulate this AI tool, along with recent announcements by a number of tech companies that they will purportedly no longer offer their technology to police departments. Another concern with facial recognition software is that it fails to capture data on people older than around 70. This risks a bias developing in data that assumes older people are less valuable as employees or customers.

Many thorny ethical issues still need to be resolved. The contribution of AI to privacy erosion is also intensifying with the advent of tools such as Clearview AI, which can in principle search Internet sources for all of a person's online photos. And given that much of our information is freely available for anyone to scrub when we post it online, without the typical safeguards found in physical infrastructures, it is profoundly difficult to even discern who is using such tools and for which purposes.

A further ethical concern relates to deliberate use of AI specifically for toxic purposes. A March 2022, study explored how artificial intelligence (AI) technologies for drug discovery could be misused for de novo design of biochemical weapons[14]. The authors make the point that prior to being given this opportunity, "We were vaguely aware of security concerns around work with pathogens or toxic chemicals, but that did not relate to us; we primarily operate in a virtual setting. Our work is rooted in building machine learning models for therapeutic and toxic targets to better assist in the design of new molecules for drug discovery. We have spent decades using computers and AI to improve human health – not to degrade it. We were naive in thinking about the potential misuse of our trade, as our aim had always been to avoid molecular features that could interfere with the many different classes of proteins essential to human life. Even our projects on Ebola and neurotoxins, which could have sparked thoughts about the potential negative implications of our machine learning models, had not set our alarm bells ringing." By modifying work they had already completed and using readily available open-source software, they found that "... In less than 6 hours after starting on our in-house server, our model generated 40,000 molecules that scored within our desired threshold. In the process, the AI designed not only VX, but also many other known chemical warfare agents that we identified through visual confirmation with structures in public chemistry databases. Many new molecules were also designed that looked equally plausible. These new molecules were predicted to be more toxic, based on the predicted LD50 values, than publicly known chemical warfare agents. This was unexpected because the datasets we used for training the AI did not include [critical] nerve agents." They go on to call for action in combatting potential misuse and argue: "Scientific conferences, such as the Society of Toxicology and American Chemical Society, should actively foster a dialogue among experts from industry, academia and policy making on the implications of our computational tools. There has been recent discussion in this journal regarding requirements for broader impact statements from authors submitting to conferences, institutional review boards and funding bodies as well as addressing potential challenges. Making increased visibility a continuous effort and a key priority would greatly assist in raising awareness about potential dual-use aspects of cutting-edge technologies and would generate the outreach necessary to have everyone active in our field engage in responsible science."

A further concern was raised in March 2023 with an article in The US Army War College's journal, "Parameters Quarterly" talking about artificial general intelligence (AGI) growing in importance. While AGI is yet to become a reality, and it still sounds a bit like science fiction, it is the concept of AI reaching a level of intelligence on par with or greater than that of humans. It is being developed as a "highly autonomous systems that outperform humans at most economically valuable work". Such systems are expected to solve problems and do complex things while adapting to their environments and improving their knowledge and skills on their own. It is believed that they will lead to the development of artificial superintelligence (ASI), which imagines systems with much greater intellectual capabilities than humans. These concepts lie behind Monash University's Robert Sparrow and the University of Twente's Adam Henschke, argument that advances in the development of AI technology could mean that AGI could be used to command human soldiers in war[15]. In the hands of those who act in bad faith, the concept is terrifying.

Trust in both AI technology and AI technology users is clearly a crucial and timely ethical issue.

AI is changing our lives in ways that are difficult to anticipate and understand. If the technology is going to be directed in a more socially responsible way, it is time to dedicate time and attention to AI ethics education."

A 2020 paper to the Computer-Human Interface conference[16] stresses the need for the ethics of AI to be relevant to developers when they say: "Many organizations have published principles intended to guide the ethical development and deployment of AI systems; however, their abstract nature makes them difficult to operationalize. Some organizations have therefore produced AI ethics checklists, as well as checklists for more specific concepts, such as fairness, as applied to AI systems. But unless checklists are grounded in practitioners' needs, they may be misused." To support this, they say "Although these systems have enormous potential for good, they can also amplify and reify existing societal biases, such as hiring systems that are more likely to recommend applicants from certain demographic groups or risk assessment systems that solidify and exacerbate patterns of racism and classism in criminal justice. When checklists have been introduced in other domains, such as structural engineering, aviation, and medicine, without involving practitioners in their design or implementation, they have been misused or even ignored. For example, commercial airline pilots misused pre-flight checklists, resulting in catastrophe, while surgeons initially refused to use surgical checklists."

Returning to the SMH report earlier in this chapter, would checklists or other interventions have resulted in different impacts on the parents? Probably not. Carissa Hessick, a law professor at the University of North Carolina who

writes about child pornography crimes is quoted in the article as saying: "....
legally defining what constitutes sexually abusive imagery can be complicated.
..." [In this case] "There's no abuse of the child," she said. "It's taken for
nonsexual reasons." In both cases discussed, the algorithm correctly identified
suspect images. In both cases the images were correctly reviewed by a human.
In both cases the images were correctly referred to the police. In both cases the
parents were exonerated by the police investigation. But also, in both the
families involved, there have been long-term serious implications.

There is a long way to go before we can have unreserved trust in AI processes. Until then, when thinking about AI, it might sometimes be helpful to
slightly rephrase Margaret Heffernan's comment when talking about Super
Chickens[17]: "AI doesn't have ideas. People do." People need to ensure that to
the greatest extent possible AI algorithms are free from the biases of their
developers and that the nuances of context are taken into account.

A 2021 paper explored the issue of ethics and algorithmic biases in the field
of artificial intelligence. Its concern was that "Despite the diversity of sources
and temporalities at the origin of these biases, the current solutions to achieve
ethical results are mostly technical. The consideration of human factors and
more particularly cognitive biases remains incomplete." This leads them to
argue "the task of designing artificial intelligence systems is conducive to the
emergence of cognitive biases".[18] They designed an initial research project that
tested the awareness of individuals who design artificial intelligence systems as
to the impact of their cognitive biases in their productions and focused on
conformity bias, confirmation bias and illusory correlation bias. They reported
that: "The first results of this pre-experimentation show that these individuals
believe that their decisions are subject to the cognitive biases of conformity,
illusory correlation and confirmation." They conclude that: "Future work
should try to understand whether there is an embodiment of these cognitive
biases in the AI system, and if so, how they are embodied."

The message is very clear. AI does not free us from biases impacting decisions and having possible adverse impact. If anything, it has the ability to
exacerbate the negative impacts of bias. Like any tool, it has the potential to be
used for positive or negative purposes – of itself AI is neutral. It is important
that every measure is taken to maximise the probability that it is used to help
achieve positive outcomes for individuals, society, and humankind itself.

Questions for group discussion:

1. "The key to growth? Race with the machines". The message is that, after
    a lag, technology enables improved productivity, significant growth, and
    societal benefits. This is particularly true when we work "with" the tech-
    nology rather than "against" it. Discuss this statement with references to
    the positive and negatives of generative AI?

2. In 2017, the British Physicist, Stephen Hawking, was speaking at the Web Summit Technology Conference in Lisbon, Portugal. As reported by CNBC, "Physicist Stephen Hawking said the emergence of artificial intelligence could be the "worst event in the history of our civilization." He urged creators of AI to "employ best practice and effective management." Why was Hawking so concerned about AI's potentials? What actions need to be taken in order to avoid this being the "worst event in the history of our civilisation"?

3. "With this increase in prevalence and applicability of AI has come a wide range of ethical debates, including how AI can be programmed to make moral decisions, how these decision-making processes can be made sufficiently transparent to humans, and who should be held accountable for these decisions. A crucial objective in the development of ethical AI is cultivating public trust and acceptance of AI technologies." What can be done to minimise bias being incorporated into AI algorithms and how can accountability for AI processes be achieved?

4. "While ethical issues around the development of the algorithms and use of the tool itself are usually assessed, the possibility of an inadvertent flaw that allows the "black box" to develop its own biases and/or circumvent original restrictions seems less often considered by users." To what extent should the user of AI be concerned about the issues raised by the example from the Home Office in UK and the concerns raised by Dattner et al? How can these concerns be addressed by users?

5. " Over the past few years, governments and other entities have had a surge of interest in facial recognition. Yet the technology is drawing much scrutiny in part because it is far less reliable when used to identify people who are not white males." Given the increasing use of facial recognition by police and security forces across the world and, in the commercial sphere, by, for example, supermarkets tracking customers from entry through to exit from the store, how do you feel about the possibility you are (or potentially could be) tracked whenever you are in a public place? What would be your reaction if you were falsely identified? How can we prevent abuse of such technology?

Notes

1 https://arxiv.org/abs/2403.00742 https://doi.org/10.48550/arXiv.2403.00742
2 https://www.abc.net.au/news/2024-02-20/australia-loss-relying-on-us-china-technology/103484844
3 https://www.theguardian.com/technology/2022/dec/04/ai-bot-chatgpt-stuns-academics-with-essay-writing-skills-and-usability
4 https://www.smh.com.au/world/north-america/a-dad-took-photos-of-his-son-for-the-doctor-google-shut-down-his-phone-flagged-him-as-a-criminal-20220822-p5bbmq.html
5 https://www.youtube.com/watch?v=3Y9Pgy5pRIo
6 https://www.youtube.com/watch?v=sod-eJBf9Y0

7 https://www.abc.net.au/news/2022-12-12/robodebt-algorithms-black-box-explainer/101215902
8 See for example, https://hbr.org/2019/04/the-legal-and-ethical-implications-of-using-ai-in-hiring, https://www.forbes.com/sites/benjaminlaker/2023/07/07/the-dark-side-of-ai-recruiting-depersonalization-and-its-consequences-on-the-modern-job-market/?sh=238419cd68c8
9 https://www.cnbc.com/2017/11/06/stephen-hawking-ai-could-be-worst-event-in-civilization.html?__source=sharebar|email&par=sharebar
10 https://www.washingtonpost.com/technology/2023/02/14/chatgpt-dan-jailbreak/
11 Ouchchy, Leila; Coin, Allen; & Dubljević, Veljko, 2020, "AI in the headlines: the portrayal of the ethical issues of artificial intelligence in the media", AI & SOCIETY (2020) 35:927–936 https://doi.org/10.1007/s00146-020-00965-5
12 https://abcnews.go.com/Technology/openai-ceo-sam-altman-ai-reshape-society-acknowledges/story?id=97897122
13 Borenstein, Jason & Howard, Ayanna, 2021, "Emerging challenges in AI and the need for AI ethics education", AI and Ethics (2021) 1:61–65 https://doi.org/10.1007/s43681-020-00002-7
14 https://doi.org/10.1038/s42256-022-00465-9
15 Robert J. Sparrow and Adam Henschke, 2013, *"Future Force, Minotaurs, Not Centaurs: The Future of Manned-Unmanned Teaming"*. https://press.armywarcollege.edu/parameters/vol53/iss1/6/
16 Madaio, Michael A; Stark, Luke; Wortman, Jennifer; HannaWallach, Vaughan, 2020, *"Co-Designing Checklists to Understand Organizational Challenges and Opportunities around Fairness in AI"*, CHI 2020 Paper CHI 2020 Paper CHI 2020 Paper CHI 2020 Paper http://dx.doi.org/10.1145/3313831.3376445
17 Organizations are often run according to "the superchicken model," where the value is placed on star employees who outperform others. And yet, this isn't what drives the most high-achieving teams. Business leader Margaret Heffernan observes that it is social cohesion – built every coffee break, every time one team member asks another for help – that leads over time to great results. https://www.ted.com/talks/margaret_heffernan_forget_the_pecking_order_at_work?language=en
18 M Cazes, N Franiatte, A Delmas, J-M André, M Rodier, et al. Evaluation of the sensitivity of cognitive biases in the design of artificial intelligence. Rencontres des Jeunes Chercheurs en Intelligence Artificielle (RJCIA'21) Plate-Forme Intelligence Artificielle (PFIA'21), Jul 2021, Bordeaux, France. pp.30–37. 6

8

BIAS AND THE LAW

2023 saw a judicial enquiry into a 2022 high-profile sexual assault case in Canberra. When the report was released, it was very critical of the then Director of Public Prosecutions (DPP) of the Australian Capital Territory (ACT). Some media were very quick to argue that this was a damning indictment of the DPP's decision to bring the initial prosecution. The DPP resigned and, a short time later, launched an ACT Supreme Court appeal against the findings. Central to the appeal was that the Judge leading the enquiry had handed his report to two selected journalists prematurely, but embargoed until released formally by the government. It became clear that one journalist was handed the report before it had even been presented to the ACT chief minister. The appeal argued that this was a potential breach of the Inquiries Act and a denial of fairness to the DPP. It argued that

> many findings against him were made unreasonably, that he was denied a fair hearing, that the inquiry breached the law through the unauthorised disclosure of material, and that he was denied natural justice due to "a reasonable apprehension of bias". He also says some of the findings made by the inquiry were outside its remit.[1]

Subsequently, in court, it was claimed that the head of the enquiry had over 55 phone discussions totalling more than seven hours on the phone to one of the media outlets to which the report was released.

For many people outside of the legal world, this may have been the first time they had heard of "apprehended bias". The legal world, however, is very aware of this concept known as "apprehended bias" which is defined as: "*An apprehension of bias will arise if courts find a fair-minded and reasonably informed observer might consider that a decision-maker might not approach their task*

DOI: 10.4324/9781003528340-9

with a sufficient level of impartiality."[2] This is one of the claims made by Donald Trump and his supporters in the various legal actions he is facing in 2023 and 2024 – they are all "witch hunts" and politically driven because the prosecutors and judges are democrats or were appointed by jurisdictions with democratic governments. This can be a powerful argument in countries such as the US where political affiliations can play a significant role in judicial appointments (think the US Supreme Court, for example). However, in countries that include Australia, New Zealand, and the United Kingdom, Trump's arguments would have less force because the Judiciary is appointed by a totally different process that is (at least in theory) independent of political affiliation and any general election process.

But bias in law goes far beyond simply the concept of "apprehended bias". In an ideal world, legal systems would ensure all laws took account of individual and societal norms and culture, be totally impartial, treat all people equally, and be readily available to all people in a timely and affordable manner. Such systems would focus on providing results that maximised the probability of all affected parties recognising that, regardless of the final decision, all parties had experienced justice. Today this is patently not the case. Whether or not we like it, the evidence is that those with power and authority are more likely to be successful in any legal activity than are those who are poor, disadvantaged, racially or culturally different, have low communication competencies, and the like. Part of the reason for this is that those with power and authority are more likely to be able to afford the very best legal advice and representation than is possible for those with fewer resources. While the legal framework in most jurisdictions does its best to remove any tendency for judges to have bias, as seen here, if bias is inherent in the system there is little they can do. Similarly, while, in the main, those involved as legal practitioners at any level may try to minimise any impact from unconscious bias, as will be argued later, it is virtually impossible to totally remove all bias.

Many years ago, outside the Court of Final Appeal, in Hong Kong, I saw a statue of Lady Justice blindfolded and holding a balance and a sword. The clear message was that "Justice is blind" – in other words, justice applies equally to all no matter their status because those sitting in judgement will, at all times, impartially weigh all evidence prior to making their decision. In most countries across the world, the judicial system claims that they operate within this maxim.

Of course, the system doesn't always operate with impartiality. The more autocratic a society's leadership, the greater the probability that those expressing views contrary to those of the leader(s) will be imprisoned or worse. Examples of this are clearly seen in Iran in 2022 following the death in custody of Mahsa Amini, and in Russia following their invasion of Ukraine where, in just one year, 23 influential people who had expressed reservations and/or opposition to the war, have died in questionable circumstances. It was seen in China with the response to the 1989 protests in Tiananmen Square (known in Chinese as the June Fourth Incident) and has been seen in Myanmar since the military coup in 2021. It can also be seen in democracies such as the USA with the outstanding example being that of Senator Lindsay Graham who, as one of those tasked with adjudicating on the impeachment of President Donald Trump, famously said he "would not pretend to be a fair juror". The refusal for some years of Republicans to take action against Representative George Santos (R-N.Y.) who, in December 2022, admitted that he lied about his job experience[3] and college education during his successful campaign for a seat in the U.S. House also raises questions about the impartiality of justice in the USA. It took a total of three years and only after an investigation by the House Ethics Committee, and the filing of federal criminal charges against Santos, that the House of Representatives finally voted to expel Santos on December 1, 2023.

Questions as to the impartiality of the judicial system are also raised when one considers the imbalance of those incarcerated in many countries – including liberal democracies. Almost without exception, the ratio of indigenous people, members of other minority groups, the unemployed, and people with addiction and mental health issues are imprisoned at rates that vastly exceed their pro-portional mix in their respective societies. Obtaining "justice" is for many, a long, convoluted, and expensive process that frequently fails the impartiality test whether in civil or criminal jurisdictions.

In just over the past 20 years, realisation of this imbalance has prompted some 100 law-specific academic studies on the issue of bias and its impact on administration of the law.

It is argued that

> Justice systems around the world are fundamentally human endeavours. As such, they rely on human cognitive systems that are subject to bias. Biases in human cognition are interesting from a psychological perspective, but in a world of legal decision making anything less than a purely objective decision can have profoundly negative ramifications, from the wrongful conviction of innocent people to failure to apprehend guilty people, to broadly felt lack of trust in the justice system. … Many legal decision-making errors result from underlying cognitive biases in the way people think about, interpret, evaluate, and integrate information. The term "cognitive bias" is quite broad and can refer to an array of psychological phenomena, including hindsight bias, outcome bias, belief perseverance, contact biases, anchoring effects, tunnel vision, and more.[4]

The authors are very clear that "cognitive bias as discussed here reflects inno-cent errors rather than malfeasance." In other words, they are arguing that the issues arising from the cognitive biases they discuss are primarily unconscious rather than conscious motivations. Their paper makes the point that the impact of unconscious bias is a serious concern:

People in all roles throughout the legal system have been shown to exhibit similar biases, from forensic scientists to police trainees to experienced detectives and police officers to expert witnesses to jurors. Further, the pernicious effects of prior beliefs regarding the suspect's guilt have numerous downstream consequences, biasing the evaluation of evidence (e.g., erroneously categorizing two fingerprints as a match) and the perceived reliability of evidence (e.g., lowering perceived reliability of belief-inconsistent evidence) and leading to behavior changes that elicit the very responses one expects (e.g., asking guilt-presumptive questions that elicit defensiveness, even from innocent suspects). These effects alone have the capacity to pervert justice. But, in fact, we argue that the negative effects of cognitive bias are even broader than this, affecting not only the manner in which single pieces of evidence are evaluated, but also the manner in which multiple pieces of evidence are integrated to reach an ultimate decision regarding the suspect.

The matter of bias impacting evidence in court is clearly an important issue.

Establishing a given bias's relevance to law requires making explicit the normative stance that establishes the bias's relevance. Much existing legal literature on cognitive heuristics and biases wrongly slides from (1) the claim that some bias influences a norm to (2) the claim that the norm should be rejected or accepted. If my argument is correct, the influence of cognitive heuristics and biases on a legal norm neither justifies automatically rejecting nor automatically endorsing that norm. Rather, the evaluation of legal norms in light of their associated biases must proceed case by case.[5]

Persad argues that, in considering the relevance of bias, it is important for a person to know "whether they define bias descriptively or prescriptively." It makes the point that "the methodology of behavioral science aims to describe how we *do* act, not tell us how we *should* act" (in other words, it is descriptive rather than prescriptive) yet much of the literature on bias and law confuses the two. When such confusion occurs, Persad says, there can be negative impacts on the arguments being presented:

Distinguishing descriptive and prescriptive definitions of bias illuminates two ways arguments can misfire:1. They attempt to infer prescriptive claims directly from the presence of bias even when bias has been defined descriptively rather than prescriptively; or 2. They fail to be clear about whether a definition of bias is descriptive.

Following extensive discussion of cases and authorities, he finally concludes:

That our decisions are subject to myriad physical, psychological, and neurological influences both from within and without should neither reassure nor disturb us: on one very plausible view, we can be fully and robustly responsible for our decisions even while those decisions are the product of internal and external influences.

He continues:

Being reassured or disturbed requires answering a further, normative question: which influences are *normatively defensible,* and which are *normatively corrosive?* Once we have a preliminary answer to the normative question, behavioral science can help us design norms that emphasize the defensible influences and avoid the corrosive ones. But behavioral scientists, though they can describe *how* we reason about the normative question, have no special expertise in answering it. That question we must answer for ourselves.

A 2015 article in the Judges' Journal[6] makes the point that:

Courts rely on expert witnesses and mostly assume that they provide impartial and objective evidence. Yet cognitive science shows that even the most dedicated and committed experts are influenced, without even realizing it, by factors unrelated to the data relevant to form their expert conclusions.

A little later they continue:

Complex cognitive mechanisms are involved in the way in which humans perceive and interpret information, make judgments, and reach decisions. These cognitive mechanisms stand at the heart of intelligence and expertise. Paradoxically, as people become experts, their brains change and develop very useful capacities, but these very mechanisms can also increase the susceptibility to bias.

They see the reason for this as being because:

cognitive science research demonstrates that judgments are shaped by a broad range of factors. For example, expectation or hope can cause tunnel vision by directing attention selectively toward certain information while ignoring other important facts. Similarly, context, motivation, and emotions can distort perception and judgments. And starting with an idea or hypothesis can cause experts to fixate and escalate cognitive commitment so much so that they do not objectively and properly consider other alternatives or identify mistakes. ... It is very important to note that cognitive biases work without awareness, so biased experts may think and be incorrectly convinced that they are objective and be unjustifiably confident in their conclusions.

An important point raised by this article is that potential for bias is generally recognised for non-expert witnesses but there is the potential for it to be forgotten when experts are involved. They note, however, that in the USA:

> Bias may be subconscious and affect perception and memory, and it is relevant in assessing witness credibility. Bias is a term used ... to describe the relationship between a party and a witness which might lead the witness to slant, unconsciously or otherwise, his testimony in favor of or against a party. (United States v. Abel, 469 U.S. 45, 52 (1984))". The relationship between domain-irrelevant information and crime scene evidence runs exactly this risk: it "might lead the witness to slant, unconsciously or otherwise, his testimony in favor of or against a party." This process is no different for expert witnesses than for lay witnesses.

But, as already seen earlier in this chapter, bias by witnesses is only one aspect of bias and the law.

The core of "the law" in most countries lies in its governing body – its constitution and its parliament. "The law" then devolves into the judicial system of courts, lawyers, and law enforcement bodies of some sort. In 2013, Dan Kahan of Yale Law School explored issues of cognitive bias and the US Constitution[7]. Kahn discusses two phenomena: cultural cognition ("a set of related mechanisms that unconsciously motivate individuals to form perceptions of risk and related facts that cohere with important group commitments") and cognitive illiberalism ("a state of affairs in which enforcement of liberal political principles is defeated, not by wilful defiance, but by cognitive bias)." In a paper for one of a Chicago-Kent Law Review series on "The Supreme Court and the American Public", he argues that

> cultural cognition is an important source of cognitive illiberalism. In the course of observing social norms and applying legal rules that implement liberal political principles, citizens and governmental decision-makers are prone to unconsciously impute harm and other socially undesirable consequences to behavior that denigrates their group's cultural outlooks.

A little later he continues that "constitutional law is effectively innocent of cognitive illiberalism, which subverts state neutrality, notwithstanding widespread commitment to it, by judges, jurors, legislators, and citizens generally."

Kahan's arguments are strong and are valid for unconscious bias. But sometimes constitutional law is not "innocent of cognitive illiberalism". Across the USA, judicial appointments have always had political overtones. The governing party in each State as well as the US Congress, evaluates judicial nominees made by the Governor or President and, more often than not, a nominee whose record accords with the philosophical stance of the governing body, receives approval. Overall, however, the system has traditionally ensured some degree of balance in both political allegiance and judicial record of appointees.

In February 2016 Justice Antonin Scalia, an icon of conservative jurisprudence, died. A few months later, in the spring of 2016, President Barack Obama named Merrick Garland, then aged 63, to fill this vacancy on the Supreme Court. Garland had long been considered a prime prospect for the high court, serving as chief judge on the U.S. Court of Appeals for the District of Columbia Circuit. Widely regarded as a moderate, Garland had been praised in the past by many Republicans. However, even before Obama had named Garland, and in fact only hours after Scalia's death was announced, Senate Majority Leader Mitch McConnell declared any appointment by the sitting president to be null and void. He said the next Supreme Court justice should be chosen by the next president – to be elected later that year. "Of course," said McConnell, "the American people should have a say in the court's direction. It is a president's constitutional right to nominate a Supreme Court justice, and it is the Senate's constitutional right to act as a check on the president and withhold its consent." At that point it was widely accepted that Donald Trump could win the forthcoming Presidential Election and McConnell wanted to heighten the probability that a nominee acceptable to Republican sensibilities would be appointed. This stance was supported by the 11 Republican members of the Senate Judiciary Committee who signed a letter saying they had no intention of consenting to any nominee from Obama. No proceedings of any kind were held on Garland's appointment.

Following Trump's success, it was easy for him to fill this vacancy and, with the death of Justice Ruth Ginsberg a short time later, the Republican dream of a Supreme Court that was dominated by people acceptable to Republican sensibilities was achieved. McConnell's stance was motivated not by unconscious cognitive bias but by conscious cognitive bias. The earlier mentioned statement by Senator Lindsay Graham about "not even pretend to be impartial" in relation to the impeachment of Donald Trump was totally consistent with conscious bias. So, too, could be seen the current (January 2023) unwillingness of Republicans to take action against then Representative-elect, George Santos (R-N.Y.) in relation to information he provided when seeking election. Sometimes illiberalism in legal matters is deliberate.

The impact of bias affects both lawyers and clients[8]. Weinstein shows that

> these often-subtle mental biases can lead to pervasive errors in decision making by causing us to ignore important information and make inaccurate predictions. They may lead a client to underestimate the risk of litigation. They may also lead a lawyer to miscategorize a client's value choice as a misjudgement of fact.

He defines cognitive biases as "also known as cognitive illusions, are systematic errors in judgment and prediction" and goes on to state: "Although technical insight into cognition can improve lawyering, legal decision making cannot, and should not, be reduced to a mathematical calculus." In other words, the emphasis should be not on trying to eliminate bias but rather to recognise its reality and then to manage it.

However, while the literature is clear about the reality of bias relating to law enforcement activities by police, prosecutors, defenders, witnesses, judges and the like, there appears to be far less discussion of bias on legal systems per se.

There are five main approaches to legal systems. These tend to be grouped under the headings of civil law, common law, customary law, religious law, and hybrid or mixed systems. Civil law has its origins in Roman Law and uses comprehensive legal codes as the basis for system with case law providing guidance but not precedent. It is found in, for example, Europe, Japan, Russia and their one-time colonies. Common Law is the body of law built through case law i.e. accumulation of judge-made binding precedents. It originated in England and then was adopted by the British colonies including the USA and the British Commonwealth. In this system, judges interpret the law and apply it to individual cases. Customary law is the legal system that existed across societies since pre-historical days and is found, inter alia, in societies such as the Aboriginal nations of Australia and the Americas. It has, sometimes, a partial underpinning of religious or theocratic legal systems. Religious or theocratic law is based on religious doctrines or principles such as Islamic (Sharia) law and is found in countries such as Iran, Iraq, Afghanistan and the Arabian countries. Hybrid or mixed systems have mixed legal systems incorporating common, civil, religious, and customary law systems. In the USA, the state of Louisiana uses some common law, but it also utilizes a civil law system for much of its state law and procedures because of its origins as a French territory. The Philippine system includes French civil law, US-style common law, sharia law, and Indigenous customary law due to its history while many African countries include a parallel tribal or ethnic legal system to adjudicate family law matters.

In at least the civil and common law jurisdictions, for criminal law, there is an underlying premise of guilt or innocence of an accused with prosecutions having to "prove beyond reasonable doubt" that an accused is guilty (for the presumption of innocence) or the defence having to prove that an accused is "not guilty" (for the presumption of guilt). In the Australian legal system, the presumption of innocence is a crucial component of criminal law. However, it can have unintended consequences that impact negatively on all parties involved.

An example of this was found in Australia during 2022. In a high-profile rape trial held in the ACT (Australian Capital Territory) Supreme Court, over a period of twelve days and involving twenty-nine witnesses, the alleged victim was subject to intensive examination over every part of her testimony. The defence lawyer, in accord with normal practice, was ruthless in highlighting any and every inconsistency in her evidence so that "reasonable doubt" could impact the jurors' decision. At the conclusion of the prosecution case, as was totally permissible, the defence chose not to call any witnesses – not even the defendant. Accordingly, there was no opportunity for the defendant to be subject to any questioning as to the events of the evening in question. After five days of deliberation the jury had not been able to reach a decision and it was then discovered that at least one juror had possession of a research paper on sexual assaults that was not included in the trial. Supreme Court Chief Justice Lucy McCallum then aborted the trial. The biases here could include belief perseverance, halo effect, and anchoring effects. That one of the only two parties who actually knew what transpired that night was able to avoid having their account tested while the other party had their life laid bare produced an inequitable situation in which the best possible interpretation of the result is that the alleged offence was "not proven". As a result, regardless of whatever the truth may be (and I certainly am not seeking to impugn either party), the stigma of being charged with rape will continue to impact the defendant while the trauma of merciless cross-examination will continue to impact the plaintiff. With the decision of the ACT Attorney General to then not proceed with a retrial, the only recourse now available to either party was to take costly civil action to clear their name – an action that was later taken by the original defendant (Bruce Lehrmann) who sued a television channel and one of its journalists for defamation.[9]

A further complicating factor when considering bias and the law is the issue of timeliness in cases (whether criminal or civil) coming to Court. The oft stated maxim of "Justice delayed is justice denied" is frequently quoted and, in most jurisdictions, every effort is made to ensure cases are heard promptly, but the courts are frequently forced to delay hearings simply because of the volume of cases. Another issue relating to bias is that courts are subject to laws made by governments. And governments, at least in democracies, can be strongly influenced by various pressure groups such as the media, policing organisations, and concerned citizens who have a somewhat myopic view of, usually, criminal activity. The result can be the enactment of laws that focus solely on apprehension and punishment of offenders rather than seeking to adequately address the causes of such activity. We concentrate on having "an ambulance at the base of the cliff rather than on placing a fence at the top". Invariably emphases such as "war on drugs", "three strikes", "zero tolerance", and other "tough on crime" approaches serve primarily to attend the interests of "the haves" rather than addressing the needs of "the have-nots". Invariably this means concentrating on relatively minor offences to the point where the ratio of indigenous people, members of other minority groups, the unemployed, and people with neurological and/or addiction issues are imprisoned at rates that vastly exceed their proportional mix in their society – and the Court time required for this reduces the Court time available for dealing with major offenses. In many countries today, Australia included, it can take months or years rather than days or weeks for a case to be heard and that can be problematic.

Of course, if this is to be addressed and remediated, we need to acknowledge that dealing with this requires that those in authority are not locked into the "status quo" bias – in other words, they need to have the insight and courage to confront what is urgent and important rather than allowing urgency as dictated by various pressure groups to dominate.

Questions for group discussion:

1. "Whether or not we like it. The evidence is that those with power and authority are more likely to be successful in any legal activity than are those who are poor, disadvantaged, racially or culturally different, have low communication competencies, and the like." What are the biases that underlie this break down of what legal systems should be? How did these arise? How can they be managed?

2. "Questions as to the impartiality of the judicial system are also raised when one considers the imbalance of those incarcerated in many countries – including liberal democracies. Almost without exception, the ratio of indigenous people, members of other minority groups, the unemployed, and people with addiction and mental health issues are imprisoned at rates that vastly exceed their proportional mix in their society." What does this say about commonality of biases across local and international jurisdictions? Why? What is your reaction to this statement? Why?

3. "Justice systems around the world are fundamentally human endeavours. As such, they rely on human cognitive systems that are subject to bias. Biases in human cognition are interesting from a psychological perspective, but in a world of legal decision making anything less than a purely objective decision can have profoundly negative ramifications, from the wrongful conviction of innocent people to failure to apprehend guilty people, to broadly felt lack of trust in the justice system." What are the biases most likely to impact? Given what we know about the interplay of emotion and cognition dominating all decision making, what can be done to minimise the impacts of these biases?

4. "The core of 'the law' in most countries lies in its governing body – its constitution and its parliament. 'The law' then devolves into the judicial system of courts, lawyers, and law enforcement bodies of some sort." … "Courts are subject to laws made by governments. And governments, at least in democracies, can be strongly influenced by various pressure groups such as the media, policing organisations, and concerned citizens". How can bias arising from pressure groups be managed across all areas of law and legal systems?

5. At what stage should a country's legal system change its architecture for corporate governance and insist what behaviours should not be acceptable in the workplace?

Notes

1 https://www.theguardian.com/australia-news/2023/sep/21/shane-drumgold-challenge-to-sofronoff-inquiry-bruce-lehrmann
2 https://law.unimelb.edu.au/__data/assets/pdf_file/0004/3606538/Groves-442-Advance.pdf
3 https://nypost.com/article/tracking-george-santos-lies/
4 Charman Steve, Douglass, Amy Bradfield, Mook, Alexis, 2019, *Psychological Science and the Law*, edited by Neil Brewer, Amy Bradfield Douglass, The Guildford Press, Chapter 2

5 Persad, G., 2014. When, and how, should cognitive bias matter to law. *Law & Ineq.*, 32, p.31.
6 Dror, Itiel E, McCormack, Bridget M, Epstein, Jules, 2015, Cognitive Bias and Its Impact on
  Expert Witnesses and the Court, The Judges' Journal, Volume 54, Number 4, Fall 2015. © 2015 by the American Bar Association,
7 Dan M. Kahan, Cognitive Bias and the Constitution, 88 Chi.-Kent L. Rev. 367 (2013). Available at: https://scholarship.kentlaw.iit.edu/cklawreview/vol88/iss2/7
8 Ian Weinstein, *Don't Believe Everything You Think: Cognitive Bias in Legal Decision Making*, 8 Clinical L. Rev. 783 (2002–2003) Available at: http://ir.lawnet.fordham.edu/faculty_scholarship/422
9 This action, in effect, forced the parties to engage in a de facto criminal trial that required a lower standard of proof than would have been required in a criminal court. On April 15, 2024, the decision in the defamation action was released. In a 324-page decision, Federal Court Justice Michael Lee dismissed Bruce Lehrmann's case and found that the respondents' "truth" defence was valid. He declared that, on the basis of probability, Lehrmann had raped the original complainant. Justice Lee stressed that his decision was based on the civil standard of proof, not the criminal standard, emphasising the "substantive difference" between the two. A key difference here was that, by initiating the defamation action, for the first time in any Court, Bruce Lehrmann was required to give evidence and was subject to cross examination by the respondents' legal teams. At the time of writing, it is unknown whether this decision will be appealed.

9
BIAS AND CONFLICT

We live in a world where fear and anger are manifest every day. Anger abounds in our politics, in our social discourse, and in our expectations for the future. The finger of blame can be pointed at the usual suspects: Dictators, populists, malcontents and online trolls, but its misuse is far more widespread. Fear sharpens the mind, which is why fear is used in campaigns, whether it's public health, whether it's to change people's attitude to things like climate change or national security. While fear and anger can help positive social change by fostering a thirst for justice and even revolution, it is more frequently used to create new biases or to reinforce existing biases – whether such biases be conscious or unconscious.

While we tend to equate fear-based leadership with totalitarianism or populism, there are many instances in democratic countries where politics is polarised – coloured by the use of fear as a blunt tool of coercion, and it has also been on the rise in corporate and organisational management. This use as a management tool is somewhat unsurprising as it is not too many years since a major publisher asked me to review a proposal for a book entitled "Management by guilt" which proposed attaining results by making employees afraid of punishment. When fear is pervasive in a system – and it's pervasive in all of our systems – we lose dynamism, we lose innovation, and we avoid seeking creative approaches for resolving intractable issues such as are at the heart of "wicked" problems. As we see in matters such as the Israeli-Palestinian conflict, the Ukraine-Russia conflict, and the rise of China as a major geo-political player, anger, fear, hatred are certainly very important components of what happens when we focus on differences rather than on what we have in common.

At the time of writing (April 2024) across Australia, 25 women have been killed by acts of domestic violence. Domestic homicide victims made up over one-third (35% or 78) of all homicide victims (220 victims) in 2020–21 in the

DOI: 10.4324/9781003528340-10

National Homicide Monitoring Program (NHMP) (AIC 2023). The majority of domestic homicide victims are killed by an intimate partner. 40 were killed by a family member with: 14 killed by a parent. One of the factors contributing to this is the status quo bias. There are many men whose mindset is stuck in an era in which women were considered less than equal with men.

One of the concerns around status quo bias is that it may indicate a fixed mindset (see the work of Dweck in Chapter 16) and a possible consequence of this is falling into what Beck and Cowan (see Chapter 13) call the "gamma trap" – a situation in which, by largely unsuccessfully trying to make the world change to suit them, a person suffers a downward spiral of emotions and anger dominates. Ultimately this downward spiral can result in such frustration that activities such as self-violence (including suicide), domestic and other social violence, or even war becomes an option.

One of the biases that many of us ignore is the status quo bias. Status quo bias is an emotional bias; a preference for the maintenance of one's current or previous state of affairs, and a preference to not undertake any action to change this current or previous state. There is a sense in which this bias has an almost insidious influence at all levels of human activity because it has the ability to underpin international issues on a daily basis – influence perhaps out proportion relative to other biases we do acknowledge. It certainly plays a significant role in influencing our world views. It also underpins many of the more obvious biases that are in play when we consider issues around conflict. When coupled with other biases it can exacerbate such problems as prejudice and discrimination For example:

- Most people have relatively strong views about the Israeli-Palestinian conflict. In this situation, status quo bias is an important contributor: we see Israel seeking to maintain two aspects of the status quo. The first aspect is the security of the State of Israel – a country which arose from the 1917 Balfour Declaration (a public statement issued by the British government) announcing its support for the establishment of a "national home for the Jewish people" in Palestine (which was, then, an Ottoman region). This Declaration became a reality on May 14, 1948, when David Ben-Gurion, the head of the Jewish Agency, proclaimed the establishment of the State of Israel.
- The first complication of this status quo bias is found in Israel being able to exert control over not only Israel per se, but also over every aspect of life in the adjoining Palestinian Territories. The second aspect is the desire by significant political groups in Israel for a return to the idealised ancient status quo of "the Promised Land" with far greater land territory than was annexed in 1948 and 1973. This second aspect has led to the establishment of Jewish settlements in Palestinian occupied territories – an activity declared illegal by the United Nations.
- Simultaneously with these Israeli actions we see the Palestinians seeking a return to the previous status quo in one of two ways. First are the

Palestinians seeking withdrawal of Israel to the internationally agreed borders as existed prior to the October 1973 Yom Kippur war. (When the Arab coalition jointly launched a surprise attack against Israel on the Jewish holy day of Yom Kippur) and the establishment of the State of Palestine. Second are the Palestinians seeking a return to the status quo prior to the 1948 proclamation. This group wants to destroy the State of Israel.

- Both Israelis and Palestinians have every right to exist, and their people have every right to live in peace and safety. However, currently, entrenched political and religious views, coupled with a significant power imbalance, mean that any resolution of the conflict is fraught with complexity. It is a classic "wicked problem" in which the probability of a "solution" cannot easily be calculated.
- Second, consider the Russian invasion of Ukraine in 2022. Again, people hold divergent views as to the rights and wrongs of this. At least for those strongly supporting Ukraine, many seem to focus on the issue of President Putin's desire for power and control with only minimal attention paid to the deeper, underlying influence of status quo bias. In this conflict, we see Russia invading Ukraine as they seek to revert to the status quo prior to 24 August 1991 in which they controlled land that was, until Ukraine officially declared itself an independent country, part of the USSR – the forerunner of the current Russian State. Following the collapse of the Soviet Union, Ukraine became independent. Ukraine seeks to maintain the status quo of being an independent country.
- Third, consider the rise of China as a major geo-political power. In the current tensions between the US (and its allies) and China, we see "the West" as typified by the US, seeking to maintain the status quo of "the rules-based order" under which "the West" seeks to maintain the rules, institutions and values of the late 20th century enforced by US power. China, however, sees that "the rules-based order" was always a Western-dominated order – an order that favoured the West – whose rules were made and broken by Western powers. China recognising and exercising its own re-emergent military and economic strength is now a serious challenge to US dominance, China seeks to establish a new status quo – one in which western powers are, at best, only at parity with "the East" – and which restores China to a position of international influence similar to that of earlier centuries.

Of course, these examples are not instances of status quo bias only – this is but one of the biases in play. Reframing these tensions under the influence of status quo bias doesn't remove the tensions or resolve the bloodshed that either is currently occurring or could occur. It does, however, enable us to see them from a slightly different perspective and such a change, perhaps, might enable us to find more inclusive means of resolution than actual or potential violence. Because of their impact on public opinion, the media (both traditional and social) has an important role to play in this.

In 2020 researchers from UCLA and Yale universities studied the influence of media on public opinion[1]. They explored the role of partisan media[2] on voting behaviour. As is stated in their paper: "Partisan media impacts voting behavior, yet what changes in viewers' beliefs or attitudes may underlie these impacts is poorly understood." And, as can be seen by even the most casual observer, partisan media seeks constantly to either advocate for whatever status quo is supportive of its political, social, and economic philosophies.

Earlier, the issue of bias in the media was explored and particular attention was paid to the role of Sky News in promoting Donald Trump's claim that the 2020 election for the US presidency had been stolen from him. As stated, eventually the Courts will (at least indirectly) adjudicate on Trump's claim per the action taken by, for example, Dominion Voting Systems, which, in a $1.6bn suit, had accused Fox News and its parent company, Fox Corporation, of maligning its reputation. This action focuses attention on specific instances of high-profile media conflating their role to report news with that of being a source of influence intended to achieve a particular result. Fox wanted to maintain the status quo of benefitting from Trump's support.[3]

A range of studies since 2014 has indicated that partisan media meaningfully affects voting behaviour and impacts elections, however little was known about what changes in viewers' beliefs, attitudes, or priorities may underlie these shifts in voting behaviour. The question of permanence of any such changes was also largely unexplored. The 2022 paper by Brookman and Kalla considered the differing approaches by CNN and Fox News to reporting on issues such as Covid and Biden in the lead up to the 2020 Presidential election. These were chosen because

> CNN provided extensive coverage of COVID-19, which included information about the severity of the COVID-19 crisis and poor aspects of Trump's performance handling COVID-19. Fox News covered COVID-19 much less. The coverage of COVID-19 Fox did offer provided little of the information CNN did, instead Fox gave viewers information about why the virus was not a serious threat. On the other hand, Fox News extensively but highly selectively covered racial issues, and its coverage of these issues provided extensive information about Biden and other Democrats' supposed positions on them and about outbreaks of violence at protests for racial justice in American cities. CNN provided little information about either. The networks both covered the issue of voting by mail, but again covered dramatically different information about it (in addition to offering different frames).

Brookman and Kalla partnered with a media analytics company to recruit individuals who regularly watch Fox News to a survey panel. These were people identified through data on their households' actual television viewership. At baseline, these Fox News viewers were nearly all very conservative and strong Republicans. Brookman and Kalla then, during September 2020, incentivised these Fox News viewers to watch CNN instead and implemented a monitoring process that would minimise fabrication of stated viewing behaviour by using real-time viewership quizzes. Their study found that the opinions of the research group were impacted: "changing the slant of their media diets impacted their factual beliefs, attitudes, perceptions of issues' importance, and overall political views." The authors argue that these effects stem in part from a bias they call "partisan coverage filtering" – a process in which partisan outlets selectively report information, leading viewers to learn a biased set of facts. They note that "participants concluded that Fox concealed negative information about President Trump. Partisan media does not only present its side an electoral advantage – it may present a challenge for democratic accountability."

While their study found

> participants were much more likely to see issues covered on CNN (COVID-19) instead of on Fox News (racial protests) as important. … (We) also found evidence of manifold effects on viewers' attitudes about current events, policy preferences, and evaluations of key political figures and parties. For example, we found large effects on attitudes and policy preferences about COVID-19. We also found changes in evaluations of Donald Trump and Republican candidates and elected officials.

Brookman and Kalla then conducted an endline survey several weeks later that found "these impacts largely receded as treated participants primarily returned to their prior viewership habits" – the participants had returned to their normal pattern of watching Fox News. In other words, permeance of change was impacted by in-group influence.

Earlier Davidio et al. was quoted as saying "We need to consider how social structure impacts biases across social institutions …" Brookman and Kalla's study highlights the importance of this statement. We have already explored the role of social media and have commented that it is not subject to the checks and balances that have traditionally existed in mainstream printed, audio and television news and opinion. However, it is important to remember that all media influences how and what people think, and every mainstream mass media outlet has its own editorial biases. This influence is what the pioneering study by Brookman and Kalla examined and showed that even people with entrenched opinions, can be influenced (at least temporarily) by mass media presenting an alternative.

Also, as discussed, it is important to note that there is no such thing as a totally neutral media – whether traditional mass media or social media. All media organisations have their political orientations, and these are reflected in the framing and reporting of news and opinions. This is important if we want a democratic society in which there is exposure to a range of opinions so that debate is encouraged. In societies where only one opinion is allowed (or is strongly encouraged), the invariable result is that the ruling political elite are supported (at least nominally) and dissent (even if not initially) becomes a criminal activity. From a societal perspective it is, to say the least, unhealthy for a single media group or mogul to dominate in any community.

It follows that, in order to demonstrate its social responsibilities and to maintain its credibility, mainstream mass media needs to be very clear as to what is "news" and what is "opinion". While that reported as "news" will always be framed in a manner sympathetic to the organisation's political orientation, as "news" it should be objectively verifiable and even a casual reader/listener/viewer should be able to note commonalities of detail across competing sites. After all, "news" is seeking to inform as to what has happened or is happening. Depending on how it is framed and what is selected as being "newsworthy", news may or may not have an influence on how people think. "Opinion", however is different. "Opinion" is a conscious effort to influence how others think. Generally, it makes no apology for being biased nor does it have any need to. "Opinion" may be objectively verifiable to some extent, but even this is not a necessity. It is presenting one side of a case and inviting debate. It can (and should) help develop, reinforce, or challenge social and individual biases. Unfortunately, today it is not uncommon to find this "news" vs "opinion" line at least blurred and often crossed. To further the political orientation of an organisation or mogul, "opinion" gets dressed up as "news" with "opinion" then encouraging shifts to more extreme views at either end of the spectrum.

But, as already demonstrated, influencing bias is not limited to the activities of mass media and social media. Culture is a key source of influence whether national, religious, political, business, or any other. Social norms cannot be ignored. And social norms are particularly powerful in influencing issues around reverting to a previous, or maintaining the current, status quo. It is a powerful voice against those that would seek change for the future.

As will be discussed later, experience and research make clear that the provision of "bias training" interventions have little long-term impact on behaviour because they fail to address the environment in which bias is developed, reinforced, and is practiced. The poet John Donne said, "no man is an island"[4]. He continues: "every man is a peece of the Continent, a part of the maine; if a clod bee washed away by the Sea, Europe is the lesse". In other words, we cannot act as though individuals are independent of their environment and culture. And, as discussed, because we are all members of a variety of different cultures, often simultaneously, addressing this multiple influence is critical in facilitating behavioural change. Later this will be addressed in more detail.

Status quo bias is also impacted by various international conventions and agreements. For most of us, it is too easy to forget that, behind much of what happens in every country are international agreements and conventions. These may develop from a variety of stimuli. For example, the state of Israel emerged from the Balfour Declaration after the First World War and Ukraine emerged following the collapse of the Berlin Wall and subsequent break up of The USSR along with, at least in part, from reaction to oppressive regimes coupled with increasing globalisation. Such conventions are initiated by the United Nations and/or agreements between independent sovereign states. But they also emerge from trade, economic and/or security agreements between various sovereign states. Examples of these would include the EU, NAFTA (North American Free Trade Agreement) etc. Whatever the stimulus, the way in which these are subsequently portrayed in the media also has an impact on our biases. We learn that a particular convention has been ratified by our country and we then, quite understandably, largely ignore it until and/or unless it then impacts directly on us. If we think of it at all, we simply take it for granted.

The almost insidious thing about the status quo bias is that we become so accustomed to something being part of our everyday existence that questioning whether it is appropriate is deemed redundant. Alternatively, as we encounter a challenge to our current world view, we seek a return to a previous (usually selectively recalled) status. As was stated above, status quo bias has a very strong influence on our mental models or world views and can underpin other biases.

One such international agreement is especially pertinent to the Russia-Ukraine situation. In 1998 the Rome Statute of the International Criminal Court (ICC) was established by the UN. In 2002 this was reconstituted as a permanent international criminal court to "bring to justice the perpetrators of the worst crimes known to humankind – war crimes, crimes against humanity, and genocide,"[5] when national courts are unable or unwilling to do so. Currently there are 123 countries that are members of the Court. Also in 2002, however, the United States, in a position shared with, among others, Israel and Sudan, having previously signed the Rome Statute formally withdrew its signature and indicated that it did not intend to ratify the agreement[6]. This withdrawal arose from mixed reactions within the US. There were those who criticised the ICC for lack of jury trials; allegations that retrials were allowed for errors of fact; allegations that hearsay evidence is allowed; and allegations of no right to a speedy trial, a public trial, or reasonable bail. There was also strong opposition from some US groups on the grounds that US participation in the ICC treaty regime would be unconstitutional because it would allow the trial of U.S. citizens for crimes committed on U.S. soil, which are otherwise entirely within the judicial power of the United States. (The Supreme Court has long held that only the courts of the United States, as established under the Constitution, can try such offences.) Simultaneously, supporters of the ICC said that, with the exception of the right to jury trial, the ICC Statute contains the due process rights found in the U.S. Constitution and were now well recognized in international standards of due process in Article 67 of the Rome Statute.

In March 2023 the role of the ICC became major news with the notification that they had issued an arrest warrant for President Putin of Russia[7]. The ICC website states:

Mr Vladimir Vladimirovich Putin, born on 7 October 1952, President of the Russian Federation, is allegedly responsible for the war crime of unlawful deportation of population (children) and that of unlawful transfer of population (children) from occupied areas of Ukraine to the Russian Federation (under articles 8(2)(a)(vii) and 8(2)(b)(viii) of the Rome Statute). The crimes were allegedly committed in Ukrainian occupied territory at least from 24 February 2022. There are reasonable grounds to believe that Mr Putin bears individual criminal responsibility for the aforementioned crimes, (i) for having committed the acts directly, jointly with others and/or through others (article 25(3)(a) of the Rome Statute), and (ii) for his failure to exercise control properly over civilian and military subordinates who committed the acts, or allowed for their commission, and who were under his effective authority and control, pursuant to superior responsibility (article 28(b) of the Rome Statute).

Ms Maria Alekseyevna Lvova-Belova, born on 25 October 1984, Commissioner for Children's Rights in the Office of the President of the Russian Federation, is allegedly responsible for the war crime of unlawful deportation of population (children) and that of unlawful transfer of population (children) from occupied areas of Ukraine to the Russian Federation (under articles 8(2)(a)(vii) and 8(2)(b)(viii) of the Rome Statute). The crimes were allegedly committed in Ukrainian occupied territory at least from 24 February 2022. There are reasonable grounds to believe that Ms Lvova-Belova bears individual criminal responsibility for the aforementioned crimes, for having committed the acts directly, jointly with others and/or through others (article 25(3)(a) of the Rome Statute).

Pre-Trial Chamber II considered, based on the Prosecution's applications of 22 February 2023, that there are reasonable grounds to believe that each suspect bears responsibility for the war crime of unlawful deportation of population and that of unlawful transfer of population from occupied areas of Ukraine to the Russian Federation, in prejudice of Ukrainian children.

Outside of (mainly) Russia and Belarus, across the world there was widespread endorsement of the ICC's action. The response from the US was supportive although possibly muted with BBC.com reporting that "US President Joe Biden has welcomed the International Criminal Court's issuing of an arrest warrant against his Russian counterpart, Vladimir Putin."[8] In the US, CNN simply stated that "US President Joe Biden, when asked by a reporter, "should Putin be tried for war crimes," he replied, "he's clearly committed war crimes," indicating Putin unsurprisingly would not be welcome in the US."[9]

Across the world, all countries have subscribed to international agreements and conventions that influence what may or may not be acceptable behaviour – they have promoted a different "status quo" or have reinforced an existing status quo. In some, whether the country has ratified the protocol seems irrelevant. For example, non-member states of the ICC can, on application of a member, be investigated. The Putin arrest warrant and the US responses to the investigation of Israel are illustrative of this. Condemnation of Russia's invasion is appropriate and the issue of an arrest warrant for Putin is an important action, but there needs to be equal treatment of protagonists – treating Russia differently from how the US and the Coalition of the Willing was treated indicates bias. As the ICC response to the invasion of Iraq makes clear, relative power dominance of aggressor nations means that conventions are not always applied equally. As previously stated, all too often, "rules-based order" has proved to be an order that favoured the West, whose rules were made and broken by Western powers.

However, it is informative to compare this action against Putin with what happened in relation to leaders of US and the "Coalition of the Willing"[10] following the invasion of Iraq in 2003. As is now widely acknowledged, the invasion of Iraq was based on information that sought to provide justification for political ends rather than accurately presenting facts. In a March 2023 interview on Fox News, Condoleezza Rice, who was George W Bush's national security adviser at the time, was asked about Russia's aggression, "when you invade a sovereign nation, that is a war crime?" She replied: "It is certainly against every principle of international law and international order."[11] The seventh of the Nuremberg Principles, which, ever since Russia's invasion of Ukraine have been widely cited in calling for Russian prosecutions, points out that "complicity" in a war of aggression "is a crime under international law". Today, it is widely acknowledged that the 2003 invasion of Iraq met the Nuremberg definition. Despite this, no ICC investigation was ever commenced – let alone any of the key protagonists being charged.

Perhaps this contrast also helps explain the response by the US in March 2021 when the Prosecutor of the International Criminal Court (ICC), confirmed the opening of an investigation into the Israel-Palestinian situation. In this instance Antony J. Blinken, Secretary of State issued a statement saying:

> The United States firmly opposes and is deeply disappointed by this decision. The ICC has no jurisdiction over this matter. Israel is not a party to the ICC and has not consented to the Court's jurisdiction, and we have serious concerns about the ICC's attempts to exercise its jurisdiction over Israeli personnel. The Palestinians do not qualify as a sovereign state and therefore, are not qualified to obtain membership as a state in, participate as a state in, or delegate jurisdiction to the ICC.[12]

In February 2024 an interim ruling by the ICC on a case brought by South Africa against Israel, again highlighted status quo biases. South Africa's submission alleged that Israel has committed, and is committing, genocide against Palestinians in the Gaza Strip, in violation of the Genocide Convention, and placed the charges in what it describes as the broader context of Israel's conduct towards Palestinians, including what South Africa described as a 75-year apartheid, 56-year occupation, and sixteen-year blockade of the Strip. South Africa requested that the ICJ render immediate provisional measures of protection by issuing an order to Israel to immediately suspend its military operations in and against Gaza.

Israel characterised South Africa's charges as "baseless". They argued that it is conducting a war of self-defence in accordance with international law following the Hamas-led attacks on its territory on 7 October 2023. Approximately 1,200 people, most of them civilians, were killed in these attacks. Israel pointed to ongoing firing of missiles at civilian population centres, the kidnapping and holding of Israeli hostages in Gaza, and contended that its war cabinet and military authorities' directives showed no genocidal intent. While acknowledging the high incidence of civilian casualties, Israel attributes them to Hamas and other militant groups using civilian infrastructure as cover for their military assets and operations. They asserted compliance with international law and claims to facilitate humanitarian aid into the territory.

On 26 January 2024 the Court issued an Order in relation to the provisional measures request in which it ordered Israel to take all measures to prevent any acts that could be considered genocidal according to the 1948 Genocide Convention. The court said, "at least some of the acts and omissions alleged by South Africa to have been committed by Israel in Gaza appear to be capable of falling within the provisions of the [Genocide] Convention". The Court did not order Israel to suspend its military campaign in the Gaza Strip, which South Africa had requested. The court also expressed "grave concern" about the fate of the hostages held in the Gaza Strip and recognized the catastrophic situation in Gaza "at serious risk of deteriorating further" prior to a final verdict.

Predictably, the key supporters of both Israeli and Palestinian positions were quick to interpret the decision as a "win" for one or the other side and subsequent actions taken at the UN General Assembly and the Security Council have been unable to make progress in bringing peace to the region. While the final judgement of the Court will take considerable time to decide, as with other ICC decisions it is unlikely that the situation in Gaza, any more than the situation in Ukraine, will be soon resolved. In the interim, innocent people suffer dislocation from their homes, destruction of their property, and an inability to get food, shelter, medical and other essential services. The result is that many die because of intransigence by the key protagonists and delaying actions by their international supporters.

The way in which all international agreements and/or conventions are policed has the ability to impact national and individual world views or mental models and can influence the cognitive biases we all hold. Unbalanced policing and/or blind adherence to any international or local convention can have just as much influence on our conscious and unconscious biases as can any other "in-group – out-group" scenario. In the case of status quo bias, the in-group endorses "our" status quo" while the "out-group" challenges it in some way. As discussed above, the law needs to be applied equally to all parties, regardless of their power and influence, if there is to be justice.

The media plays an important role in keeping us informed. Their framing of such information can help us either to support or to challenge our status quo bias when we consider our response to international conflict. This is a further key reason why acknowledging and addressing bias in the media is so important.

Questions for group discussion:

1. "Reframing these tensions under the influence of status quo bias doesn't remove the tensions or resolve the bloodshed that either is currently occurring or could occur. It does, however, enable us to see them from a slightly different perspective and such a change, perhaps, might enable us to find more inclusive means of resolution than actual or potential violence." Make a list of the various biases (both national and international) that impact conflicts such as the examples. How can these biases be addressed and what role can international pressure have on these?

2. "Partisan media impacts voting behavior, yet what changes in viewers' beliefs or attitudes may underlie these impacts is poorly understood." In your consideration of conflicts around the world – northern Europe, Africa, the Middle East, China, the Americas, Caribbean etc – to what extent have your personal views as to the rights and wrongs of all parties involved been impacted by partisan media? Why? How?

3. "There needs to be equal treatment of protagonists – treating Russia differently from how the US and the Coalition of the Willing was treated indicates bias. As the ICC response to the invasion of Iraq makes clear, relative power dominance of aggressor nations means that conventions are not always applied equally. As previously stated, all too often, "rules-based order" has proved to be an order that favoured the West, whose rules were made and broken by Western powers." What do you believe are the biases that mean "conventions are not always applied equally"? Is this a sustainable situation if we are seeking to minimise international conflict? What actions can be taken to encourage equal application? What can actions can you personally take to try and reduce negative impacts of the biases that drive this situation?

4. "In order to demonstrate its social responsibilities and to maintain its credibility, mainstream mass media needs to be very clear as to what is 'news' and what is 'opinion'." Is the difference between "news" and "opinion" really important in relation to conflicts? Why? What changes could media organisations make in order to neutralise perceptions of bias?

5. "Culture is a key source of influence whether national, religious, political, business, or any other. Social norms cannot be ignored. And social norms are particularly powerful in influencing issues around reverting to a previous, or maintaining the current, status quo. It is a powerful voice against

those that would seek change for the future." Why is this the case? To what extent do your primary cultural identifications impact your views relating to the various tensions and conflicts extant today? How do these same factors impact on all other conflict situations that personally affect you?

Notes

1 Brookman, David and Kalla, Joshua, The manifold effects of partisan media on viewers' beliefs and attitudes: A field experiment with Fox News viewers*, 2022, https://osf.io/jrw26/. The authors note that this was an initial study and there are explicit in stating further studies should be done: we only considered the effect of shifting Fox News viewers to CNN. While our theoretical argument would expect similar effects among viewers of other partisan media networks, future work should attempt to replicate this (e.g., shift MSNBC viewers to Fox News).

2 "Partisan media engages in both traditionally-emphasized forms of media influence (agenda setting and framing) as well as a form of influence we call partisan coverage filtering. Partisan media also engage in an underappreciated practice we call partisan coverage filtering: selectively reporting information about selectively chosen topics, causing its viewers to learn more information favorable to the network's partisan side and potentially changing viewers' attitudes and political evaluations as a result"

3 Attention is drawn to the earlier noted report from Reuters. This case was never heard in Court. According to the news agency, Reuters, on April 19, 2023: "Fox News on Tuesday disposed of one legal threat with its $787.5 million defamation settlement with Dominion Voting Systems, but the network still faces a $2.7 billion lawsuit from another voting technology company, Smartmatic USA, over its coverage of debunked election-rigging claims." (https://www.reuters.com/legal/fox-resolves-dominion-case-bigger-election-defamation-lawsuit-looms-2023-04-19/)

4 Donne, John, 1624, "Meditation 17", from Devotions Upon Emergent Occasions

5 *Human Rights Watch (July 2008). Courting History: The Landmark International Criminal Court's First Years. New York.*

6 Countries not members of the ICC include United States, Russia, China, Israel, Libya, Qatar.

7 Situation in Ukraine: ICC judges issue arrest warrants against Vladimir Vladimirovich Putin and Maria Alekseyevna Lvova-Belova https://www.icc-cpi.int/news/situation-ukraine-icc-judges-issue-arrest-warrants-against-vladimir-vladimirovich-putin-and

8 https://www.bbc.com/news/world-europe-64998165

9 https://edition.cnn.com/2023/03/18/europe/putin-icc-arrest-warrant-analysis-intl-cmd/index.html

10 Coalition of the willing referred to the US-led Multi-National Force – Iraq, the military command during the 2003 invasion of Iraq and much of the ensuing Iraq War. The coalition was led by the United States.

11 https://www.facebook.com/QudsNen/videos/when-you-invade-a-sovereign-nation-that-is-a-war-crime-fox-news-presenter-said-t/347605783931775/

12 https://www.state.gov/the-united-states-opposes-the-icc-investigation-into-the-palestinian-situation/

10

BIAS AND DISSEMINATION OF KNOWLEDGE

In the Introduction to this book, I stated: "It is this issue of bias's impact that needs to be addressed. As I do so, it is certain that many of my own biases will be revealed – even if I have no intention of making such revelations nor even know that I have that bias. I will try to be neutral." One of the key issues we all face is determining the extent to which anything we see, read or hear is impacted by the biases held by authors, presenters, editors, etc and their associated sources of the information provided. Today with a 24/7 news feed from traditional media coupled with the plethora of social media broadcasts the relationship between our biases and the dissemination of knowledge is increasingly important.

In the information science field, there is a taxonomy known as the DIKW pyramid[1], which refers loosely to a class of models for representing purported structural and/or functional relationships between *data, information, knowledge*, and *wisdom*. Typically information is defined in terms of data, knowledge in terms of information, and wisdom in terms of knowledge. The key thing to note about this is the flow from data to wisdom – each level is reliant on its predecessor but underlying everything is data.

Data is defined as "facts and statistics collected together for reference or analysis". They are not a set of assumptions or personal opinions or some other collection of thoughts. It is something that can be independently verified and which, when collated and interpreted, provides information that can be used to further one's knowledge. Much of what is today promulgated as "information" lacks verifiable data as its source. The 24/7 news cycle means that organisations often rely on press releases and other promotional material as sources for their "information" despite the purpose of a press release being to ensure that what is published is framed in a manner designed by some public relations authority. They are invariably biased in some way. Of course, for material available on

DOI: 10.4324/9781003528340-11

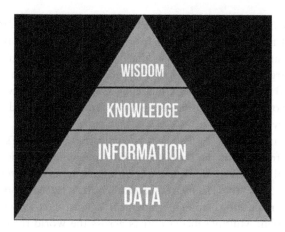

FIGURE 10.1 The DIKW Pyramid

social media, the issue of verifiable data is seldom of concern – assumptions, personal opinions or some other collections of thoughts are promulgated with no other intent but to further the objectives of their initiator. The potential for misinformation to be confused with information is high and, as already discussed, a key problem with misinformation is that, once it enters our brain, it remains there and influences our processing of all subsequent material.

In general parlance no such taxonomy is usually found. Almost anything and everything can be considered information – critical thinking is seldom applied to verify what is seen, read and/or heard. The result is that knowledge and wisdom can be very subjective because both may be independent of the quality of information available and the data on which this information is based. Biased knowledge can quickly become the norm. Misinformation can run rife. "Things are seldom what they seem, skim milk masquerades as cream" wrote WS Gilbert in HMS Pinafore! This can create serious problems for the victims.[2]

For the mainstream media, generally some attempt is made to check information before publishing but seldom are there checks and balances in social media. This gives rise to two aspects of bias in what is generally considered "information". The first is the biases underpinning the material provided: the second is the biases of the receivers that determines which sources they access and the elements of critical thinking they apply to what these sources.

First, bias in the sources.

As previously mentioned, in January 2021, Dominion Voting Systems filed now-settled, defamation lawsuits against former Trump campaign lawyers Sidney Powell and Rudy Giuliani, seeking $1.3 billion in damages from each. During subsequent months, Dominion filed suits seeking $1.6 billion in damages from each of Fox News, Newsmax, OANN and former Overstock.com CEO Patrick Byrne, while also suing Mike Lindell and his corporation, MyPillow. Their case was that Donald Trump and various surrogates were promoting conspiracy theories, which falsely alleged that Dominion was part of an international cabal that stole the election from Trump, and that it used its voting machines to transfer millions of votes that had been cast for Trump instead to Biden. They argue that there was no evidence supporting these claims, which were debunked by various groups including election technology experts, government and voting industry officials, and the Cybersecurity and Infrastructure Security Agency (CISA).

The consistent response by Fox was to claim that Dominion's lawsuit is an attack on the freedom of the press (the First Amendment of the US Constitution) because all they were doing was reporting on important events.

In February 2023, the Delaware superior court released Dominion Voting Systems' brief requesting summary judgment against Fox News for defamation – and $1.6bn. Multiple media outlets across the world then reported that the 192-page document makes it clear that senior figures at Fox News from Rupert Murdoch down knew immediately after the election that claims of voter fraud, in particular those aimed at Dominion, were false. In sworn depositions obtained by Dominion Voting Systems, senior figures at Fox News from Rupert Murdoch down make clear that they knew immediately after the election that claims of voter fraud, in particular those aimed at Dominion, were false. The depositions reveal that Rupert Murdoch, the billionaire owner of Fox News, acknowledged under oath that several Fox News hosts endorsed Donald Trump's lie that the 2020 election was stolen from him. They also reveal that key presenters such as Tucker Carlson called Trump's claims "ludicrous" and "off the rails": Sean Hannity texted about "F'ing lunatics": and a senior network vice-president called one of the stories "MIND BLOWINGLY NUTS".

The depositions show that Murdoch himself dismissed Trump's claims, describing the former president's obsession with proving the election was stolen as "terrible stuff damaging everybody" and he admitted that he could have ordered the network not to platform Trump lawyers such as Sidney Powel.

Subsequently, a Harvard law professor, Laurence Tribe, was widely reported as saying: "I have never seen a defamation case with such overwhelming proof that the defendant admitted in writing that it was making up fake information in order to increase its viewership and its revenues. Fox and its producers and performers were lying as part of their business model." The Court filing makes clear that fear of losing supporters was a key driver behind Fox giving prominence to Trump's claims – the quest for profits took precedence over all else.[3]

While it has long been acknowledged and accepted that all media outlets frame their reporting to suit their particular philosophical, religious, and/or political orientation, it has also been understood that, within this orientation, they would rigorously check the veracity of material presented and, wherever possible, they would not place undue emphasis on a single source. This was claimed to be a clear distinction between mainstream media and social media.

The issue of bias being rampant in social media has been recognised for almost as long as social media platforms have been available. While, as indicated, bias in traditional media has been widely recognised, in the past, issues around access, distribution, diverse publications and time meant that societal impacts have, generally, emerged more slowly and have affected fewer people than is the case with social media.

In 1964 a Canadian professor of English literature, Marshall McLuhan, proposed that a medium itself, not the content it carries, should be the focus of study[4]. He said that a medium affects the society in which it plays a role not only by the content delivered over the medium, but also by the characteristics of the medium itself: there are personal and social consequences of any medium. McLuhan says (Ch 1) "... the "message" of any medium or technology is the change of scale or pace or pattern that it introduces into human affairs. ... it is the medium that shapes and controls the scale and form of human association and action."

McLuhan used his book title to draw attention to his claim that "a medium is not something neutral, it does something to people, it takes hold of them, it roughs them up, it massages them, it bumps them around in the same way that a chiropractor manipulates a body in order to reposition muscles." His view was that the general roughing up that any society gets from a medium, especially a new medium, is that on which we should focus.

In his Introduction to the first edition of his book, McLuhan wrote:

> In the mechanical age now receding, many actions could be taken without too much concern. Slow movement insured that the reactions were delayed for considerable periods of time. Today the action and reaction occur almost at the same time. We actually live mythically and integrally, as it were, but we continue to think in the old, fragmented space and time of the pre-electric age.

McLuhan wrote this in 1964 when the world was still in the relatively early stages of embracing telephones, radio and television as essential everyday items that could be owned and/or accessed by everyone. How much more prescient are his words in these early decades of the twenty-first century – this digital age? Today we live in a society where almost everyone (at least in the developed world and frequently in the third world) has some form of communications device that connects to the internet of things and gives instant access to everything happening and being said everywhere in the world.

In the Introduction to the second edition, McLuhan makes the point that "any technology gradually creates a totally new human environment. Environments are not passive wrappings but active processes." Again, in this digital age we have ample evidence of the truth of his statement. Every day in virtually every place on earth people are moving around paying more attention to their mobile communication devices than they are to anything else. This includes all too often, failure to pay attention to their own personal safety and well-being. The result is sometimes tragic when such behaviour is accompanied by interaction with motor vehicles and the like. McLuhan made the point that any medium has the power of imposing its own assumption on the unwary! He says: "The effects of technology do not occur at the level of opinions or concepts but alter sense ratios or patterns of perception steadily and without any resistance."

In the 1930's it was Joseph Goebbels who made transformational use of media. He was particularly adept at using the relatively new media of radio and film for propaganda purposes. Aware of the value of publicity (both positive and negative), he deliberately provoked beer-hall battles and street brawls, including violent attacks on the Communist Party of Germany. Goebbels adapted recent developments in commercial advertising to the political sphere, including the use of catchy slogans and subliminal cues. He formulated the strategy that fashioned the myth of Hitler as a brilliant and decisive leader. He arranged massive political gatherings at which Hitler was presented as the saviour of a new Germany. In a major new approach, Goebbels oversaw the placing of movie cameras and microphones at key locations to accentuate Hitler's image and voice. Such events and manoeuvrings played a major role in convincing the German people that their country would regain its honour only by giving unwavering support to Hitler. Goebbels was a master communicator who ensured that the use of media would never again return to primarily print for its major impact.

When McLuhan speaks of the "electric media" he is talking primarily of film, wireless technology, radio, television, the telephone, tele printers, and the relatively early stages of computer usage. However, as he points out, these "electric media" ensured that complex data could be processed faster than at any previous period in history; that stories could be accompanied by recent film of events; and that information from one location could be available virtually anywhere else in the world within a matter of hours or days rather than weeks. What was more, when desired, this material could be edited and reused easily so that particular political messages could be emphasised. The news cycle was reduced from weeks to days and currency of information became a competitive advantage. Through the insights of Goebbels media had changed.

At that time McLuhan never foresaw the rise of the internet and social media. However, everything he says of "the electric" media is even more pertinent today. As we have moved from "the electric age" through "the electronic age" to "the information age" our quest for information immediacy has accelerated from days or weeks to micro-seconds. Today something happening anywhere in the world can be viewed in real time by anyone in any other part of the world. And this dissemination of events can be done by anyone without the need for sophisticated recording and broadcasting resources – the attack on the Twin Towers of the World Trade Centre in New York on 9/11 and the terrorist attack of March 2019 in Christchurch, New Zealand that resulted in the tragic deaths of some 50 people provided clear evidence of that. Our news cycle is continuous. With the widespread use of social media, stories can be promulgated without any of the previous checks and balances designed to ensure balanced, honest and accurate reporting. "Fake news" can be promulgated along with "real news" and, for many, the only criterion for assessing veracity lies in the frequency and vehemence with which a story is broadcast. The potential for enhancing rather than reducing bias is exacerbated – and social media such as Twitter, Meta (previously Facebook) and the like aid and abet this promulgation of bias. It is pertinent to recall the comments by Richard Sima[5] earlier about the more we see something repeated, the more likely we are to believe it to be true. This "illusory truth effect" arises because we use familiarity and ease of understanding as a shorthand for truth; the more something is repeated, the more familiar and fluent it feels whether it is misinformation or fact. ... "There is only typically one true version of a claim and an infinite number of ways you could falsify it, right?" said Nadia Brashier, a psychology professor at Purdue University who studies why people fall for fake news and misinformation. "So, if you hear something over and over again, probabilistically, it's going to be the true thing." Misinformation thrives because, as Sima also says: "We are also more susceptible to misinformation that fits into our worldviews or social identities, and we can fall into confirmation bias, which is the tendency to look for and favor information fitting what we already believe."

One of the most prominent users of social media to promulgate inaccurate information and encourage bias was (and, at the time of writing, still is) past President Donald Trump – and, as the Dominion Voting Systems material makes clear, he has been aided and abetted by media that includes Fox News. Although cracks sometimes appear in official Republican support[6], Donald Trump continues to deliver the message he wants to deliver to the people who matter to him – the everyday voting Americans who will determine the next election. The result is that at July 2024, Trump is clearly almost certainly going to be the Republican candidate for the 2024 presidential elections. Disaffected Republicans and the "elite" may complain and try to ensure a balanced approach is given but, in a society that now responds to superficial soundbites rather than to in-depth analysis and discussion, Trump has mastered the communications war. Whatever he wants others to believe he says loudly, and he says it often. Whether or not others like it, Trump has ascertained the best medium for communicating with his target audience.

Evidence of the bias promulgated and reinforced was seen in the events of January 6, 2020 and the subsequent activities of the Republican Party and Trump adherents to oppose any investigation that might dent the aura around Trumpism. Even though the Supreme Court refused to intervene in the order releasing Trumps tax returns and the Federal Bench overturned the appointment of a Special Investigator to vet the material seized in the FBI raid on Trump's Florida home, there is still considerable support for Trump from "ordinary" Americans. Throughout 2023 and early 2024, in the various court cases where Trump has been the defendant, no matter what the courts' decisions and judgements, court processes have become rallying calls to his supporters. Politics in the US (as in many other countries) has degenerated into a conflict between diametrically opposed tribes – neither of which, because of their biases, can admit to any fault on their own part or any good in the other.

The other key users of social media to promulgate questionable (if not completely false) "information" are extremists. Whether from "the left" or "the right" there are those who use social media to promote their own ends regardless of any impact on individuals or society. A prominent name in such misinformation is "QAnon" – a political conspiracy theory and political movement. It originated in the American far-right political sphere in 2017 and centres on false claims made by an anonymous individual or individuals known as "Q". Those claims have been relayed, developed and supplemented by numerous communities and influencers associated with the movement. The core QAnon theory is that a cabal of Satanic, cannibalistic sexual abusers of children operating a global child sex trafficking ring conspired against former U.S. President Donald Trump during his term in office. QAnon has direct roots in Pizzagate, an internet conspiracy theory that appeared one year earlier; it also incorporates elements of many other theories.

QAnon is but one of a myriad conspiracy theories. Many relate to clandestine government plans and elaborate murder plots. Key to conspiracy theories is to deny consensus or to making claims that cannot be proven using established verification methods. They are not always false by default however they are often discredited because of their cumbersome and improbable nature. Psychologists have suggested that they arise from (and appeal to) a form of cognitive bias called "illusory pattern perception". What they all have in common is that they seek to undermine trust in governments, official accounts of events, and of traditional mass media. Each claims to have some secret "insider" knowledge of malfeasance by those with power. While they have existed for decades, it is today's growth and ready availability of social media platforms that has enabled them to gain their now very significant amount of influence and supporters.

Second, bias in the source user.

There are many people who focus only on media and other information sources that conform with their world view. Rather than seeking information per se, they are seeking confirmation of what they already believe or would like to believe. They will not even entertain the possibility that other views may be valid. This helps explain the rate at which material such as extremist material is disseminated as well as the rise in conspiracy theories. "If I read/see/hear it here, it must be correct and it must be important, so I'll make sure all my contacts and friends are aware of it."

In 2020, Ofir Turel of California State University Fullerton and Alexander Serenko[7] of Ontario Tech University argued that:

> Many theoretical accounts of addictive behaviors, including models of
> Internet use disorders, implicate cognitive biases in the formation and

maintenance of excessive behaviors. Yet, little empirical evidence regarding the role of such biases, including implicit attitude, in the development and maintenance of excessive use of social media exists.

Turel and Serenko developed the "Facebook Implicit Association Test (FIAT)" and employed it in a sample of 220 Facebook users. Their interest was related to the possibility of social media usage being a form of addiction and they argue that: "… the rewarding nature of such use, and especially the variability in the schedule of rewards (e.g., 'likes'), can lead to repeated, difficult to control use of social media sites. …. Indeed, the excessive use of social media can manifest itself in typical behavioral addiction symptoms." They are careful to make the point that

> While excessive social media use has not been formally recognized as an addiction disorder by the American Psychiatric Association and the World Health Organization … a plethora of evidence suggests that some social media users have poor control over their use patterns, which can disrupt normal functioning in school, family, and workplace domains.

If one of our dominant milieus is found in social media groups then it is highly likely that we will choose the groups that reinforce rather than challenge our cognitive biases.

Earlier we discussed how cognitive biases develop through our formative years and made the point that "from birth our environment – family, community, school etc – consciously and unconsciously impacts to form our mental models. As we age, these early influences are supplemented by other factors." Clearly the media – especially social media – is potentially one of these "other factors" and, the greater one's use of social media platforms, the higher the probability that sites supporting our world view will be those most accessed. The result is, particularly if, as argued by Turel and Serenko, use of social media has the potential to be addictive, one's existing world view becomes increasingly resistant to change of any form. This will be discussed further in later chapters.

A 2021 work[8] considers "the role that social media plays in spreading misinformation, widely described as 'Fake News'." The authors identify "… five themes that explain the fake news phenomenon: the dissemination process, spreading channel features, outcomes, fabricated legitimacy and attitudes." They point out that "… in the US, Spain, Italy and the UK the majority of adults now receive their news from social media" and "… Fake news can instil misleading beliefs in people who will subsequently base their decision on those false beliefs." Given the earlier comments by Turel and Serenko, it appears clear that those most frequently using social media channels such as Facebook, are those most likely to both be influenced by and, in turn, seek also to influence others in relation to world views that may or may not bear any relation to reality.

Such a view is supported in another 2021 paper[9] which argues that "social media has played a pivotal role in polarising views on politics, and climate change, and more recently, the Covid-19 pandemic. Social media induced polarisation (SMIP) poses serious challenges to society as it could enable 'digital wildfires' that can wreak havoc worldwide." The authors explored how manifestations of confirmation bias contributed to the development of "echo chambers" at the height of the Covid-19 pandemic. They point out that:

> On one hand social media helps in communicating individuals and organizations about their products, services and developing network of communities that can be helpful to share the information on real time basis and create the awareness on a specific issue such as health during Covid-19 ... On the other hand, social media is full of possibilities of fake and misleading content such as Covid-19 variants and their cure along with role of vaccination in fighting Covid-19, along with cyber risks.

A little later they point out that: "The devastating effect of SMIP on communities, businesses, and governments has been identified by the World Economic Forum (2018) as the greatest threat to society due to the speed at which 'digital wildfires' spread on a global scale." They see a key reason for this "wildfire" spread of "information" as being the role of social media as an "echo chamber". They say:

> Echo chambers refer to the situation where people 'hear their own voice' ... In the context of social media, it refers to situations where users consume content that expresses the same point of view that users hold themselves .... As social media platforms largely rely on algorithms to generate large quantity of content, which can lead to the emergence of conspiracy theories, other forms of distorted information, and even extremist groups with a shared ideology, which further lead to the emergence of echo chambers ...

The message is that biases impact both the means of communication used and the material that is shared either as an original posting or as the reposting or other endorsement of material posted by others. Given Di Domenicoa et al.'s comment about the majority of adults in US, Spain, Italy and the UK now receiving their news from social media, concerns about "information" that is obtained from sources lacking significant evidence of objective reporting and comprehensive forms of fact checking looks like being an on-going one.

Given the ease by which social media platforms can be accessed and used, it is almost certainly impractical to expect postings on such platforms to provide balanced views on any issue. As Modgil et al. point out, they readily become an echo chamber in which partisan views can be promulgated and in which any dissenters can be attacked and neutralised. The situation is different for traditional, mainstream media. If traditional media are to maintain their relevance and value it is increasingly important that they use balanced information drawn from a cross section of resources and that they are rigorous in the fact checking and accuracy of message.

Questions for group discussion:

1. "It has long been acknowledged and accepted that all media outlets frame their reporting to suit their particular philosophical, religious, and/or political orientation, it has also been understood that, within this orientation, they would rigorously check the veracity of material presented and, wherever possible, they would not place undue emphasis on a single source. This was claimed to be a clear distinction between mainstream media and social media." Is there still a clear distinction between mainstream and social media in relation to bias and is it important? Why? Why not?

2. "… the 'message' of any medium or technology is the change of scale or pace or pattern that it introduces into human affairs. … it is the medium that shapes and controls the scale and form of human association and action." Thinking about the transformation of media and forms of mass communication over the past 30 or so years, has trust grown or diminished in the information generally available from all sources? Why? What biases have these changes engendered and how are these demonstrated?

3. "[There are] many theoretical accounts of addictive behaviors, including models of Internet use disorders, implicate cognitive biases in the formation and maintenance of excessive behaviors. Yet, little empirical evidence regarding the role of such biases, including implicit attitude, in the development and maintenance of excessive use of social media exists." Is this lack of empirical evidence important? Why? Why not? What are the potential positive and negative impacts on societal biases from such potentially addictive behaviours?

4. "The more we see something repeated, the more likely we are to believe it to be true. This 'illusory truth effect' arises because we use familiarity and ease of understanding as a shorthand for truth; the more something is repeated, the more familiar and fluent it feels whether it is misinformation or fact." What is the real responsibility of all forms the media to fact check material and what biases impact their current behaviour? What can individuals do to avoid the problems associated with "illusory truth"?

5. Modern new generations have immediate access to data through access to media. The first observation on an issue remains in the memory, even if it lacks legitimacy. How do we guard/inform our precious new minds? Should media be made to organise its data so that every "data set" found from a search must have an alternative opposite data search? How do we guard against intrusion into a new life, and how do we honour the role of parents?

Notes

1 The origin of the DIKW pyramid is uncertain and it is also known as the DIKW hierarchy, wisdom hierarchy, knowledge hierarchy, information hierarchy, information pyramid, and the data pyramid.

2 https://www.abc.net.au/news/2024-04-15/how-misinformation-spread-after-bondi-junction-stabbing/103708210
   https://www.smh.com.au/business/companies/man-misidentified-as-bondi-junction-killer-hires-lawyers-to-sue-seven-20240417-p5fkfk.html

3 It must be noted that this case was never heard in Court. According to the news agency, Reuters, on April 19, 2023: "Fox News on Tuesday disposed of one legal threat with its $787.5 million defamation settlement with Dominion Voting Systems, but the network still faces a $2.7 billion lawsuit from another voting technology company, Smartmatic USA, over its coverage of debunked election-rigging claims." (https://www.reuters.com/legal/fox-resolves-dominion-case-bigger-election-defamation-lawsuit-looms-2023-04-19/)

4 McLuhan, Marshall, 1964, *Understanding Media: The Extensions of Man*. Originally published in 1964 by Mentor, New York; reissued 1994, MIT Press, Cambridge, Massachusetts

5 https://www.washingtonpost.com/wellness/2022/11/03/misinformation-brain-beliefs/

6 See, for example, comments by Republican Senator Cassidy on May 21, 2023: https://www.theguardian.com/us-news/2023/may/21/republican-senator-bill-cassidy-trump-lose-2024-race

7 Turel, Ofir & Serenko, Alexander, 2020, "**Cognitive biases and excessive use of social media: The Facebook implicit associations test (FIAT)**", Addictive Behaviors, Volume 105, June 2020, 106328,https://doi.org/10.1016/j.addbeh.2020.106328

8 Di Domenico, Gian Domenico, Sita, Jason, Ishizaka, Alessio and Nunan, Daniel 2021. Fake news, social media and marketing: A systematic review. Journal of Business Research 124, pp. 329–341. http//dx.doi.org/10.1016/j.jbus res.2020.11.03 7 >

9 Sachin Modgil, Rohit Kumar Singh, Shivam Gupta, & Denis Dennehy, 2021, "A Confirmation Bias View on Social Media Induced Polarisation During Covid-19", Information Systems Frontiers
   https://doi.org/10.1007/s10796-021-10222-9

11

BIAS AND HISTORY – A SYSTEMS APPROACH

In previous chapters I have referred to events such as the US invasion of Iraq, Russia's invasion of Ukraine, and Israel's response to the October 7 terrorist attack by Hamas. I have shown that these all involve some aspect of status quo bias, and I highlighted the role played by history in the development of this bias and in the decision-making heuristic employed. Although not necessarily recognised by the protagonists, President Bush's response to September 11's attack on the USA was impacted by his father's response to Iraq's invasion of Kuwait in 1990. President Putin's invasion of Ukraine was impacted by the history of the USSR, and the Israel-Palestinian conflict is impacted by the events of and subsequent to the establishment of the State of Israel.

It is widely recognised that historians must be selective in what they record and that, as a consequence, there can be a bias in how a particular history is slanted. In the main such biases even themselves out as different historians explore the same data. It is a slightly different aspect of bias that is more commonly found today. This is the bias that ignores uncomfortable historical information which, if explored, may provide a valuable framework for assessing current events.

One of the most common biases impacting human behaviours is that of immediacy. This is the brain's built-in mechanism that makes people focus on immediate concerns despite their importance. It is related to the "Immediacy" Effect (also called "Hyperbolic Discounting" or "Present Focus Bias") where people prefer an instant reward over attaining something of potentially more value in the future. This devaluing of something that is delayed can be explained by our modern desire for immediate gratification: our brains are wired to prefer the instant and immediate over the future possible so that present rewards are valued more highly than future ones. It is also found, albeit in a slightly different form, when we prefer to deal with the present regardless of

DOI: 10.4324/9781003528340-12

the past or the future. It has lead to the oft encountered situation where people focus on dealing with what is "urgent" regardless of whether it is important. In this situation there tends to be habitual procrastination on confronting issues and/or making decisions until the "urgent" point is reached and, if challenged, we can claim a poor decision was prompted by the need to make a decision "now" and we didn't have time to consider the bigger picture. We live in the present with little regard for the past or the future.

One of the downsides of this behaviour is that all too often, the problems we face today have arisen out of the solutions we provided yesterday. We find this, for example, in the workplace and elsewhere where, initially, small acts of inappropriate behaviour go unchecked or inadequately addressed until, eventually, the behaviour becomes a major issue that may even involve litigation and/or criminal activity. (See Chapter 16) It often means that we see each activity as a discrete activity rather than as part of a pattern. We fail to recognise that it is part of an overall historical narrative because we are not using systems thinking.

Systems thinking requires understanding interconnectedness[1]. This 2015 study shows: "Systems, if ever they were separated, are indomitably moving towards interconnectedness as we hurtle into a globalized future. ... All of these systems feed into each other to produce extremely complex, unpredictable effects. Or, do they?" .... "With the exponential growth of systems in our world comes a growing need for systems thinkers to tackle these complex problems." It goes on to comment:

> According to the Merriam-Webster dictionary, a system is defined as a regularly interacting or interdependent group of items forming a unified whole (Merriam-Webster's online dictionary, n.d.). .... a requirement for a complete systems thinking definition should be that it defines the latter as a goal oriented system. To accomplish this, the definition must contain all three of the aforementioned kinds of things (elements, interconnections, and a goal or function)". After exploring the literature regarding definitions of systems thinking, Ross and Wade go to define systems thinking as "a set of synergistic analytic skills used to improve the capability of identifying and understanding systems, predicting their behaviors, and devising modifications to them in order to produce desired effects. These skills work together as a system.

Another source has a similar emphasis but puts it a little differently. They state:

> Systems thinking is also a sensitivity to the circular nature of the world we live in; an awareness of the role of structure in creating the conditions we face; a recognition that there are powerful laws of systems operating that we are unaware of; a realization that there are consequences to our actions that we are oblivious to.[2]

As already indicated, however, our biases frequently prevent us from seeking and/or recognising the links between events and activities. We witness history but fail to see events as parts of a comprehensive system and so see each on as a discrete unit to be addressed.

Since the turn of the century, especially since the 9/11 event in the USA, there has been increasing international angst about religious extremism, terrorism, the rise of China as a superpower and, more recently with the invasion of Ukraine, and the October 7, 2023 attack on Israel, the possibility of a third world war. Along with this, time and again people in Iraq, Iran, Afghanistan and similar places have been labelled "barbarian" or worse because of their religious intolerance and aggressive expansion of territory. We are caught in the "us" versus "them" conundrum.

The philosopher, essayist, poet and novelist George Santayana (1862–1952) once said: "Those who cannot remember the past are condemned to repeat it."[3] There is also a commonly encountered aphorism (often attributed to Winston Churchill) that "history is written by the victors". When considering the relationship between bias and history, it can be useful to remember these.

It is certainly true that historical accounts can be subject to the personal bias of the writer which leads academic historians to emphasise that knowledge about our past, certain figures and events, is based only on a relatively few sources and furthermore, our understanding of history is never static and unchanging. History is, in truth, written and rewritten by all sorts of people with different agendas. This reality needs attention and will be addressed below.

Most people are not serious students of history. With the exception of events directly impacting on them, people are far more likely to watch films depicting historical events and/or to read historical novels or populist accounts than they are to work through academic tomes. But even if we do work through academic tomes, the sheer volume of material available means that we tend to be selective – and often such selection is influenced by our immediate culture and environment. The result is that we develop a bias in terms of our "history awareness". Our mental framework relating to history then heavily impacts what we remember and what we think about both past and current events.

Which is where it is appropriate to remind ourselves of what we have been told about the past. International conflict caused by forces such as nationalism, colonisation, extremism and associated violence are not new phenomena nor restricted to any particular faith, nationality or society.

Ancient texts are replete with stories of violence as nations vie to maximise their power and influence in various locations. Read such ancient Greek works as "Jason and the Golden Fleece by Apollonius of Rhodes.", "The Trojan Women and Other Plays" by Euripides, "The Histories" by Herodotus, "Republic" by Plato, "Greek Lives" by Plutarch, "The Anabasis" by Xenophon, or the works of Sophocles and violence is a frequent subject. Extremism and violence are also found in works sacred to Jews, Christians, and Muslims although, for many people, these are considered as significantly different from what is usually termed "Greek Mythology".

A well-known example of this is the story of Israelite conquest of Canaan. Although probably not reduced to writing until at least around 400 BCE, the biblical book of Joshua is the written record of an oral history dating back hundreds of years. In Joshua Chapter 6, verse 21 we read an example of what is an oft repeated story as the Israelites advanced and sought to eliminate those of a different nationality and faith. Speaking of the Israelites destruction of Jericho we read: "Then they utterly destroyed all in the city, both men and women, young and old, oxen, sheep, and asses, with the edge of the sword." (Revised Standard Version) While, as stated earlier, the Bible is not history as we now understand it and while archaeology may raise serious doubts as to many "facts" it records, whether Jericho was destroyed as per the biblical account, is irrelevant. The fact of the Bible being widely understood as an authoritative religious work means that, from this passage and many others like it, there are people who develop a belief that extreme violence is acceptable in the pursuit of religious goals. They then allow this bias to impact their behaviour. And this is regardless of whether the religious goals arise from Judaism, Christianity, Islam, Hinduism or any other faith or philosophical teaching.

Moving to more recent events, consider the history of the Christian Church. From the 12th through to the early 19th centuries, a group of institutions within the Catholic Church whose aim was to combat heresy, conducting trials of suspected heretics. Studies of the records have found that the overwhelming majority of sentences consisted of penances, but convictions of unrepentant heresy were handed over to the secular courts, which generally resulted in execution or life imprisonment. The term usually associated with this is "the Inquisition" and information was frequently obtained from the accused by torture and violence.

Lest religious bias be suspected, it is important to note that the Protestant Christian Church is not exempt from such extreme behaviour. Consider the actions of many Protestant Missionaries when going to newly acquired countries such as the Americas, Asia, Africa and Australasia. Existing cultures were frequently targeted in all areas including food, clothing, family relationships and faith with those reluctant to conform being threatened with physical violence and eternal damnation unless they converted. This forced conversion was made even more complicated by the competing claims of the Catholic and Protestant versions of Christianity with those who "chose" the "wrong" version often being then "encouraged" to make a further change.

Over the centuries there was also the rise of what, since the 19th century, has been known as antisemitism. (It is important to note that the behaviours associated with antisemitism had already been extant for well over 1000 years. Instances of persecution of Jews includes the Rhineland massacres preceding the First Crusade in 1096, the Edict of Expulsion from England in 1290, the 1348–1351 persecution of Jews during the Black Death, the massacres of Spanish Jews in 1391, the persecutions of the Spanish Inquisition, the expulsion from Spain in 1492, the Cossack massacres in Ukraine from 1648 to 1657, various anti-Jewish pogroms in the Russian Empire between 1821 and 1906, the 1894–1906 Dreyfus affair in France, the Holocaust in German-occupied Europe during World War II and Soviet anti-Jewish policies.) It is important, however, that legitimate criticism of Israel's current behaviour regarding the Palestinian territories and treatment of Palestinian people who are resident in Israel per se, is not conflated with antisemitism. Similarly, "Hamas" should not be conflated with "Palestinian". "Hamas" is an organisation that is different from "Palestinian" per se. Punishing the Palestinian people under the guise that Hamas has imbedded itself inside Palestinian organisations and buildings is disingenuous. All people and every person should be accorded unconditional respect regardless of any differentiating factor – but inappropriate, excessive, and/or illegal behaviour will always need to be addressed. As has been amply demonstrated in the 20-plus years since George Bush declared a "war on terrorism", no ideology can be defeated by violence.

As previously stated, the issue is not unique to any particular faith or philosophy. No faith is exempt from criticism. In the history of virtually every society and faith we can find examples of violence and, often, religious intolerance in order to "encourage" conversion.

Today we may well deplore the restrictive activities and violence of religious fundamentalists in Iran, Saudi Arabia, Iraq, Afghanistan and other Islamic countries plus many of the laws being enacted in strongly conservative parts of the USA and Europe, but what we see happening in these places now is little different from what conservative, fundamentalists of all faiths have practiced in earlier years. Our cognitively biased recall of history seeks to rationalise and/or justify what "our" group has done while condemning that done by the "other" groups. The activities of all rigidly conservative religious groups tend to be different only in the brand of faith they support.

What about terrorism? "Terrorist" tends to be the term we apply to people using violence for (usually) political purposes and with whom we vehemently disagree.

Modern day terrorism has its genesis in the resistance movements of the Second World War. Across Europe, Germany's invasion of countries was met not only by military opposition but, long after Germany had obtained military victories, by the resistance of ordinary local citizens who sought to sabotage and destroy both occupiers and their infrastructure. The same was seen in Asia with the resistance to Japanese occupiers and, post 1945, the desire for autonomy by Vietnam and other Indo-China nations. The occupiers saw such resistance as terrorist activity. Those opposing Germany and Japan (and, later France and the USA) saw the same people as heroic freedom fighters. It was widely recognised that when otherwise powerless because of oppressive and exploitive occupation, any activity that damaged the occupiers was legitimate. The post second world war activities of Jews against British occupiers in Palestine and the activities of various nationalistic forces across Africa, India, Malaya, Indonesia, Northern Ireland and other countries are now widely seen in a similar light. The same individual may be seen as a terrorist or a freedom fighter depending on the vantage point from which he or she is observed. A "4 Corners" episode on Australia's ABC television channel of March 11, 2024 is illustrative of this. When a previous senior member of Israel's Shin Bet was asked about how he would react if he was a Palestinian under Israel's control, he replied that he would oppose Israel with everything he had.

A similar situation pertains with the rise of China as a world power and the Russian invasion of Ukraine. Is it possible that our celebration of "capitalism" over "communism" in post 1990 Europe – a celebration that has sought to impose a bias towards "western" values across the world – has been a significant contributory factor in the Russian invasion? Is it possible that some at least of our disquiet about a resurgent China arises out of a bias (be it conscious or unconscious) that only those in the west have any right to be a "world power" and that we consider it horrific that countries, which were once our colonial outposts, could now be at least our equals?

This is not to condone any terrorist activity no matter the "brand". Nor is it an apologetic for any violent act including wars and other acts of aggression. Every act of terrorism and aggression is a scourge that needs to be eliminated, but, when we consider such activity, we need also to recall the bigger picture and to ask whether our biases are preventing treatment of causes by concentrating on "us" versus "them". We then concentrate on resolving "symptoms" and wonder why the past is repeated.

That we so seldom consider this more comprehensive picture is not necessarily a matter of neglect. More often it is because of what might be termed a version of "dealing with the urgent rather than the important". In other words, the issue encountered is of sufficient magnitude to warrant immediate responsive action. Lives are threatened or lost and/or there are seriously injured people, and there is serious property damage. It is vital to attend to this. First responders are focused on providing whatever help they can, and administrators are focused on seeking to ensure that all requisite services are supported. This is appropriate and essential. However, in too many cases, this is where things stop. To quote Shakespeare, "We have scotched the snake, not killed it." (Macbeth, Act 3, Scene 2) We may have dealt with the immediate evidence of an underlying problem, but we have not addressed the underlying cause. Because we tend to be short-term, action orientated, it is easy to fall into the trap suggested by the American journalist, H.L Mencken, who said: "There is always an easy solution to every human problem – neat, plausible, and wrong."[4] We need to develop the ability to deal with the degrees of complexity and ambiguity involved if we are going to deal appropriately with what is both "urgent and important". Unfortunately, all too often, our bias for immediacy, limits our ability to provide the quality of response that is really needed.

Earlier it was stated that:

> It is certainly true that historical accounts can be subject to the personal
> bias of the writer which leads academic historians to emphasise that

knowledge about our past, certain figures and events, is based only on a relatively few sources and furthermore, our understanding of history is never static and unchanging. History is, in truth, written and rewritten by all sorts of people with different agendas.

A 2002 study[5], addresses this issue when it explores the issue of bias and history and says:

> There are four common ways in which historical writing can be biased. First, historians sometimes misinterpret evidence, so that they are not justified in asserting that the inferences they draw about what happened in the past are true. For example, they may attend to evidence that suggests that a certain event occurred but ignore evidence that shows it to have been impossible. Second, when historians compile an account of a historical subject, be it a person, an institution, or an event, what they say about it might be justified and credible, but the account might omit significant facts about the subject so that it is unbalanced, or what I call *unfair*. For instance, it might elaborate upon people's virtues but ignore their vices, giving an unfair impression of their character. The third kind of bias is that of a general description of the past that implies facts which, on the evidence available, are known to be false. Thus, a Marxist might describe a revolution as a class struggle when there were no classes involved in it at all. A fourth common form of bias in history occurs in providing causal explanation of historical events when some but not all of the important causes are mentioned, so that the reader gets a misleading impression of the process by which the event came about.

McCullagh makes the point that in many cases such bias is accidental – caused by an oversight – and draws a distinction between this and deliberate bias. He sees deliberate bias as being where the historian seeks the outcome produced to further certain interests held. He says:

> Mistakes in biased history are motivated, not accidental. ... The social group to which a historian belongs can cause a historian to prefer one general theory of human nature to another: liberals think people are normally motivated by reason and principle; Marxists think they are normally motivated, often unconsciously, by socioeconomic self-interest. The inferences they draw about people's motives for action will vary accordingly. ..."

In other words, an issue of bias exists in the historian and may, consciously or unconsciously, impact their work.

This then adds another level of complexity to our discussion on bias and history. If our information sources lack appropriate checks and balances, our own individual biases may be amplified by the biases found in these information sources. For example, the framing of the same event may be (and usually is) different when recorded across media be the media traditional mass media or contemporary social media. McCullagh points out that one of the benefits of peer reviewing of academic works means that, usually, accidental bias is identified and corrected, and that deliberate bias is at least identified and noted. The issue for most people is that they do not read academic journal articles for general information but, rather, are reliant on mass media with both its strengths and shortcomings. And we all tend to concentrate our information sources from those media that are most compatible with our underlying biases – those that most closely conform to and reinforce the mental models we have developed during our most formative years. Rather than challenging us to reconsider and confront our unconscious and/or conscious biases, they further consolidate them. No matter which end of the political, social, cultural or any other spectrum to which we orientate, the impact of bias in history can have serious consequences for us and for society as a whole. There is a need for more of us to develop the ability to understand complexity and ambiguity when considering current and historical events – to develop the systems thinking that will encourage us to challenge our biases.

This issue of the need to deal with complexity and ambiguity was addressed some years ago by Elliott Jaques[6]. Jaques made the point that leaders need to have the skills of greater conceptual ability, and a better ability to deal with complex information, than do their followers. Jaques made it very clear that, if they are to provide an environment in which others can be successful, the more senior one is in any organisation, the more imperative it is that you have the ability to deal with large amounts of ambiguity and complexity. Although not addressing the issue of bias (Jaques was writing on effective organisational management), his point that an inability or unwillingness to explore and manage increasing amounts of data and the plethora of other external stimuli, will lead to organisational demise is pertinent. If we are locked into a short-term view that fails to consider both the greater historical picture and the potential consequences of our actions, then we heighten the probability of lurching from crisis to crisis. A comprehensive systems approach is imperative if we are to minimise the negative potentials of our unconscious and conscious cognitive biases. George Santayana's comment is as relevant today as it ever was.

Most of us have a very relaxed view the neutrality of the history we read. We are not historians, and we largely accept what is provided. But this relaxed approach can create problems when we treat current events as discrete activity rather than as part of a pattern. Part of dealing with ambiguity and complexity requires that we recognise the larger context within which events occur – a systems approach – in which we seek to understand the bigger picture – both past and possible future – and the patterns that this reveals. This is true whether we are dealing with a recalcitrant child, workplace misbehaviour, national or international conflict or any other event of concern. Such an approach enables us to understand what is really "important" and to then prioritise dealing with what is "urgent and important" – causes and effects – rather than simply trying to resolve symptoms. History provides context.

Of course, if we are to develop our ability to deal with complexity and ambiguity, it may mean that we need to rethink our understanding on common sense and our self-belief of behaving in a rational manner.

Questions for group discussion:

1.   "One of the most common biases impacting human behaviours is that of immediacy. This is the brain's built-in mechanism that makes people focus on immediate concerns despite their importance. It is related to the 'Immediacy' Effect (also called 'Hyperbolic Discounting' or 'Present Focus Bias') where people prefer an instant reward over attaining something of potentially more value in the future." Considering your own decision-making process, to what extent are you impacted by the immediacy bias? What is your record on problems faced today having arisen out of the solutions you provided yesterday? Why? Why not? How important has this been in relation to your history of "good" decision-making?

2.   "Our biases frequently prevent us from seeking and/or recognising the links between events and activities. We witness history but fail to see events as parts of a comprehensive system and so see each on as a discrete unit to be addressed." How often do you try to consider decisions from a systems perspective (i.e. how the current problem/issue fits into a bigger picture) rather than treating it as a discrete event? Why? Why not? Has this approach created any subsequent problems for you?

3.   Every act of terrorism and aggression is a scourge that needs to be eliminated, but, when we consider such activity, we need also to recall the bigger picture and to ask whether our biases are preventing treatment of causes by concentrating on "us" versus "them". What biases impact your response to all forms of aggression, inclusive of terrorism and domestic violence? What action can you take to manage these biases?

4.   "We need to develop the ability to deal with the degrees of complexity and ambiguity involved if we are going to deal appropriately with what is both 'urgent and important'. Unfortunately, all too often, our bias for immediacy, limits our ability to provide the quality of response that is really needed." To what extent has this failure to adequately consider the complexity and ambiguity surrounding the decision caused you subsequent problems?

5.   If you could restate the end goal of your university study, how important to you would it be to return to the community that raised you and spend your nest 20 years giving your new knowledge back to them, instead of pursuing instant career gratification?

Notes

1 Arnold, Ross D and Wade, Jon P, 2015, "A Definition of Systems Thinking: A Systems Approach", Procedia Computer Science 44 (2015) 669–678, 2015 Conference on Systems Engineering Research, doi: 10.1016/j.procs.2015.03.050
2 https://thesystemsthinker.com/systems-thinking-what-why-when-where-and-how/
3 George Santayana, The Life of Reason, 1905. From the series Great Ideas of Western Man.
4 H.L Mencken, 1917, The Divine Afflatus
5 McCullagh, C Behan, 2002, "Bias in Historical Description, Interpretation, and Explanation", Wiley Online Library, https://doi.org/10.1111/0018-2656.00112
6 *Requisite Organisation* Elliott Jaques, 1998, Cason Hall & Co

12

BIAS, COMMON-SENSE AND RATIONALITY

For at least the last 200 years there have been those who have expressed concern about emotions. People who admit to allowing their emotions to drive decisions and behaviour (or who are assumed to do this) have frequently been denigrated by a bias that ignores the reality of emotion almost always being involved to some extent in every human activity.

Earlier, Jonathan Lehrer[1] is quoted as saying that our conscious actions are not totally under control. Quoting the neuroscientist, Joseph LeDoux, he says: "But consciousness is a small part of what the brain does, and it's a slave to everything that works beneath it."

Most people like to believe that they have common sense and that, in the main, they act in a rational manner. We see this "acting in a rational manner" as one of the factors that distinguishes humans from other members of the animal kingdom. While lower species respond instinctively to their stimuli, we believe that, as humans, we respond differently because of our higher cognitive competence. Edith Ackerman[2] supports this when, quoting the 1944 work, "An Essay on Man"[3] she says: "man is set above animals, not because he possesses higher sensibility, longer memory, or an ability for quicker association, but because of his power to create and manipulate symbols – to endow things with meaning and with life."

Mildenberger[4] argues that the

> reason to be rational is that if an agent complies with rational requirements the people around him, as well as he himself, will be able to explain and predict his attitudes. Rationality allows us to make sense of an agent's attitudes in terms of his other attitudes. This form of explainability is valuable, because it provides us with greater comprehension as regards an agent's attitudes.

DOI: 10.4324/9781003528340-13

However, JS Evans[5] suggests that there are two types of rationality – rationality of purpose and rationality of process – and that we may be biased as to which of these are involved when we consider being "rational". It may be perfectly rational to determine purpose but that is no guarantee that we will adopt rational processes to attain it.

This earlier study is later developed further[6] when it is argued that "views of human rationality are strongly affected by the adoption of a two minds theory in which humans have an old mind which evolved early and shares many features of animal cognition, as well as new mind which evolved later and is distinctively developed in humans. Both minds have a form of instrumental rationality – striving for the attainment of goals – but by very different mechanisms. The old mind relies on a combination of evolution and experiential learning and is therefore driven entirely by repeating behaviours which succeeded in the past. The new mind, however, permits the solution of novel problems by reasoning about the future, enabling consequential decision making. I suggest that the concept of epistemic rationality – striving for true knowledge – can only usefully be applied to the new mind with its access to explicit knowledge and beliefs. I also suggest that we commonly interpret behaviour as irrational when the old mind conflicts with the new and frustrates the goals of the conscious person." His point is that there are two qualitatively distinct forms of cognitive processing: an "old mind" approach tends to operate in a fast, automatic, high capacity, intuitive manner that is strongly influenced by the past while a "new mind" approach allows for a slow, controlled, low-capacity consideration of multiple factors. Neither is necessarily "right" or "wrong" but each has elements of bias. There are similarities here to the earlier discussed (Chapter 3) "Red Zone – Blue Zone" concept of our brain's locus of control.

A further overlay is in a 2013[7] study considering the field of economics, which argues that an underlying assumption is that "people act so as to satisfy best their preferences" and that in this instrumental model of rationality, "reason is cast in the role of selecting the best means to an end, the satisfaction of preferences." This, of course, takes no account of "the character of people's preferences" which "can be selfish, altruistic, honourable, admirable, spiteful, etc." In other words, a person may claim to be acting rationally to achieve results but what is considered "rational" may be (and probably is) impacted by underlying biases of which the person may or may not be aware.

Hulpke et al[8] alludes to this matter of underlying bias when considering the current emphasis on evidence-based decision making. While they acknowledge that such a process certainly aids in rational decision making, they go on to note that "a rational fact-based [approach] might not give sufficient credit to instinct and feelings. Decision-makers should take into account facts, evidence, when making decisions, but not ignore intuition, hunches and feelings." This has implications for the interaction of rationality and bias. What they are saying is that it is important to recognise the role of the processes underlying our consciousness (Joseph LeDoux – Chapter 3) rather than assuming we will get best results by ignoring or downplaying them.

In 2019 Fogal[9] argued for "two threads in our thought and talk about rationality, both practical and theoretical" – substantive rationality and structural rationality. He illustrates them thus: "... it's rational to exercise regularly as well as look both ways before crossing the street, but irrational to spend your life memorizing telephone numbers or bet everything you have on a fair coin landing heads. In this sense, to be rational is to be reasonable. Call this substantive rationality." He contrasts this with rationality as a

> a matter of coherence, or having the right structural relations hold between one's attitudinal mental states – one's beliefs, intentions, preferences, hopes, fears, and the like – independently of whether those states (henceforth, "attitudes") are reasonable or justified. ... coherence is thus a broad and broadly normative one, encompassing a range of different combinations of attitudes that intuitively clash, or fail properly to 'fit' together, where the lack of fit needn't involve logical inconsistency. Call this structural rationality.

This "structural rationality" is the focus of his paper. The author discusses the standard approaches to structural rationality which he sees as being "associated with a distinctive set of rules or requirements that mandate or prohibit certain combinations of attitudes, and it's in virtue of violating these requirements that incoherent agents are structurally irrational." He then continues that "rather than corresponding to a distinctive set of lawlike requirements, structural rationality should be seen as corresponding to a distinctive kind of pro tanto rational pressure or force – that is, something that comes in degrees, having both magnitude (strength) and direction (for/against). Call this the pressure-based account of structural rationality." The pressure to which he is referring is that of an individual's personal values, belief systems, and attitudes. He sees these as impacting significantly on one's behaviour. The relevance to bias is clear. We may think we are acting in a rational, neutral manner, but our conscious and/or unconscious biases are impacting on our behaviour, regardless of whether we are aware of this, and this pressure will take precedence over, or at least significantly impact, our rationality. Here we have strong overtones of both Hargreaves Heap and of Hulpke and Fronmueller.

Evidence of this can be seen every day. Amongst the most obvious examples are those of the political realm. Consider the rise of Donald Trump from often ridiculed contender for the 2016 US Presidential elections through to being the dominant force in the Republican party and, at the time of writing (July 2024) the presumptive republican candidate for the 2024 US presidential election. In the early stages of his 2016 presidential campaigning there were scathing assessments of him from other republican candidates. Prominent among these was an American lawyer and politician serving as the senior United States senator from South Carolina – Lindsey Graham. Graham was an outspoken critic of Trump's 2016 candidacy and repeatedly said he did not support Trump yet, after a March 2017 meeting with Trump, Graham became a staunch Trump ally, often issuing public statements in his defence. Key among these supportive statements was Graham's comment in December 2019 where he stated he would "not pretend to be a fair juror" at Trump's Impeachment hearing and, in April 2022, warning of "riots in the street" if Trump were to be charged of criminal activity.

The world of 2016 was a world in which the gap between rich and poor had widened further. In the nineteen-eighties and nineties the promises made by politicians and business leaders stated that globalisation, small government, minimal regulation, free trade, and other aspects of neoliberalism would result in a better quality of life and improved economic conditions for everyone. By 2016 these promises had been shown to be empty, and across the world people used elections to show their dissatisfaction. Increasing numbers of people across the globe were showing that they believed the system to be broken and that traditional ways of repair could no longer work. They seemed to have listened to the adage that "insanity is doing the same things and expecting different results"! Trump positioned himself as a non-establishment "outsider" who would "clean out the swamp" of Washington and restore true democracy to the USA and, with this, improve the lot of ordinary struggling Americans. His approach worked.

As is common knowledge, in January 20, 2017 Donald John Trump became the 45th President of the United States of America. During the period of Trump's presidency, the media, like the general US population, became increasingly polarised around political inclinations. The Republican Party became, in effect, the Trump Party, and, as Graham recognised, a successful career as a Republican Senator, was often dependent upon Trump's endorsement. However, in 2020 Trump lost the election and, on January 6, 2021, Joe Biden became US President. Trump, who has a strong need to be always perceived as a "winner" has consistently refused to acknowledge he was the loser. In August 2022, Lindsey Graham continued his support for Trump and following the exercise of a search warrant on Trump's home in Florida, stated that there will be "riots in streets" if Trump was prosecuted over classified records that were found there. Evidence based rationality that would consider the facts in order to make decisions has, for both men, been compromised by the structural reality of personal value systems – for Trump, the fear of being a "loser" and for Graham, the belief that supporting Trump will continue to enhance his power and influence. Throughout this, Trump did not change – rather Graham, along with almost all of the US Congress republican members and would-be members, changed his stance based on the structural reality of the influence Trump had with in excess of 75 million Americans.

Rizzo et al's 2018 study[10] makes the point that:

> The rationality norms accepted by neoclassical economists and applied by behavioral economists are static. The individual is either "rational" or he is not. His preferences are either completely ordered, consistent through time, and transitive, or they are not. In the neoclassical version of rational choice theory, actual behavior conforms to the static axioms of preference.

They argue that this approach misses "misses an important aspect of human decision-making" and that "If we only take a snapshot of the individual at a moment in time, we will fail to see how the individual's decision-making evolves. We may simply have a picture of it in an inchoate state." (Shades of lacking a systems approach!)

It is not just economists who see rationality in this binary, static way. Across all strata of society, there is a general perception that people either act in a rational manner or non-rational manner – we try to "pigeonhole" them. Invariably this perception is based on isolated actions rather than on what occurs over time. Such an approach ignores the range of biases that could influence an individual over time and the behavioural changes that these could facilitate. It also ignores the reality that, over time and with psychological growth, the relative importance of our values framework is subject to change – the relative importance of our values when aged around 10 (primarily focused on family and friends) is almost certainly different and more nuanced when we are aged 20 and we focus on our own place in the world. It is possible that the same individual makes both rational and non-rational decisions in different situations and under differing conditions (see Chapters 13 and 16).

So, if even what we usually believe to be rational behaviour is tainted with bias, what about the much-vaunted appeal to "common sense"?

In January 1776, an article by the English-born American political activist, philosopher, political theorist, and revolutionary (Thomas Paine) was published[11]. In the opening clauses Paine writes: ".... A long habit of not thinking a thing *wrong* gives it a superficial appearance of being *right*, and raises at first a formidable outcry in defence of custom. But the tumult soon subsides. Time makes more converts than reason. ..." In other words, "common sense" is often little more than unquestioning acceptance of the status quo. Throughout the article he continues to challenge people to question the accepted status quo and to apply a reformed common sense by seeking independence from British rule.

A 2000 study[12] suggests that "how [*this*] pamphlet persuades its readers is an object lesson in the workings of modern democratic culture." It argues that Paine's article has

> ... crucial rhetorical ingredients for another reason: they have made the pamphlet all things to all people. Every brand of American politics seems to find some justification in its pages, and the glass that Paine so

beguilingly offers can, in consequence, be either half empty or half full as each occasion or cause commands.

This is, in part, because "Time and again, Common Sense succeeds in having it both ways on debates that will consume the later body politic." and that "Paine orchestrated ideological unities out of fragments, and he knew how to wrap his readers in the sincerity of his claims."

While Ferguson is actually discussing Paine's pamphlet itself rather than "common sense" per se, what he makes clear is that how discussions are framed is crucial in determining how one decides exactly what is "common sense" at any specific point in time and in relation to any specific situation encountered.

The 2014 study by Watts[13] suggests that bias arising from "common sense" has potential to influence even academic research. He looks at the field of sociology and says:

> ... sociologists rely on common sense more than they realize. Moreover, this unacknowledged reliance causes serious problems for their explanations of social action, that is, for why people do what they do. Many such explanations, it is argued, conflate understandability with causality in ways that are not valid by the standards of scientific explanation. ...

Watts points out [common sense] "is generally associated with the practical knowledge of ordinary people, deployed in everyday situations and, as such, is distinct from the style of theoretical knowledge to which sociologists aspire." and that

> much of what passes for common sense is inconsistent and even contradictory. More generally, sociologists have also pointed out that what common sense treats as "facts" – self-evident, unadorned descriptions of an objective reality – often disguises value judgments that depend on the subjective experience of the person making the evaluation as well as on the supposedly objective nature of the thing being evaluated.

Watts' case is that

> common sense reasoning pervades sociological theorizing in a fundamental way – at the level of sociological theories of action. In particular, I argue that many such theories – most prominently rational choice theory, but also the many variants of individualism that have pervaded sociology over the past century, as well as more recent additions such as Bourdieu's field theory and Gross's pragmatist theory – are all descendants of the same ancestor "theory," which for the sake of argument I will call rationalizable action – the claim that actions, whether individual or collective, can be explained in terms of the intentions, beliefs, circumstances, and opportunities of the actors involved.

Perhaps all this helps us understand why, as is so often expressed, "common sense is a very uncommon phenomenon". We want to be rational, and we want to show common sense, but we do not want to confront the possibility that what we see as being rational and what we see as being common sense, are both impacted by our mental framework, of intuition or reflection, our value systems, our biases, and the way in which the situation faced is framed. Is it really any wonder that, at least across the western world, there are so many people dealing with mental health issues and why there is so much unethical behaviour?

Questions for group discussion:

1. "There are two types of rationality – rationality of purpose and rationality of process – and that we may be biased as to which of these are involved when we consider being 'rational'." Thinking about your past decision-making, which of these two has dominated? Has that always been appropriate? Why? Why not? How do you know?
2. "The old mind relies on a combination of evolution and experiential learning and is therefore driven entirely by repeating behaviours which succeeded in the past. The new mind, however, permits the solution of novel problems by reasoning about the future, enabling consequential decision making." What are the biases that encourage us to mainly operate from "the old mind"? How valid are these biases and how can we manage them?
3. "A person may claim to be acting rationally to achieve results but what is considered 'rational' may be (and probably is) impacted by underlying biases of which the person may or may not be aware." To what extent has "the character of [your] preferences" (which "can be selfish, altruistic, honourable, admirable, spiteful, etc.") been allowed to impact? How has your choice of heuristic been impacted by bias affecting your preferences?
4. "How discussions are framed is crucial in determining how one decides exactly what is 'common sense' at any specific point in time and in relation to any specific situation encountered." When was the last time your decision-making impacted by bias arising from "common sense"? How did this affect the quality of your decision?
5. "Common sense is often little more than unquestioning acceptance of the status quo." What is your reaction to this statement? What are the potential negative implications of applying "common sense" rather than exploring alternatives? To what extent do you think it is really viable to challenge the status quo in everyday decisions? Why?

Notes

1 Lehrer, Jonah op cit

2 Ackerman, Edith 2011, "The Craftsman, the Trickster, and the Poet: "Re-Souling" The Rational Mind", https://www.academia.edu/2281722/The_craftsman_the_trickster_and_the_poet_Re_souling_the_rational_mind_2011_

3 Cassirer, E. *An Essay on Man*. New Haven, CT: Yale University Press, 1944

4 Mildenberger, Carl David, 2019, "A reason to be rational", INQUIRY, 2019, VOL. 62, NOS. 9–10, 1008–1032. https://doi.org/10.1080/0020174X.2018.1470570

5 Evans, J. S. B. T. (1993). Bias and rationality. In K. I. Manktelow & D. E. Over (Eds.), *Rationality: Psychological and philosophical perspectives* (pp. 6–30). Taylor & Frances/Routledge

6 Evans, Jonathan St. B. T., 2014, "Two Minds Rationality", Thinking & Reasoning, 2014 Vol. 20, No. 2, 129–146, http://dx.doi.org/10.1080/13546783.2013.845605

7 Hargreaves Heap, Shaun P, 2013, "Rationality", in *Handbook on the Economics of Reciprocity and Social Enterprise* (Bruni, Luigino & Zamagni, Stefano eds) pp277–284

8 Hulpke, John F, & Fronmueller, Michael P, 2021, "What's not to like about evidence-based management: a hyper-rational fad?", Organizational Analysis Vol. 30 No. 7, 2022, pp. 95–123

9 Fogal, Daniel, 2019, "Rational Requirements and the Primacy of Pressure", Mind, Vol. 129. 516. October 2020 doi:10.1093/mind/fzz038

10 Rizzo, Mario J & Whitman, Glen, 2018, *Rationality as a Process, Review of Behavioral Economics, 2018, 5: 201–219*

11 National Humanities Center Thomas Paine, *Common Sense*, 1776, 3d ed., full text incl. Appendix

12 Ferguson, Robert A., "The Commonalities of Common Sense", 2000, The William and Mary Quarterly, Jul., 2000, Vol. 57, No. 3 (Jul., 2000), pp. 465–504

13 Watts, Duncan J., 2014, "Common Sense and Sociological Explanations", AJS Volume 120 Number 2 (September 2014): 313–51

13

BIAS AND ETHICS

Chapter 1 looked at the issue of judgments and decision making (JDP) and discussed the work of Daniel Kahneman and Amos Tversky who introduced the concept of heuristics being vital to decision making.

In mid-May 2022, during a speech in Dallas, former President George W Bush condemned the "decision of one man to launch a wholly unjustified and brutal invasion of Iraq" …. "Whoops! I mean of Ukraine," he added a second later, as laughter rang out in the room. The mistake was widely reported across the world but very few media outlets fully considered the magnitude of what Bush had said. The 2003 invasion of Iraq was, in fact, no different from the actions of Vladimir Putin against Ukraine – both were done for political reasons and used fabricated reasons for justification. Both deconstructed their cases for invasion on a simplified approach that, in effect, said "We are the good guys. We are invading the bad guys, and we're doing it to protect our nation and our people."

Bush's "Freudian" slip makes clear that, deep down and no matter what he may say, there may be some level of recognition that his decision to invade Iraq was wrong – it was no different from that of Putin with Ukraine (although both Bush and Putin are highly unlikely to ever admit this). Bush's decision led to the failure of the State of Iraq together with the death and injury of thousands of innocent civilians as well as of military personnel from all "Coalition of the Willing" nations and from the Iraqi military. Iraqi prisoners of war – many of whom were innocent people who were arrested by mistake – appear to have been violently tortured by US and allied troops. Hundreds of thousands of civilians died. The entire country was left in ruins. And the suffering in Iraq continues long after the occupying forces have left.

Today (early 2024) the world is already calling for Putin to be tried as a war criminal and the West has placed severe international restrictions on Russia's

DOI: 10.4324/9781003528340-14

economy. We, rightly, see that his actions must not go unpunished – but we have never taken any action against Bush and the leaders of other nations who so willingly sided with him in 2003 – although some of the military personnel were convicted of crimes relating to torture of Abu Ghraib prisoners, the people who were really in charge have faced no consequences whatsoever. There is a glaring hypocrisy in our different responses to almost identical crimes. Of course, we justify this be claiming that we are on the side of "good" while Putin (and/or Saddam Hussein) was not. A similar scenario applies to the Israeli response to the terrorist attack of October 7, 2023. The attack by Hamas was (and is) unforgiveable; action by Israel to defend its borders and to minimise the probability of future terrorist attacks is totally justifiable. But when such defence results in total devastation of Gaza's infrastructure, demolition of homes and hospitals, dislocation of virtually all its population, and the deaths of some 30,000 civilians (many of whom are children), then ethical questions must be asked.

The purpose of this example is not to demonise Israel's current activities (and it is certainly not antisemitism) or Bush and the Coalition of the Willing nor to justify Putin's invasion of Ukraine. The purpose of the example is to illustrate the problem in using inappropriate and/or inadequate processes when making decisions. As discussed in Chapter 1, if our decision process is based on a priori assumptions (i.e. reasoning or knowledge which proceeds from theoretical deduction rather than from observation or experience – intuitive responses), it becomes possible to "justify" virtually any decision no matter how illegal or immoral it may be.

Much earlier I quoted Haselton et al.[1] who see bias as something that has evolved. They suggest bias is the situation in which human cognition reliably produces representations that are systematically distorted compared to some aspect of objective reality. They explore why biases often seem to be implemented at the cognitive level, producing genuine misperceptions, rather than merely biases in enacted behaviour. They argue "perhaps the most commonly invoked explanation for bias is as a necessary by-product of processing limitations – because information processing time and ability are limited, humans must use shortcuts or rules of thumb that are prone to breakdown in systematic ways." In other words, we need heuristics because, without them, we would be drowned in an ocean of data and stimuli so great that we could not function – they are a critical component for our survival.

The question we need to confront relates to the legality and ethics of our heuristics and the extent to which our choice of heuristic is impacted by our biases.

In most liberal democracies, the legality of our biases can be readily tested. Many jurisdictions have laws that specifically proscribe any activity that is discriminatory of a person on a wide range of grounds that includes gender, sexual orientation, marital status, age, ethnicity, colour, religious affiliation, physical and/or mental handicap. Where any such factor influences our decision making or any other behaviour, there is potential for us to be prosecuted and, in some instances, imprisoned if found guilty in a court of law.

The ethical constructs are not so clear-cut.

In the making of decisions, there are two key sets of factors – instrumental and normative. Instrumental factors are those in which the drive to make decisions comes largely from the decider's own perspective. In this sense they may, in a business context, relate to what product can be made because of demand in the marketplace, financial capital and resources available. By comparison, the normative factors are those in which the driver of decisions comes largely from the perspective of those impacted. In this way, a normative approach to the decision about what to produce would be largely determined by what product or services are demanded by customers and what harms or benefits arise throughout the process of creating or providing it. In other words, there is a link between one's values system and the heuristic used in decision making.

The relationship between personal values and the ethical dimension of decision making receives attention in a 2007 work[2]. The study found "a significant positive contribution of altruistic values to ethical decision making and a significant negative contribution of self-enhancement values to ethical decision making." The study reinforced earlier works in which can be found general agreement that values influence behaviour. It confirmed that personal values are a major component of an individual's personal traits influencing the ethical dimension of her/his decision behaviour. In context, their study was considering employment criteria and they concluded that "the findings of this study indicate that, when hiring, one might tend to prefer employment candidates with altruistic values to one's demonstrating self-enhancement values." However, their research is relevant to this discussion on heuristics and cognitive biases because of the connection they make between individual values and behaviour. If the decider is driven by self-enhancement values, it appears more likely that a heuristic supporting personal advancement is chosen than one in which personal interest may be negatively impacted.

This contention is reinforced by a more recent study which found:

> In a sample of 263 senior-level undergraduate business students, survey results suggested that hypercompetitiveness was generally associated with "poor ethics" and PD (personal development) competitiveness was linked with "high ethics". For example, hypercompetitive individuals generally saw nothing wrong with self-interested gain at the expense of others, but PD competitors viewed such activities as largely inappropriate. Hypercompetitive people also tended to be highly Machiavellian but not ethically idealistic. In contrast, PD competitors tended to be ethically idealistic but not Machiavellian.[3]

The consistent message is that deciders operating from an altruistic or systems approach values system are more likely to seek heuristics promoting normative decision-making approaches than are those operating from a values system in which the advancement of personal interests is dominant.

Rogers and Schill (2021)[4] make the point that:

> Ethics is a generic term that covers several different ways of examining, understanding, and applying moral principles that guide behavior and actions to address specific problems or dilemmas. Ethics are the standards of right and wrong that guide behavior. An ethical framework or code provides guidance for how people reason, problem-solve, and respond. ... Ethics connotes a dynamic process of discussion and debate among individuals involved in the decision-making process. An ethical approach requires multidisciplinary cooperation and collaborative participation to arrive at a course of action infused with trust and integrity.

Their point is that the application of our personal ethical constructs is influenced by the environment within which such application is found. If we are in an environment that strongly supports a particular view, we are very likely to be influenced by this regardless of our personal beliefs.

At the core, ethics is all about what we "should" do. It contrasts with law which sets out the legal constraints within which we "must act" if we are to avoid legal consequences for our behaviour. Effectively, "law" is the absolute base line for behaviour rather than the totality. The problem is that what we "should" do is largely determined by our underlying value systems – our mental models – and these are strongly influenced by familial and social inputs during our formative years. The result is that each and every one of us looks at the world through a different set of lenses. We see, or more accurately perceive, the world in our own unique way. We each perceive a very different view of the life that we imagine surrounds us. As the research discussed earlier in this chapter make clear, such perceptual differences impact our behaviour.

This perception then impacts on what we learn and how we interpret it. As we have experiences, we generate memories, and we compare our present situation with the memory of the last time we were in a similar situation. This is done continually in the subconscious part of our brain; the part we are not aware of. At one level we learn to recognise danger and develop survival skills and at the other, we develop likes and dislikes, preferences and aversions. In turn, this means that, in many ways, our experience of "now" is a limited and distorted view as it has passed through two distinct groups of filters. The first filters are shaped by the nature of our senses and their intensity and accuracy. The second set of filters is built upon a model of our past and our previous experiences. Our life experiences and the conditions of life that we have encountered dictate our view of our own reality. This will not be the same interpretation of reality as experienced by somebody with more or less acute senses and a different experience of the past. The result is that we all have our own views as to what we *ought* to do when confronted by ethical conundrums.

We assemble likes and dislikes. We think of things as being good or bad, pleasant or unpleasant, safe or threatening. These judgements are based on our experiences. There is simply nothing else to assemble them from, other than the behaviour of those around us and the messages we receive from television, social media, books and other sources that we use to tell us stories about the nature of life. This information provides the filtering that is the second way in which we effectively distort and selectively react to the information we receive from the outside world. Our sense of the world is fundamentally unique to us. We have created our own rules for viewing the world based on the experiences we have been through. We see this as who we are and our truth and this influences our perception of what is (and what is not) ethical.

Today it is generally agreed that the main different approaches to ethical considerations are:

- The Utilitarian Approach – an ethical theory that determines right from wrong by focusing on outcomes. It is a form of consequentialism. Utilitarianism holds that the most ethical choice is the one that will produce the greatest good for the greatest number. The question of determining which "greatest number" should be our focus, can lead to very subjective judgements.
- The Rights Approach – the best ethical action is that which protects the ethical rights of those who are affected by the action. It emphasises the belief that all humans have a right to dignity.
- The Fairness or Justice Approach – has its roots in the teachings of the ancient Greek philosopher Aristotle, who said that "equals should be treated equally and unequals unequally." The basic moral question in this approach is: How fair is an action? Again, the question of who are "equals" vs "unequals" can lead to very subjective judgements.
- The Common-Good Approach – regards all individuals as part of a larger community. As such, we share certain common conditions and institutions upon which our welfare depends. For society to thrive, we need to safeguard the sustainability of our community for the good of all, including our weakest and most vulnerable members.
- The Virtue Approach – the idea of "community". A person's character traits are not developed in isolation, but within and by the communities to which he or she belongs, including family, church or religious group, school, workplace, and other private and public associations.

These five are generally grouped into what are known as deontological approaches and teleological approaches. In very broad terms, deontology is any approach to ethics which adheres to the theory that an end does not justify the means (i.e. the process is as important as the result) while teleology is any approach to ethics that adheres to the theory that the end always justifies the means. Whether we espouse a deontological or a teleological approach will be influenced strongly by the world view we have developed in our earlier years – our unconscious biases will impact both our own preferred ethical construct and also how we view those who espouse a different ethical construct. The result is that, depending on our own position, we will tend to view the decision-making heuristics of others as, from an ethical perspective, being either appropriate or inappropriate.

The question this raises relates to the appropriateness of any ethical system used. Is it a case of "right approach" versus "wrong approach" or something similar? In Chapter 3 the matter of a person's "world view" impacting their behaviour was discussed. A further (and still very relevant) understanding of "world views" and how they impact was developed by Clare Graves in 1965, Professor of Psychology, Union College, Schenectady, New York who said[5]:

> With the development of a system point of view, authorities have been taking a new look at both value systems and the relationship of these to managerial problems. One authority, Pepper, directed attention to the possibility that the problem of ethics is not what system of ethics is the right system, but it is quite another problem. He said: "… there are a number of normative 'ethical' systems that have been adequately described and verified; thus the central problem 'of ethical behavior' is how choices are made among them, 'or' do some natural 'ethical' norms have precedence over others or under some condition - - -?"
>
> That a number of ethical systems have been adequately described and verified is, I think, beyond question, but since I don't agree completely with Pepper as to why certain ethical norms take precedence over others, and since we are now interested in ethical norms as they effect the viability of organization I will present some additional hypotheses as to the conditions, under which certain ethical norms take precedence over other ethical norms and some hypotheses as to how these ethical norms effect the viability of organizations. … A business cannot operate viably independent of the values of the people imbedded in it. Business to be viable must be managed such that its managerial practices are congruent with the values of the people who must implement through actions the goals of the organization. The answers to questions like, "How hard should a man work? How much can we expect a man to invest in his job? What kind of punishments can a company use to direct behavior?" can be found predominantly within the firm. They depend on what managerial control system is dictated by the values of management and on how congruent this chosen control system is with the values of those in the firm who are managed. If managerial decisions, which stem from the values of managers, are out of harmony with the values of the managed the company may find itself at a competitive disadvantage because other managers who use controls congruent with the values of those whom they manage will tap reserves of human energy which simply are not available otherwise. …

Some years later, in 1970, Graves elaborated on this concept of differing value systems[6]. He said:

> Today, in the minds of many, there is a passionate certitude as to what is wrong with man. He is simply breaking apart at his moral seams. From every direction fingers point with certainty to the evidence that he is becoming ethically decrepit. From one direction, "the establishments", the finger points at the psychedelic and confrontational behavior of youth, while from youth's direction it points at the callous exploitation of our environment by established businessmen and the older generation's failure to live by the values vocally professed. Business managers see a breakdown of the work ethic in the "make-work" phenomena and careless practices of their employees but the public points to shoddy engineering and merchandising practices of the employers as evidence of value sickness in the businessman's behavior. Dissenters are called immoral because, in the name of "Civil rights," they have frightened many of their fellow citizens. Yet these same dissenters point to the immoral activity of those who use "civil rights" and shield as they carry on vicious and even murderous attacks upon those who are dissenting. These and countless other value problems are cited as the signs of rampant immorality and unethical behavior in our people, our country and our world.

Graves went on:

> ... man's troublesome behavior can be seen as a sign of growth rather than as a sign of decay, as a sign of reaching for a better form of existence rather than as a sign of the disintegration of all that is good, as a sign of the emergence of that which is better, which is more human in man rather than as a sign of a break through of the worst that is in him.

He then went on to argue:

> a. That man's nature is not a set thing, that it is ever emergent, that it is an open system, not a closed system. b. That man's nature evolves by saccadic, quantum-like jumps from one steady state system to another. c. That man's values change from system to system as his total psychology emerges in new form with each quantum-like jump to a new steady state of being.

Graves posited an open ended spiral comprising at least eight levels of values systems or, in terms used throughout this book, "the world view" through which we filter our decisions and activities: our behaviour. Each level reflects a world view based on increasing levels of complexity and ambiguity. The driver for changing levels comes from a recognition that one's current world view is inadequate for confronting the reality of the current world situation. At this point an individual can choose to form a more appropriate world view or to remain in their current state. There is never any external compulsion to change. Each level will have its own impact on whether decisions are made using instrumental or normative factors – and each will consider the constructs used to be "ethical".

Graves moved the discussion as to whether an ethical construct was "right" or "wrong" to one which considers the ethical constructs applied in terms of a person's position in this open system of world views. He made clear that different world views will perceive "being ethical" in different ways. In other words, the ethical construct used tells us something about the world view held by any person. In terms of what was discussed in the Introduction to this book, Graves is urging us to consider the mental framework from within which a person operates and how this has impacted their ethics. The question is not a black and white "right versus wrong", but one of how our mental mindsets impact our behaviour. Our cognitive biases are integrally linked to our mental framework.

Graves argued that humans move in their world views from instinct, through safety, power, order, success, people, process, and synthesis approaches[7]. These represent rising levels of openness and ability to deal with complexity and ambiguity. For the first six of these a person can see only that approach (effectively a monochromatic perspective) while they are in that world view and this temporarily limits the options they consider when dealing with any issue. So, as an example, for a person operating out of what Graves' terms the level of family or tribe, ethical options will be considered in relation to those people I consider "mine" and any detrimental impact on others will be of little or no concern. Only at the process or integrated systems level (Grave' second tier) does a polychromatic perspective become possible so that a greater variety of options become apparent. In other words, only at the process level does a person become fully willing and able to consider in depth options that involve greater levels of ambiguity and complexity in relation to resolving otherwise intractable problems. Only at the process level and above can a person more appropriately choose how and when they use different world views.

Under Graves' concepts, during their lifetime a person develops (or not) along a spiral depending on their response to things they encounter. When they realise that their current worldview is failing to provide the solutions they need, a person can choose to stop where they are, pause and consider before taking action, or make the move freely to the next stage. At any point the person continues to have access to, and to use, the earlier stages of the spiral – the important thing is to understand the strengths and limitations of each stage and, as much as possible, to access them appropriately. Graves portrayed the interactions between these levels in a helix form similar to what is usually associated with DNA. Some of the key elements of Grave's approach can be summarised:

Identification	Common Characteristics & Value System	Identifying Slogan
Level 1.1	Purely animalistic survival. Individual survival is paramount. Found very seldom in society except in babies and very ill people who have regressed to infantile states.	"I will survive at the most basic level"
Level 1.2	A concern for other worldly powers which might be found in traditional religions or in astrology, new age concepts such as crystals, the occult etc. People are bonded in an almost tribal fashion depending on their adherence to the particular belief system, but follow and have allegiance to the chief or elder. This is also the level that bonds together a close family or group such as may be seen in a religious community.	"The family that prays together stays together"
Level 1.3	Aggressively seeking what is wanted, *NOW*. No guilt and or sense of commitment except to those who are "on my side" and support me. The most powerful person becomes the leader and allegiance is based on having and holding power. Seen extensively in gangs and much antisocial individualistic behaviour. Money and other commodities are pursued for their power component rather than for themselves. On the positive side, red indicates risk takers, entrepreneurs, explorers, researchers breaking new ground, etc.	"Might is right" "Kick the door in" "Make it happen"
Level 1.4	At the next system, people recognise the need for and value of law and order. Everything has a place and everything should be done decently and in order. Those who adhere to the "right way" are assured of benefits in the future with the result that delayed gratification is acceptable. A person can "put up" with all sorts of perceived injustices because "that's the rule" and, in the long term, things will even out. This tier also supports perfection, craftsmen, conservatism, skill development, is used by coaches, teachers, lawyers, and police.	"This is the way. Walk ye in it" "Keeps me safe."
Level 1.5	Competition is both good and necessary. We should strive to encourage individual responsibility and individual wealth. Ultimately the weak should go to the wall, as market forces should dictate what survives and distribution of wealth. Economic rationalism is paramount and we encourage people to look after their own education, health services, retirement, etc. This tier also provides a better life, rewards risk takers, seeks alternatives as the better way, etc.	"Greed is good" "Things can be better."

Identification	Common Characteristics & Value System	Identifying Slogan
Level 1.6	The attainment of material gains is, ultimately, self-destructive. "Vanity of vanities," saith the preacher, "all is vanity". We have a responsibility that is beyond ourselves to the socially and economically disadvantaged as well as to those who are powerless to care for themselves in our world – whales, oceans, the ozone layer, forests, etc. We should be concerned about the world we are bequeathing to our children and our children's children. This tier also works for the growth of teams, seeks equality, and works for the end of "isms" such as racism, sexism, ageism, etc.	"We must be socially responsible"
Level 2.1	The next tier is a quantum leap from the Level 1.6 approach and is the first system at which all preceding systems are truly seen as "just different". People operating primarily at this system are able to recognise and use all preceding systems of complexity as valid and useful tools and/or understandings of the way by which humanity confronts and deals with the life conditions we encounter.	"Let's look at the total system"
Level 2.2	Understanding of this is still developing and there are very few (if any) proven examples of extensive Level 2.2 thinking. It appears to recognise the reality of powers and forces that are beyond our understanding, but these are seen simply as gaps in our knowledge rather than mysterious "other" such as would be believed by people operating primarily from an earlier system.	"An holistic view"

In 1991, one of Graves' past students, Donald Beck, applied this theory when working to help South Africa's transition out of the Apartheid era[8]. This and other experiences while working across a variety of organisations, led Beck and another of Graves' past students, Chris Cowan, to move from the alpha numeric coding used by Graves to a colour labelling for each level[9]. The changes were driven by the realisation that many people saw the alpha-numeric coding in a "right or wrong" or "better than" framework rather than simply as being "different". They went on to consider the ethical constructs most likely to be used in the first seven levels or tiers as shown below. In this table it is easy to see how each level promotes an increased level of willingness and ability to deal with complexity and ambiguity.

The link here to one's choice of heuristic when considering action, is clear. People with different mental models will use different ethical constructs in their choice. It is not a case that one choice is "right" and other is "wrong" but different mental models orientate to different approaches and, for each person, their choice is "right" because of how they see the world. Coming from this

TABLE 13.1 Beck & Cowan's Spiral Dynamics Summary (first 7 levels)

Colour	Emphasis	Ethical Behaviour
Beige	Survival such as found in babies and people with dementia	No ethical constructs
Purple	Family or Clan/group/tribe/gang	Do what the family want you to
Red	Short-term guilt-free, raw power that gives immediate satisfaction	Do whatever is necessary to extend or maintain my power and get what I want
Blue	Only one best way; adherence to rules, regulations, law	Do what is legal. If in doubt, don't do it
Orange	Short-term competition-driven success	If others are doing it successfully, so can I
Green	Search for harmony and equality	Do what is best for everyone
Yellow	Big picture, long-term orientation that accepts chaos and change as inevitable and natural	Actively seek to bring about a better global world that is developing healthy societies and planet

perspective it then becomes possible to have a mutually beneficial discussion on different world views rather than a confrontational argument in which each seeks to convince the other of their errors. This is important when considering how to manage biases.

Such a discussion then makes it possible for shifts in mental models to occur – something Beck and Cowan address in discussing the possibility of personal development. This concept has much in common with the concept of growth mindsets (see Chapter 16). Beck and Cowan make the point, as Dweck would also later emphasise, that shifting between levels (utilising a growth mindset) is not automatic nor compulsory. It is a personal choice that confronts any person when they realise that their existing mindset is not adequate for the world situations currently being encountered. Having a fixed mindset or a growth mindset is optional.

Beck and Cowan illustrate the change process by showing how many of the changes occur without any difficulty: a person recognises the need to change some aspect of their world view in order to function more effectively and, without too much debate, makes the necessary adaptation. However, for all of us, there are some changes that we are reluctant to make: we have very strongly held views and we see any challenge to these as being an attack on our integrity. Beck and Cowan show that, in such instances, it is possible that this reluctance to change can impact our mental health. The call this "the Gamma trap".

"Gamma" is explained as being "a state of anxiety, fear, and frustration because problems are apparent but there seems no way to do anything about them." In other words, our reluctance (or refusal) to adapt our world view can cause problems in our relationships and other aspects of everyday living. Beck and Cowan make the point that when a person realises that their current world view is not adequate for the issues currently being faced but decide that their view is "right" and that change is required from everything else (in other words, you must change to suit my world view) it is possible for a downward spiral of frustration to develop. This may be demonstrated by anxiety, depression, and the like with, at the extreme, violent antisocial and anti-establishment behaviours to emerge. Perhaps this concept of "the Gamma trap" helps explain why sometimes biases that have developed into prejudice, stigma, and discrimination can result in domestic violence and other criminal behaviours including murder – even war. Perhaps it also helps us understand the examples with which this chapter opened.

This need to consider changing of one's world view as being optional is reinforced by Korteling et al.[10]. Earlier it was argued that the brain is not like a conventional repository or hard disk that can take up and store any information that is provided, almost indifferently of its characteristics. Instead, it is an associative network that requires new or additional information to be compliant or consistent with its existing state. What is associatively selected, processed, and integrated is not only determined by stimulus characteristics like the saliency of a target in its context, but also by the compatibility (match) with the brain's momentary state and connectionist characteristics. Although we know that the brain has plasticity (in other words neural connections can change) this tends to be a very long and complex process as can be seen in people who are recovering from a neural injury[11].

Korteling suggests the principle of compatibility in neural information processing implies a compulsion to be consistent with what we already know, think or have done, resulting in a tendency to ignore or overlook relevant information because it does not match with our current behaviour or mindset. Accordingly, in any confrontational argument, the issue of changing world view will be seen as an attack that must be resisted and overcome. In contrast, a respectful discussion on different world views can take into account the similarities between the existing and potential world views in a way that influences change and brings about recognition of the need for change as well as an understanding of how this change can occur.

Beck and Cowan argue that for systemic values-level (what they describe as "memes") change to occur, there is the need for a person to meet six conditions: potential in the brain or brain syndicate, the possibility that solutions to the problems can be found; dissonance in relation to both the current situation and the future; identification of current change barriers and how to manage them; insight into alternative forms and means of addressing the problems; consolidation and support for the person during the transition process.

Of course, it is important to note that changing our world view does not mean that bias is eliminated. Bias is present in every one of Graves' levels. What the meme-change means is that one set of biases is replaced by a new set that is more compatible with the world view of the new level and is better able to positively deal from a systems perspective with the levels of complexity and ambiguity being faced.

As noted in Chapter 1, while our underlying value system or mindset will influence our heuristic choice, it is important to be reminded that a heuristic is not a cognitive bias. A *heuristic* is a rule, strategy or similar mental shortcut that one can use to derive a solution to a problem. It is important also to note, however, that while the use of heuristics can reinforce existing biases, not all biases are impacted by the heuristics used. It is the choice of heuristic that determines the action: our biases are what impact our choice of heuristic. And it is our underlying value systems that, through our world view, ultimately drive this choice of heuristic. As indicated, our underlying value systems are impacted by the past – and our unwillingness and/or our inability to develop our value systems and change our world view, can have seriously negative personal consequences.

Questions for group discussion:

1. It has been argued that the ethical constructs we use at any time are impacted by our world view and that, as we mature, our world views are subject to change. Considering your personal development over the past 5–10 years, have your world views changed/developed and what has been the impact on the ethical considerations you now make in decision-making?

2. "Bias is the situation in which human cognition reliably produces representations that are systematically distorted compared to some aspect of objective reality." What biases impact you personally when differences between your personal opinions and evidence from some aspect of objective reality collide? How can you manage the impact of these biases?

3. "[The brain's] is an associative network that requires new or additional information to be compliant or consistent with its existing state. What is associatively selected, processed, and integrated is not only determined by stimulus characteristics like the saliency of a target in its context, but also by the compatibility (match) with the brain's momentary state and connectionist characteristics." When making decisions, how frequently do you challenge any considerations of consistency with past decision-making processes? Does this indicate any potential unconscious biases that may need attention?

4. Do you have a tendency to ignore or overlook relevant information because it does not match with your current behaviour or mindset? What problems can arise from this? How can you change your thought processes so as to minimise this bias?

5. If you were 45 with a successful career, spouse and children and investments but your external circumstances changed dramatically, would you sell everything material so that your family could continue to survive? Effectively sacrificing everything you'd built up over that time?

Notes

1 Martie G. Haselton, Daniel Nettle, Damian R. Murray 2015, *"The Evolution of Cognitive Bias"* The Handbook of Evolutionary Psychology, First published: 18 November 2015 https://doi.org/10.1002/9781119125563.evpsych241
2 David J. Fritzsche & Effy Oz, "Personal Values Influence on the Ethical Dimension of Decision Making", 2007, Journal of Business Ethics (2007) 75:335–343, DOI 10.1007/s10551–006–9256–5
3 Peter E. Mudrack, James M. Bloodgood, and William H. Turnley 2012, "Some Ethical Implications of Individual Competitiveness", J Bus Ethics (2012) 108:347–359. DOI 10.1007/s10551–011–1094–4
4 Rogers, B.; Schill, A.L. Ethics and Total Worker Health®:Constructs for Ethical Decision-Making and Competencies for Professional Practice. Int. J. Environ. Res. Public Health 2021, 18,
    10030. https://doi.org/10.3390/ijerph181910030
5 Graves, Clare W., 1965, "Value Systems and their Relation to Managerial Controls and Organizational Viability", Conference papers of the College of Management Philosophy, The Institute of Management Sciences, in San Francisco
6 Graves, Clare, 1970, "Levels OF Existence: An Open System Theory of Values", Journal of humanistic psychology, 1970 journals.sagepub.com
7 This material is briefly discussed in Long, DG, "Third Generation Leadership and the locus of control, 1988, Routledge Publishing, UK. A comprehensive explanation of the concept is found in Beck, Don Edward, & Cowan, Christopher C., 1996, "Spiral Dynamics: mastering values, leadership, and change", Blackwell Publishers Inc, Cambridge, Massachusetts
8 Beck, Don & Linscott, Graham, 1991, "The Crucible: Forging South Africa's Future", New Paradigm Press. Denton, Texas
9 Beck, Don Edward, & Cowan, Christopher C., 1996, "Spiral Dynamics: mastering values, leadership, and change", Blackwell Publishers Inc, Cambridge, Massachusetts. See also https://spiraldynamics.org/
10 Korteling et al., op cit
11 See Norman Doidge, *"The Brain That Changes Itself"*, op cit

14

BIAS AND MENTAL HEALTH

When people encounter dissonance between their existing value systems and the behaviours resulting from this, and the reality with which they confront on a daily basis, the options are really to change the way in which one thinks and generally behaves or to maintain one's existing approach while seeking to force the world to adapt to me. As we saw above, Beck and Cowan[1] called this the "gamma trap" which, in too many instances, leads a person to anxiety, depression, and other mental health issues.

The impact of bias on mental health has two distinct elements. First, there is a long-held stigma associated with mental health. Because it directly impacts how a person behaves and this is often manifest in antisocial behaviour, there can be a reluctance to acknowledge one has mental health issues. Second, the medical profession is often reluctant to try mental health treatments that are different from mainstream approaches.

Clearly, one of the most misunderstood issues faced by people in every society is that of mental health. Since time immemorial it has been seen in a completely different manner from physical health issues and physical injury. For much of recorded history, behaviour that is different from that of the majority has been considered supernatural and a reflection of the battle between good and evil. When confronted with unexplainable, irrational behaviour and by suffering and upheaval, people have reacted with fear. This fear has led to isolation and alienation through to serious physical restraint, imprisonment, and death of those affected.

Today, despite the widespread recognition of mental health issues being on a par with physical health issues, the impact of history means that many people are ashamed of acknowledging they are experiencing a mental health event. While they would readily acknowledge a physical health event and seek treatment, with mental health, for many people the fear of some form of discrimination still dominates.

DOI: 10.4324/9781003528340-15

Since the 1960's, deinstitutionalisation has generally occurred in the West, with isolated psychiatric hospitals being closed and replaced by community mental health services. Despite the claimed benefits of this shift including the importance of community-based care, all too frequently, inadequate services and continued social exclusion have led to many experiencing mental health episodes being homeless or in prison. It has also led to serious problems with care of the aged and those suffering dementia. Far too frequently, inadequately trained carers – often contractors or casual employees with little in-depth knowledge of the individuals for whom they are caring – encounter situations with which they are ill-equipped to cope. The result is over medication so as to minimise "disruptive" behaviour, physical restraint, or the calling of police or security personnel to apprehend "offenders". In Australia this was tragically illustrated by the May 2023 tasering of a frail 95-year-old woman with dementia who, while carrying a serrated steak knife, and using a walker, was approaching slowly towards police officers.[2] Police stated that she was tasered after "refusing an instruction to drop the knife"! She later died in hospital. (Without prejudging any court decision, it should be noted that the police officer involved is, as at April 2024, facing criminal charges in relation to his actions.)

In August 2022, the American Psychiatric Association website notes that

> More than half of people with mental illness don't receive help for their disorders. Often, people avoid or delay seeking treatment due to concerns about being treated differently or fears of losing their jobs and livelihood. That's because stigma, prejudice and discrimination against people with mental illness is still very much a problem.

They continue:

- **Public stigma** involves the negative or discriminatory attitudes that others have about mental illness.
- **Self-stigma** refers to the negative attitudes, including internalized shame, that people with mental illness have about their own condition.
- **Institutional stigma** is more systemic, involving policies of government and private organizations that intentionally or unintentionally limit opportunities for people with mental illness. Examples include lower funding for mental illness research or fewer mental health services relative to other health care.

Stigma not only directly affects individuals with mental illness but also the loved ones who support them, often including their family members.

They argue that

"Effects can include:
reduced hope

lower self-esteem
increased psychiatric symptoms
difficulties with social relationships
reduced likelihood of staying with treatment
more difficulties at work"

For many years, mental health professionals, governments and the media (at least in the developed economies) have largely sought to remove much of this stigma. This is important because, as the Australian Department of Health says: "Almost half of all Australian adults will face mental ill-health during their lives. Suicide was the main cause of death for Australians aged 15 to 49 years in 2019."[3] Similar statistics apply in many other countries.

Research suggests that one of the factors underpinning failures in mental health treatment is found in what the American Psychiatric Association listed as their third stigma: "**Institutional stigma**, is more systemic, involving policies of government and private organizations that intentionally or unintentionally limit opportunities for people with mental illness. Examples include lower funding for mental illness research or fewer mental health services relative to other health care."

The 1960's start of a move away from mental health institutions, evidenced with isolated psychiatric hospitals being closed and replaced by community mental health services, was concurrent with the move to the current economic paradigm of neoliberalism (see chapter 4). This is described by Britannica.com as an

> ideology and policy model that emphasizes the value of free market competition. Although there is considerable debate as to the defining features of neoliberal thought and practice, it is most commonly associated with laissez-faire economics. In particular, neoliberalism is often characterized in terms of its belief in sustained economic growth as the means to achieve human progress, its confidence in free markets as the most-efficient allocation of resources, its emphasis on minimal state intervention in economic and social affairs, and its commitment to the freedom of trade and capital.

It emphasises a "user pays" approach in which services are privatised with governments and society having minimal responsibility to care for those in need. Neoliberalism also encourages consumerism and when people adopt materialistic values, they are more likely to have symptoms of anxiety and depression with poorer relationships and lower self-esteem.

A direct result of this move to a neoliberal approach has been limited amounts of public money being available for all health services – arguably with mental health services being among the most seriously impacted because of the long treatment times that are often required. In turn this has led to many health professionals being forced to alleviate symptoms rather than having the resources available to identify and treat causes. The use of drugs such as antidepressants as a first resort is not uncommon with those presenting to a general practitioner.

The early 21st century has seen increasing research attention paid to a more comprehensive approach. Researchers are arguing that blending established mental health practices with complementary approaches has considerable benefits for all stakeholders.

A 2009, paper entitled *"Perceived need for mental health care: findings from the 2007 Australian Survey of Mental Health and Wellbeing"* drew the conclusion that:

> More than 2.2 million people in Australia have perceived needs for mental health care, and more than a million Australians regard themselves as having that need met by services. In response to a decade of mental health-care reforms, we can tentatively say that progress appears to have been made. Undoubtedly, there are major gaps that still remain, and of note approximately 400,000 Australians have unmet needs for mental health care. It appears that the relative disparity between need for care and actual care may be larger in areas outside of the conventional mental health service domains of medication and psychotherapy or counselling, where perhaps greater progress may have been made in enhancing service provision.[4]

As at April 2024 the situation appears to be very little different – apart from consistent media reports that the number of people with "unmet needs for mental health care" having increased significantly.

It is reported[5] that

> Mental illness refers to more than 400 diagnosable mental disorders including Major Depressive disorder, Bipolar disorder or Schizophrenia. These are mental health conditions that disrupt a person's psychological functioning, and are characterized by alterations in thoughts, emotions and behaviors. The often-severe impact that mental illness has on people's lives highlights the need for effective treatment approaches and access to delivering services. Uptake of recommended treatment however can be challenged by social stigma, the cost-intensive nature of many therapies, and difficulties in adhering to treatment and accessing mental healthcare services.

The report explores the concept of "human flourishing" and argues that, in relation to this "… opportunities have so far been largely underexplored in the context of promoting the mental health of people suffering from mental health problems." They go on to suggest that provision of mental health initiatives could include Computerized & Online Therapy, Mobile Systems for Self-Management, Concept of Mental Wellbeing, and Design for Mental Wellbeing. In the third category they nominate as critical components: Hedonia: Pleasure, Eudemonia: Realizing One's Potential, (which includes *Positive Sense of Self,*

Purpose & Growth, Mental Balance, Social Wellbeing). In the fourth category they include *Design for Pleasure, Design for a Positive, Strong Sense of Self, Design for Mental Balance: Mindfulness, Design for Social Wellbeing*. Their study emphasises the need to focus on the person rather than on the illness and the human rather than the technology. Their conclusion is that "HCI for mental health must explicitly incorporate positive approaches in the design and evaluation of technology mediated interventions."

In a later report (2016), Thiem et al.[6] showed that "Research and design for people suffering from significant mental health problems and who are hospitalized is very rare" and "highlighted the value of our approach to working with MHPs for identifying new possibilities for a personal and accessible mental health design that avoided an over-reliance on traditional healthcare procedures."

Thieme et al.'s study receives some support from other 2015 papers. In 2015, Jurewicz[7] reported that

> In the era of an ageing population, young adults on medical wards are quite rare, as only 12% of young adults report a long-term illness or disability. However, mental health problems remain prevalent in the younger population. In a recent report, mental health and obesity were listed as the most common problems in young adults. Teams set up specifically for the needs of younger adults, such as early intervention in psychosis services are shown to work better than traditional care and have also proven to be cost effective.

She concludes

> ... In response to the mental health needs of young people, there has been a movement to develop psychiatric services specifically for young adults. If there is similar development for medical needs of young people, there needs to be a recognition of their psychological as well as physical needs.

In other words, her study made clear that mental health service for young people need to take a holistic approach.

This need to take a holistic approach is also advocated by other researchers[8] who argue:

> In the rapid-fire world of health care, mental illness and its impact on physical health can all too easily be overlooked or undermanaged. With heavy case loads, crowded hospital emergency departments, and busy primary care practices, there can be a tendency to take an episodic approach, focusing solely on the primary diagnosis or condition. What is needed is a holistic approach that looks at the whole person, including one's physical and mental health. With a greater understanding of the interconnection

between the two – for example, depression as a comorbidity to chronic illnesses and life-altering injuries, conditions, and disabilities – professional case managers can devise and implement comprehensive care plans that tap the expertise of a diverse transdisciplinary care team.

They made the point that

By the year 2020, depression is projected to be the second leading cause of disability throughout the world, trailing only ischemic heart disease. Depressive disorders are also present as comorbidities, triggered or exacerbated by acute and chronic conditions, injuries, disability, or other health episodes

and that "If a depressive disorder goes undiagnosed and untreated, there is a high risk that the individual will not progress as planned or desire to attain his or her overall health goals, such as maximum medical improvement following an injury or disability, as well as life goals including employment."

A 2016 study[9] makes clear that such a "multilevel framework consists of five central components: (1) holistic health, (2) cultural and socioeconomic relevance, (3) partnerships, (4) collaborative action-based education and learning and (5) sustainability."

In the USA, a 2007 report[10] reviewing the historical tension concerning the integration of religion and the science of mental health; explored current social trends that are creating new opportunities and pressures to move in multi-level direction and discussed strategies for the integration of religion and spirituality in mental health services and practice. Linking this to aspects of traditional and ethnic approaches to mental health, it argues that

Today's mental health system is largely a product of western science. Like a one-eyed giant, it has great power, but it lacks the wisdom which makes life sacred and meaningful. The challenge for today's mental health system is to unite East and West; to integrate wisdom and science; to make room for the sacred as well as the practical.

It saw that

Since the 1970s, a small but determined group of mental health professionals have worked to bring religion into professional discourse and programs and to introduce cultural perspectives on religion into clinical training. In part due to their efforts, psychiatry has formally endorsed a "bio-psycho-social-spiritual model".

She notes that (in the USA) "The Joint Commission on the Accreditation of Healthcare Organizations now requires that a spiritual assessment be conducted with mental health and substance abuse patients (JCAHO, 2005), and several screening tools exist." A little later she comments that "For mental health practitioners, a basic level of familiarity with alternative cultural approaches is essential if their practice is to remain relevant." She shows that "Research data increasingly support the effectiveness of religiously-based mental health treatments."

It is important to note, however, that Blanch makes clear there are dangers in such recognition because of the potential for abuses such as proselytising and promoting a particular religious or spiritual approach to the exclusion of others. She suggests very strong guidelines for controlling such religious/spiritual inclusion but argues that, despite the potential for abuse, for some people the interaction can prove a very valuable variable in mental health treatment.

A study[11] in 2015 saw

> ...that a traditional or complementary system of medicine is commonly used by a large number of people with mental illness". They continue and make the point that "collaborative engagement between traditional and complementary systems of medicine and conventional biomedicine might be possible in the care of people with mental illness. The best model to bring about that collaboration will need to be established by the needs of the extant mental health system in a country.

Given the complexity of multi-cultural society in many countries today, the 2020 study by Ilse Blignault and Arshdeep Kaur[12] of the Translational Health Research Institute, Western Sydney University, Australia is pertinent. They explored approaches in mental health care in Pacific Island Countries and argue that "Mental health is determined by a range of interrelated factors: physical, psychological, social, cultural and spiritual. In the Western Pacific Region, which encompasses the Pacific Island Countries (PICs), more than 100 million people are affected by mental disorders." They note that:

> Traditional medicine has a long history. It has been defined as the sum total of the knowledge, skill and practices based on theories, beliefs and experiences, indigenous to different cultures, whether explicable or not, used in the maintenance of health, as well as in the prevention, diagnosis, improvement or treatment of physical and mental illness.

They conclude that

> Collaborative and integrated approaches offer several potential advantages. Cultural acceptability, accessibility, reduced stigma and a more holistic model of care can lead to better engagement with and utilisation of services. Integrated treatment approaches may also be more cost-effective. Integrative mental health care that recognises the importance of traditional

beliefs also shifts the emphasis of care from treatment to prevention and self-healing and community wellness.

Referring to the World Health Organisation, a 2021 paper[13] pointed out that the WHO's "2003–2020 Mental Health Action Plan called for government health programs to include traditional and faith healers as treatment resources to combat the low – and middle-income country treatment gap." They go on to argue that one of the problems with any such integration is that "Well-meaning attempts such as culturally adapted psychotherapy and cultural competence have focused more on the biomedical therapies of conventional psychotherapists rather than the indigenous, 'culturally commensurate' therapies offered by indigenous healers." They conclude that "Ultimately, understanding the contributions and value of traditional healing to individual, family, and societal wellbeing and mental health is crucial before these resources are potentially sidelined or lost in the march to reduce the biomedical treatment gap."

Listening to and acting on the messages from this research may go a long way to reducing the stigma associated with mental health issues and its treatment. There is, however, a further element raised by Wilkinson & Pickett[14]. They argue that some 50 years of research demonstrates there is "a very strong correlation between the prevalence of mental illness and inequality." They point out "that governments may spend either to prevent social problems or, where income differences have widened, to deal with the consequences." Comparing international data with that collected across the 50 states of the USA, they found that those countries and states with high levels of equality performed better on every factor – including economic – than those with the low levels of equality. They also found that although prejudice against minorities – ethnic divisions – may increase social exclusion and discrimination, "ill-health and social problems become more common the greater the relative deprivation people experience – whatever their ethnicity." They argue that "downward discrimination" (class or status bias) along with racial bias and prejudice is lower and mental health better in societies with low levels of inequality. This is particularly the case with self-harm and suicide – the support that comes from an equitable community and sense of society encourages mental health rather than mental illness.

Across the world, most people know individuals with mental health issues. What all this research makes clear, is that eliminating the bias that sees mental health issues as on different plane from other health issues and being willing to broaden mental health treatment practices can go a long way to improving the lot of everyone – whether or not they ever experience a mental health incident. Ultimately, without a healthy society the economy suffers.

Questions for group discussion:

1. Today, despite the widespread recognition of mental health issues being on a par with physical health issues, the impact of history means that

many people are ashamed of acknowledging they are experiencing a mental health event. When was this last true of you? Why? How were you impacted by bias arising from the three stigmas? What has been the impact?

2.   "The WHO's 2003–2020 Mental Health Action Plan called for government health programs to include traditional and faith healers as treatment resources to combat the low – and middle-income country treatment gap." What are the biases that impact on this approach being implemented in your country/society? Why is this? How can these be managed?

3.   "What is needed is a holistic approach that looks at the whole person, including one's physical and mental health. With a greater understanding of the interconnection between the two – for example, depression as a comorbidity to chronic illnesses and life-altering injuries, conditions, and disabilities – professional case managers can devise and implement comprehensive care plans that tap the expertise of a diverse transdisciplinary care team." What are the professional, political, economic, and social biases that create difficulties in providing a truly holistic approach to mental health care? How can these be addressed in order to facilitate change?

4.   "Governments may spend either to prevent social problems or, where income differences have widened, to deal with the consequences." What are the heuristics commonly used by governments in determining expenditure on social problems? What biases underpin these heuristics and how can these be managed?

5.   An individual that needs help with mental unwellness might not be in a position to decide rationally to search out and accept help. In a workplace, this can bring complications for the company, division, team and the individual. What is a proactive way for modern organisations to care for their employees in this respect?

Notes

1 Beck, Don Edward, & Cowan, Christopher C., 1996, "Spiral Dynamics: mastering values, leadership, and change", Blackwell Publishers Inc, Cambridge, Massachusetts
2 https://www.bbc.com/news/world-australia-65642974. This was not the first instance of NSW Police using violence against people with dementia. See also https://www.abc.net.au/news/2023-05-22/elderly-woman-handcuffed-by-nsw-police-nursing-home-in-2020/102374334
3 https://www.health.gov.au/health-topics/mental-health-and-suicide-prevention
4 Meadows, GM & Burgess, PM, 2009, "Perceived need for mental health care: findings from the 2007 Australian Survey of Mental Health and Wellbeing" Australian and New Zealand Journal of Psychiatry 2009; 43:624_634
5 Anja Thieme, Jayne Wallace, Thomas D. Meyer and Patrick Olivier, 2015, " Designing for Mental Wellbeing: Towards a More Holistic Approach in the Treatment and Prevention of Mental Illness" British HCI 2015, July 13–17, 2015, DOI: http://dx.doi.org/10.1145/2783446.2783586
6 Anja Thieme, John McCarthy, Paula Johnson, Stephanie Phillips, Jayne Wallace, Siân Lindley, Karim Ladha, Daniel Jackson, Diana Nowacka, Ashur Rafiev, Cassim

Ladha, Thomas Nappey, Mathew Kipling, Peter Wright, Thomas D. Meyer and Patrick Olivier, 2016, "Challenges for Designing new Technology for Health and Wellbeing in a Complex Mental Healthcare Context", Mental Health in Technology Design and Social Media https://doi.org/10.1145/2783446.2783586

7 Jurewicz, I 2015 "**Mental health in young adults and adolescents – supporting general physicians to provide holistic care**", Clinical Medicine 2015 Vol 15, No 2: 151–4, Royal College of Physicians 2015

8 Carter Jolynne Zawalski Sandra, Sminkey Patrice V., Christopherson Bruce 2015, Assessing the Whole Person: Case Managers Take a Holistic Approach to Physical and Mental Health, Professional Case Management. Vol.20, No.J, 140–146, DOI: 10.1097/NCM.0000M0000000087

9 Khenti Akwatu, Freel Stefanie, Trainor Ruth, Mohamoud Sirad, Pablo Diaz, Suh Erica, Bobbili Sireesha J, and Sapag Jaime C, 2016, Developing a holistic policy and intervention framework for global mental health, Health Policy and Planning, 31, 2016, 37–45 doi: 10.1093/heapol/czv016

10 Blanch, Andrea 2007, Integrating Religion and Spirituality in Mental Health: The Promise and the Challenge, Psychiatric Rehabilitation Journal 2007, Volume 30, No. 4, 251–260 DOI: 0.2975/30.4.2007.251.260

11 Gurej, Oye, Nortje, Gareth Makanjuola, Victor Oladeji, Bibilola D Seedat, Soraya & Jenkins, Rachel 2015, "The role of global traditional and complementary systems of medicine in the treatment of mental health disorders", *Lancet Psychiatry* 2015; 2: 168–77 https://doi.org/10.1016/S2215-0366(15)00013-9

12 Blignault, Ilse and Kaur, Arshdeep 2020 "Integration of traditional and western treatment approaches in mental health care in Pacific Island Countries" Australasian Psychiatry 2020, Vol 28(1) 11–15 https://doi.org/10.1177/1039856219859273

13 Tony V. Pham, Tony V Koirala, Rishav Wainberg, Milton L & Kohrt, Brandon A 2021 "Reassessing the Mental Health Treatment Gap: What Happens if We Include the Impact of Traditional Healing on Mental Illness?" Community Mental Health Journal (2021) 57:777–791 https://doi.org/10.1007/s10597-020-00705-5

14 Wilkinson, Richard & Pickett, Kate, 2010, op cit

15

LIVING WITH BIAS

As discussed earlier, for countless years, the dominant paradigm in almost all societies was one of males being the provider and females being the nurturer. This was then reinforced by religions of all varieties tending to develop their concepts of the divine in terms of the physical characteristics most valued – the dominant male who provided food and protection from danger. Invariably this led to a male dominated society. Over the years this evolved to become the default setting for societies across the globe. Women were largely excluded from positions of power, authority, and leadership. Similarly, for many years the advocates of slavery effectively argued that those they enslaved were a lesser species than the enslaver. Even if, perhaps, they were human, it was argued, they were a lesser species of humanity than was the slave owner because, after all, they were "defeated people". Accordingly, slaves could be treated as animals with no rights and treated as chattels.

Today, in societies such as Afghanistan under Taliban rule and most other autocratic societies, the western world widely acknowledges there is significant and obvious bias and discrimination – often against women and minority groups including LBGT+. Such bias (although frequently disguised) is also, sadly, still a wide-spread phenomenon in liberal democracies. All too often the status quo has come to mean that those in control need to be of the correct ethnicity, religion, sexual orientation, and similar characteristics. There are efforts by conservative forces (albeit often covert rather than overt) to try and maintain this status quo in liberal democratic societies including Australia, the UK, US and New Zealand – those advocating change are denigrated as "woke" or worse. The "white lives matter" movement is a symptom of this.

Over recent years there have been moves across multiple societies to deal with this issue of bias and its resultant discriminatory behaviour. Use any search engine to check on confronting biases and you will be bombarded with a

DOI: 10.4324/9781003528340-16

plethora of courses and other material on identifying and eliminating bias, fostering diversity, and moving to an integrated workplace and/or society. It is widely recognised that while people like to believe that they are rational and logical, as we have seen in earlier chapters, the fact is that people are continually under the influence of their emotions and, therefore, biases. These biases distort thinking, influence beliefs, and sway the decisions and judgments that people make each and every day.

A 2018 study[1] from the University of London argues that the current move to "unconscious bias training" is a diversity intervention based on unproven suppositions and is unlikely to help eliminate racism in the workplace. It highlights that knowing about bias does not automatically result in changes in behaviour by managers and employees: that even if "unconscious bias training" has the theoretical potential to change behaviour, it will depend on the type of racism: symbolic/modern/colour-blind, aversive or blatant. In addition, even if those deemed racist are motivated to change behaviour, structural constraints can militate against pro-diversity actions. Agency (the capacity of individuals to act independently and to make their own free choices) is overstated by psychology-inspired "unconscious bias training" proponents. They conclude that from a critical diversity perspective (sociologically influenced) the training looks pointless.

Noon's work is reinforced by research published in 2023[2]. The study directly contradicts broadly accepted recommendations that this type of behaviour can be reduced through the formal delivery of education via videos or in-person talks – a practice used regularly in different sports around the world. Denison et al. explored the use of homophobic language in men's community sport and found education campaigns run by professional rugby players did nothing to stop young players and their coaches from mindlessly using words such as "fag" and "poof" in team settings. This study is a very early attempt to explore anti-homophobia educational intervention delivered by professional athletes. It was undertaken by every under-18s and Colts (under-20s) team in Victoria (Australia), whose participants filled out surveys two weeks before and two weeks after players from the Melbourne Rebels Super Rugby team travelled around the state to deliver talks.

In the pre-training survey, 55.3% self-reported using homophobic language at least once over the previous two weeks and 77.4% perceived teammates to have used homophobic language. In the post-training survey, those numbers had risen to 61.2% and 82.1% respectively. "Use of professional rugby athletes to deliver education on homophobic language was not effective," the study reads. "Other approaches to reduce homophobic language [and other forms of discrimination] such as peer-to-peer education, and enforcement of policies prohibiting specific language by coaches, should be explored." The results do indicate that homophobia is not the primary driver behind the use of slurs, rather a means "to conform to the behavioural norms in rugby" and this is an important point: there is a psychological pressure to be part of a larger "in-group" and we try to conform to our perception of acceptable behaviour of that in-group.

Denison states that the results were "very disappointing". "The results are also hard to understand because most young men we study, including the rugby players, have positive attitudes towards gay people and would have no problem with having a gay player on their team," Denison said. "The vast majority also said they would stop others from bullying a gay teammate. Even more surprising, more than half said they have close gay friends. Despite all this, they are still using homophobic language, even after being told by professional rugby players that their behaviour is very harmful and to stop. "We aren't just talking about them using phrases like 'that's gay'. They are constantly using words like 'faggot'. This language is deeply entrenched in male sport and it will be very difficult to stop."

Cultural environment and habit are powerful influencers on behaviour!

Denison et al.'s study reinforces an earlier finding. In 2021 where a key concern with anti-bias workshops was highlighted[3]. This considered facilitated modelling (a tradition that extensively involves stakeholders in addressing complex issues) as it provides an opportunity for workshop participants to learn. In this, each brings his or her mental model about the organisation and its environment and this mental model consists of all the deeply held beliefs that individuals maintain. Engaging in a structured dialogue can lead to instances where opposing mental models are confronted with each other and if the participants manage to surface and resolve these differences, this constructive conflict leads to cognitive change. De Grooyert et al. point out that

> The potential benefits of facilitated modelling, including cognitive change and consensus forming, have been extensively described. However, the evidence that these benefits are achieved often remains anecdotical, and mainly relies on self-reported assessments. This is problematic, as self-reported measures can prove unreliable.

Their study showed experienced and observed cognitive change were not related but, for consensus forming, they did find a modest correlation between experienced and observed outcomes.

It is clear that, while workshops can have an impact, for real (i.e. long-term) change to occur, workshops alone are not enough.

The issue of racial prejudice as an unconscious bias[4] was explored in 2020. This explored the roots and ramifications of unconscious bias, from the level of the neuron to that of society. and has shown how social conditions can interact with the workings of our brain to determine our responses to other people, especially in the context of race. it found that a key factor is our social conditioning. Eberhardt's work with police in northern California illustrated that bias does not vary across racial distinctions: non-white Police Officers show similar patterns of behaviour to white Police Officers in similar situations operating in the same environment. The legacy of past policies, such as segregated neighbourhoods and mass incarceration, creates conditions that trickle down to individual brains. This reflects the point made earlier by Dovidio et al.[5] when they point out that institutional policies and cultural processes perpetuate disparities between groups and enhance bias. They say: "group competition is central to the development and maintenance of social bias."

Dovidio et al. argue that an important approach to dealing with bias is to temper the competition that exists between teams by encouraging intergroup interdependence. Quoting a 1969 work by Sherif and Sherif[6], on intergroup conflict and cooperation, they say: "... functional relations between groups are critical in determining intergroup attitudes. ... competition between groups produces prejudice and discrimination, whereas intergroup interdependence and cooperative interaction that leads to successful outcomes reduces intergroup bias". They also point out that prejudice is a mechanism that maintains status and role differences between groups as well as within groups and they argue that the reactions of individuals exacerbate this process. "People who deviate from their group's traditional role arouse negative reactions; others who exhibit behaviors that reinforce the *status quo* elicit positive responses. Dovidio et al. also make the point that

> ....unconscious associations, which are culturally shared and automatically activated, may be disassociated from expressions of personal beliefs that are expressed on self-report measures of prejudice, and these two types of measures may vary systematically. ... understanding the causes, dynamics, and consequences of contemporary forms of bias can help to identify effective strategies for combating bias. ... Approaches for dealing with the traditional form of prejudice are generally less effective for combating the consequences of contemporary forms. For example, Whites already consciously endorse egalitarian, nonprejudiced views and disavow traditional stereotypes. Moreover, the traditional approach of emphasizing social norms that proscribe the avoidance of negative behavior toward Blacks and other people of color is not likely to be effective for addressing aversive racism. People possessing this type of bias have already internalized these norms and are very guarded about overtly discriminating against people of color. Thus, contemporary forms of bias have to be combated at implicit, as well as explicit, levels.

In-groups are psychologically primary and we cross them at our own peril.

Another study on this in-group – out-group issue[7] highlights that a key factor is that individuals perceive a given out-group as more or less heterogeneous ("The same individual may have the impression that a given out-group is composed of members who are rather dissimilar from each other, or who resemble each other quite a bit") and this perceived variability of a social group is an important construct because it affects an individual's attitude towards that group. It can be conceptualised as having cognitive (stereotypes), affective (prejudice), and behavioural (discrimination) components. They argue that, once a perceiver realises that an out-group is heterogeneous, group membership becomes non-diagnostic and can no longer serve as a guide for behaviour.

While most material on bias and its manifestations such as prejudice and discrimination focus on the sociological issues, Ilan H Meyer[8] adds another dimension when considering the issue of prejudice and discrimination as stressors and assessing their impact on various health outcomes. Meyer focuses on the impact of prejudice from "the target's perspective" and how, since 1999 there has been a renewed awareness of the health issues involved: prejudice (specifically racism) is now firmly "within the stress conceptual framework". It has long been realised that stress is a significant contributor to health issues but the inclusion of bias in its various formats as a stressor provides additional reasons as to why addressing bias is of vital concern – even if, as Meyer notes, "prejudice enters any stressful life event indirectly". Meyer continues: "… there seems to be a consensus that it is insufficient to understand prejudice only as a mediator that leads to excesses in certain life events and that researchers should assess prejudice and discrimination as unique events". When this is done, then concerns about bias in its many manifestations moves beyond its direct impact on the individual to the institutional factors that generate and sustain prejudice and discrimination – often through manipulation of employment practices and the like.

A 2021 report from Wharton Business School[9] explores how companies can make more equitable workplaces a reality with the help of middle managers, who ultimately shape the environment and daily experiences of employees. They make it clear that simply providing awareness and/or even skills training is inadequate. Not only does the overt behaviours need to be addressed but so also do the mental models underlying the behaviour and the environment within which people work.

Earlier, mention was made of Corrigan's work in the early years of the 21st century. A team (of which I was a member) lead by John Corrigan was researching issues around the earnings and status of teachers[10] in Australia. A study of the available literature indicated that virtually all studies conducted in Australia and overseas sought to ascertain parent, student, and community views of teachers and teaching from the base of believing that "the system" was fine and that the problems, if any, were caused by teachers, parents, and a decline in community values. Pressure groups of teachers, parents, and others then sought to validate their own position with the result that conflict focused on peripheral or, in Deming's terms[11], "special" causes or issues such as remuneration, school conditions, funding, and curriculum rather than confronting the systems problems.

A loop had developed which resulted in a downward spiral of confidence in teachers and the state education system and allowed bodies with vested interests (such as the non-government school system) to flourish even though, in fact, the education provided by non-government schools was not appreciably (if at all) better (in real terms) than that of government schools. It became apparent that there was an underlying bias that was negatively impacting the teaching profession – especially in the state public education arena.

This study was a key contributor to the development of what has earlier (Chapter 3) been referred to as the "red zone" – "blue zone" dichotomy.

Unfortunately, because, as discussed in Chapter 3, the red zone is dominated by the amygdala it is not capable of distinguishing between real threats or imagined threats and so it reacts in the same way whether a threat actually exists. This readily leads to bias and its associated behaviours. Accordingly, from across the spectrum of the key players (students, teachers, school administrators, politicians, and parents) there was often significant resistance to considering a different approach – the thought of starting with students was not readily accepted by some. No matter their rhetoric, it was hard for many (especially at the political and departmental administration level) to accept that the underlying system was in need of radical overhaul.

When the brain's area of control is in the blue zone we have the opportunity to see things differently – to recognise and control bias. (This, of course, does not necessarily mean that because the opportunity exists we will avail ourselves of it!) Because the blue zone is dominated by the cortical brain – that part of the brain which deals with thought, voluntary movement, language and reasoning (in other words "with higher level learning") – we have the ability to see things as they actually are and to distinguish between real and imagined threats. This enables us to make a more appropriate response and to find ways of dealing with "the new" in exciting and innovative ways.

Evans' work, mentioned earlier, is relevant here. As discussed in Chapter 9, Evans[12] argues that "views of human rationality are strongly affected by the adoption of a two minds theory in which humans have an old mind which evolved early and shares many features of animal cognition, as well as a new mind which evolved later and is distinctively developed in humans." In Corrigan's terms, this "old mind" is the red zone while the "new mind" is the blue zone. Only when the "new mind" (blue zone) is fully engaged are we able to reflect on the possible presence of bias and to take account of this.

The studies by Phelps, Amodio, Torrence[13], and others referred to earlier also provide support for the need to deal with addressing bias in a comprehensive way. Rather than treating symptoms by alerting people to types of bias and developing an awareness to recognise the problems arising from bias, we need to address the issue of how we process perceived threat (even if such perception is unconscious). We need to encourage a shift from "red zone" dominance to "blue zone" dominance. We need to facilitate the role of the prefrontal cortex as the default operating system.

A further clue as to why this "two minds" concept is so important can be found in the work of Endel Tulving. Tulving[14] argues that "Although common sense endows many animals with the ability to remember their past experiences, as yet there is no evidence that humanlike episodic memory – defined in terms of subjective time, self, and autonoetic awareness – is present in any other species." Episodic memory was very loosely defined as "the kind of memory that allows one to remember past happenings from one's life." This, of course, implies that there is more than one type of memory and that such other types serve different functions from episodic memory. As Tulving makes clear, this is a departure from traditional thought "because in traditional thought, as in common sense, memory is 'unitary' in the sense that there is only one 'kind' of memory, as there is only one kind of water, or blood or forget-me-nots." However, the point is made that research in the early 1960's demonstrated that

> the laws and principles governing primary ("short-term") memory are not quite the same as those that apply to secondary ("long-term") memory. ... Today, the break between primary memory, or its more theoretically meaningful successor "working memory" on the one hand, and secondary memory ("long-term memory") on the other, is as sharp as one can find anywhere in nature. More recently, research has shown that episodic memory is one of a family of "multiple memory systems" that has "traditionally been categorized as one of the two subsystems of "declarative" (or "cognitive" or "explicit" memory, sematic memory being the other one.

While both the "old mind" and the "new mind" access both semantic and episodic memory, where episodic memory can remember the past and learn from it, semantic memory simply remembers the past while concentrating on the present. In other words, the intuitive response triggered by the "old mind" (red zone) knows what the past holds but has limited ability to consider whether the responses triggered are appropriate. It is only when humanlike episodic memory is accessed by the "new mind" (blue zone) that it is fully possible to control any cognitive bias that may be triggered. The extent of "common sense" demonstrated at any time depends on the extent to which higher brain functions (the "new mind" / "red zone") are employed.

This raises questions as to what is involved in making and implementing a conscious decision to shift from a red zone to a blue zone mental state. Adam Liete's work is relevant here. Leite[15] comments that while

> A broad tradition of thought urges that what makes an attitude properly one's own in some sense deeper than mere correctness of ascription from an external perspective – one's own as subject, we might say – is one's endorsement of it. ... however, endorsement does not forge a distinction between what properly belongs to "me" as subject and that in my psychology to which I relate only as an object of description, report, and possibly management.

In other words, it is possible to philosophically agree with a concept yet not to allow that concept impact on our behaviour. He argues that

> It is widely agreed that there is such a thing as reflectively making up one's mind and thereby shaping one's beliefs – a process of determining *what* one

believes by determining what *to* believe – and that such processes of active deliberation can take place in a fully self-conscious way. Self-conscious deliberation requires that one stand in a distinctive stance or relation to one's beliefs, one often termed "first-personal" as distinct from "third-personal" or "merely attributional". An essential first task is to characterize this stance or relation in a way that does not beg any crucial questions.

In other words, the starting point for change is that a person acknowledges their current state from a "this really is me" perspective rather than considering it from what could be called "an academic" or "third party" perspective. It requires "an episode of self-conscious deliberation". Beck and Cowan's aforementioned concept of the system of values' change and the possible descent into the "Gamma Trap" is relevant here (Chapter 13). For lasting change to occur, not just the individual's concerns but the environment within which they operate need to be addressed.

But acknowledging that "this really is me" and determining to change is not, of itself, sufficient. For change to be implemented, the environment must be not only conducive to change but must actively facilitate change – and that requires leadership.

What we know from both research and experience is that most people are only able to give their very best when they feel

- emotionally safe;
- unconditionally respected;
- believed in as individuals;
- listened to

and, in theory at least, these are the conditions that should be created when facilitating change. Unfortunately, this is often forgotten. Almost by definition, people operating in the red zone cannot feel emotionally safe because a hallmark of the red zone is, at the best, vague apprehension and, at the worst, debilitating fear. It doesn't matter what a facilitator may say, unless the facilitator's behaviour shows that the words are backed up by supportive actions, any attempt to encourage creativity through honest, upwards feedback and/or criticism has the proverbial snowball in hell's chance of success! And even if the facilitator is supportive and provides the optimal learning environment, unless there is on-going support from the person's social environment, the probability of long-term change is low.

Despite what some people seem to believe, leadership is not primarily a hierarchical concept. If leadership is defined as "*creating an environment in which people can be successful*", then any person can be a leader: age, gender, hierarchical status, and all other such variables largely are irrelevant. What is essential is that the leader is trusted by the people involved – it is all about relationships. Clearly this is a complex responsibility and one that requires significant ability to deal with ambiguity and complexity (see the earlier comments on the work of Elliot Jacques). A "leader" who is lacking in the appropriate level of ability to deal with ambiguity and complexity will invariably seek to reduce the leadership role to its most basic component – power – and may attempt to impose change on others. Immediately this occurs, the four essentials for successful change (feeling emotionally safe, feeling unconditionally respected, feeling believed in as an individual, and feeling listened to) have disappeared. The probability of successful permanent change occurring is extremely remote. The best that can be expected is instrumental compliance – in other words, acting in the desired manner when others can see what is happening, but having no personal commitment to any behavioural change. A temporary veneer disguises the reality that nothing has really changed. The highest probability of success exists when an internal desire to change results in an individual taking responsibility for their own change process. This requires openness and authenticity from all parties involved and this develops from the seeds of openness and harmony that are sown in the development of trust.

Questions for group discussion:

1. "All too often the status quo has come to mean that those in control need to be of the correct ethnicity, religion, sexual orientation, and similar characteristics. There are efforts by conservative forces (albeit often covert rather than overt) to try and maintain this status quo in liberal democratic societies." What do you see as being the "rights" and the "wrongs" involved in discussions about maintaining the traditional status quo in liberal democratic societies? What biases underly your "right" and/or "wrong" classifications? How did these impact your decisions?

2. "Knowing about bias does not automatically result in changes in behaviour by managers and employees: that even if 'unconscious bias training' has the theoretical potential to change behaviour, it will depend on the type of racism: symbolic/modern/colour-blind, aversive or blatant. In addition, even if those deemed racist are motivated to change behaviour, structural constraints can militate against pro-diversity actions." What are the key components needed for any intervention promoting effective bias management to be successful? Why? How can these be implemented?

3. "Social conditions can interact with the workings of our brain to determine our responses to other people, especially in the context of race. A key factor is our social conditioning." How has social conditioning impacted the biases you have today? If you are seeking to manage biases, what changes do you need to make in your social environment? Why? How can you make these changes?

4. "It has long been realised that stress is a significant contributor to health issues but the inclusion of bias in its various formats as a stressor provides additional reasons as to why addressing bias is of vital concern." How and

when do your biases affect your health issues because of their impact? What about for other people with whom you interact – your social environment? How can this be managed?

5. In future work roles and places, what impact will machine learning have on an employee's ability to make meaning and therefore grow professionally & personally in their career?

Notes

1   Mike Noon, 2018, *"Pointless Diversity Training: Unconscious Bias, New Racism and Agency"*, Work, Employment and Society, Vol. 32(1) 198–209, doi.org/10.1177/0950017017719841
2   https://bjsm.bmj.com/content/early/2023/02/09/bjsports-2022-105916?rss=1
3   Vincent de Gooyert, Etienne Rouwette, Hans van Kranenburg, Edward Freeman, Harry van Breen, Cognitive change and consensus forming in facilitated modelling: A comparison of experienced and observed outcomes, *European Journal of Operational Research* (2021), doi: https://doi.org/10.1016/j.ejor.2021.09.007
4   Her work is reported: https://www.science.org/news/2020/03/meet-psychologist-exploring-unconscious-bias-and-its-tragic-consequences-society
5   Dovidio, John F., op cit
6   **Social psychology** Muzafer Sherif 1906–1988.; Carolyn W Sherif (Carolyn Wood) New York: Harper & Row, 1969
7   Abdelatif Er-rafiy and Markus Brauer, 2012, Increasing Perceived Variability Reduces Prejudice and Discrimination: Theory and Application, Social and Personality Psychology Compass 6/12 (2012): 920–935
8   American Journal of Public Health | February 2003, Vol 93, No. 2, p262–265
9   Knowledge at Wharton, June 21, 2021 *"How Middle Managers Can Help Make a More Equitable Workplace"*, Wharton School of the University of Pennsylvania
10 Further information on this work is found in: Andrew Mowat, John Corrigan, Doug Long, 2009, *"The Success Zone: 5 powerful steps to growing yourself and leading others"*, Global Publishing Group, Mt Evelyn, Vic. Australia. Also in: Douglas G. Long, 2012, *Third Generation Leadership and the Locus of Control*, Gower Publishing Limited, Farnham, Surrey, UK.
11 William Edwards Deming, an American engineer, statistician, professor, author, lecturer, and management consultant was a pioneer in assisting organisations improve the quality of their products and services. He argues that there were two key factors – systems causes and special causes – with most quality problems being caused by systems issues: the overall system was not designed to incorporate high levels of product/service quality.
12 Evans Op cit
13 Phelps et al, op cit
14 Tulving, Endel, 2001, *"Episodic Memory and Common Sense: how far apart?"*, The Royal Society, *doi:* 10.1098/retb.2001.0937
15 Leite, Adam, 2018, "Changing One's Mind: Self-Conscious Belief and Rational Endorsement", Philosophy and Phenomenological Research, Vol. XCVII No. 1, July 2018, doi: 10.1111/phpr.12332

16
THE WAY FORWARD

In the early 1990's original TV adaptation of the book *To Play the King* [1], the second part of the *House of Cards* trilogy, Michael Kitchen plays a newly crowned (and unnamed) king who deeply disapproves of his Conservative government led by the Machiavellian Prime Minister Francis Urquhart (played by Ian Richardson). In his first meeting with the Prime Minister, the newly crowned king asks him to cancel the "modernist" redevelopment of an old city site. Urquhart is dismissive, saying: "The King's job is to give garden parties and to save us the bother of electing someone else president". Later, in a vicious encounter with the King, he tells him: "politics is about the attainment and use of power ... no place for a king". The King replies: "Did I miss a mention of morality in there, prime minister?" The response is telling. Urquhart replies: "Morality, sir, is the monologue of the unexcited and the unexcitable, the revenge of the unsuccessful, the punishment of those who tried and failed, or who never had the courage to try at all."

There is relevance here to the issue of bias. Clearly Urquhart is biased against the concept of morality being relevant to politics. However, until he acknowledges any bias – instead seeing his current world view as normal – nothing will change. So long as we refuse to admit that we are biased, there are very few steps that will be taken to address any problems that arise. Acknowledging that an issue exists is an essential criterion before any solution or remediation is possible. Only after acknowledgement is made can we decide whether to manage the status quo or seek to eliminate the problem. Based on the research reflected throughout this work, I suggest that total removal of all bias is impossible so we now need to address how the problem can be managed.

Earlier it was stated that every person has an absolute right to be treated with unconditional respect (which says something about my own biases). This is a premise that is sometimes misunderstood. Most people claim to treat others

DOI: 10.4324/9781003528340-17

with respect, and it is possible to be quite affronted when any suggestion is made that indicates the "respect" we show is inadequate. However, in most societies, our default way of dealing with others is that of conditional respect. In other words, "if you do what I want, then I will show you respect." The (usually) not stated corollary of this statement is, of course, "and if you don't do what I want, then I'll act in a way that makes you want to do what I want you to do." Accordingly, in order to avoid or at least minimise negative consequences, there is considerable pressure to comply – instrumental compliance is a coping mechanism to avoid negative consequences. Conditional respect is an approach in which a person and their behaviour are conflated and in which a person's sense of self-worth can readily become intertwined with how they are perceived by others. In other words, we manipulate situations in order to achieve our desired results – we use bias to our own ends. Many sociological problems can be traced back to this.

Today's dominant work-place paradigm is one of controlling people and events through various management and leadership practices. Uncertainty and an apparent inability to deal with ambiguity and complexity in an authoritative manner can be seen as "career limiting" for the ambitious young person – of any gender. The result is that ambiguity and uncertainty are ignored, disguised or reduced to some point where a relatively simple solution can be imposed. We are conditioned to demonstrate bias towards "being decisive" or "being in control" regardless of whether we are actually equipped for this – or whether the situation being faced actually requires this.

An unconditional respect approach is quite different. Unconditional respect differentiates between the person and their behaviour. Unconditional respect says

> I may not agree with your views and/or your behaviour, but, simply because of the fact of your humanity, I will treat you the same as I, myself, want to be treated. I do not need to like you and I may not want to have you as part of my social circle, but I will still interact with you in a respectful manner.

This distinction between the person and their behaviour, makes it possible to deal with inappropriate behaviour in a manner which does not demean or bully in any way. It enables discussions in which all parties can learn and grow from the interaction. It enables a positive, healthy interaction no matter who the other person is or what they have done, in which that person understands the need for, and the process of, behavioural change. It enables us to escape the bias towards total control.

This is probably best illustrated by considering the way in which most parents interact with their baby. This new little person – someone who, in almost every instance, is keenly anticipated, deeply and strongly loved, and for whom the new parent(s) wants nothing but the best – has a mind of his, her (or their!) own. When hunger hits, baby cries. When there is physical discomfort, baby cries. When there is illness or injury, baby cries. When tiredness comes, baby cries. Too cold? Baby cries. Hungry, thirsty? Baby cries. In these very early days and weeks it seems as though only two stages exist for baby – comfortable (or asleep) and quiet or something wrong and crying. And knowing what baby is trying to communicate when crying is not always easy. Asking (or demanding) that baby conforms to what suits the parent is an exercise in futility. Complaining that baby is not listening or "should" be doing something different does nothing to alleviate parental pressure. Most parents quickly understand that the baby needs to be treated with unconditional respect – to be loved and cared for despite baby's (often) antisocial behaviour. We realise that baby lacks the physical and cognitive capacity to act differently, and we adapt to that reality.

The situation of ambiguity and complexity doesn't get any easier as baby develops into an infant, child, adolescent, and young adult. Each stage is accompanied by different challenges – especially as the child starts to develop his or her own conceptual skills which may eventually move to the point of questioning the very fabric of his or her parents' value system and life practices.

When a baby is very small, unconditional respect is essential and generally very obviously provided. Baby cannot do anything for him or herself and cannot even communicate clearly and easily as to what he or she wants and needs. When dealing with a baby every aspect of care and support has to be initiated by the parent / care giver and it must always be assumed that "baby knows best". This unconditional respect says: "no matter what you do, I will always love you and care for you." Most parents have no difficulty in understanding and applying this. The situation changes as the infant starts to develop cognition. Once an infant can begin to understand something about what they are doing, something seems to change. For many parents, this change becomes most apparent with the outbreak of "the terrible two's"!

Now there is a tendency for parents to tell the child it is "naughty" when it does something different from what the parent desires. What the parent wants is total compliance with the parents' wishes – the bias towards total control. The problems, from the child's perspective, are that, first, the child may not yet fully understand what the parent is saying and, second, that the child is simultaneously developing its own sense of identity. This developing sense of identity may not be at the stage of that the parent would like. And accompanying this "naughty" complaint, many parents also provide punishments of one sort or another. The range of these punishments can be from as simple as a raised voice through to shouting and screaming, through to psychological and physical violence – not necessarily in that order. It is at this stage that, for many children, the scene is set for later becoming dysfunctional adolescents and adults. Does that parent usually genuinely care for the child no matter how the parent responds to "naughtiness"? In most cases "yes". Does the parent genuinely love the child? Again, in most cases "yes". Does the parent want to give the child that which is best for the child? Again, in most cases "yes". In other words, most times when a parent punishes a child there is nothing but love behind the action. Invariably parental such action is taken "for your own good"![2] As adults, it is all too easy to carry the same approach into all areas of our lives: we seek to change behaviour by, consciously or not, punishing what we consider to be inappropriate behaviour.

But is the punishment effective? In other words, does the punishment have the desired long-term effect of behavioural change while simultaneously encouraging mental and emotional growth and personal accountability? For most people the end result is that the main effect of such punishment is that the person being punished takes a further step along the road to "don't get caught" with every punishment received. (If you doubt this, consider the problem of recidivism (the tendency of a convicted criminal to reoffend) in most societies.) A further impact is that conditioning towards the bias for total control has commenced.

The initiation of conditional respect as the default setting is complete.

Does this mean that inappropriate behaviour should be ignored? Certainly not. It is always important to address inappropriate behaviour of any sort and at any time. However, *how* we address it is critical. If we use our default position – conditional respect – we will conflate the person with the behaviour. If we practise unconditional respect, we will make a clear distinction between the person and the behaviour[3].

Given our current approach, it is no wonder that for most people the default behavioural position seems more orientated towards avoiding punishment rather than the desire to act appropriately. The conditioning from childhood has fostered a set of biases that have become the unconscious drivers of our everyday behaviour. Accordingly, when confronting the manifestations of bias, simply providing an intervention that highlights why our behaviour is considered to be inappropriate is unlikely to bring about any significant change. We need to return to first principles and create a new environment – one that is supportive and non-judgemental – to facilitate the change required. This is the point made earlier by both Mike Noone and Vincent de Gooyert et al when considering how to deal with bias. Their studies made clear that effective bias management requires a far more complex approach than simply providing a training or educational intervention. And certainly more than simply punishing what we consider to be inappropriate behaviour!

This, of course, raises questions as to the level of complexity needed and how to address the balance between individual change and societal change.

Joydeep Baruah[4] discusses "… 'understanding' various *forms* and *nature* of 'limits' to human development in general, and those contingent on *group affiliation* and *social conditioning* in particular viewed from the capability perspective." The argument is that "human life is all about 'doings and beings' what people 'value or have reason to value' and, hence, ultimate evaluation of human life needs be carried out with respect to peoples' capability to perform valuable doings" and continues "the distinction between 'functioning' and 'capability' is elementary in capability framework. Typically, a 'functioning' is taken as an 'achievement' of an individual while the 'capability' is considered to be the embodiment of her/his 'real freedom to achieve'. Baruah suggests that this "freedom to achieve" is limited by the influence of "complex social issues", "intricate intra-group relations and interactions" that include social conditioning and group affiliation.

While not discussing bias per se, as discussed earlier, unconscious bias (and possibly conscious bias also) is impacted by social conditioning and group affiliation. While Baruah argues that human development in general is directly impacted by group affiliation and social conditioning providing limits on a person's ability to develop their full potential, it would appear a similar argument can be made for the role of bias which, as discussed, develops from the same group affiliation and social conditioning. In other words, while a behavioural intervention programme may argue that it is enabling a person to manage their biases, that person may not actually possess the "real freedom to achieve" such change until their group affiliation and social conditioning environment provides a fertile environment within which the change can take place. Individual agency (the capacity of individuals to act independently and to make their own free choices) is potentially limited by the environment that has fostered the biases. This is a point made earlier.

In theory the capability for change exists: in practice such capability may be seriously limited. If this is so, then it is clear that both individual change and societal change need to be addressed in tandem. Failure to address both heightens the probability that a person will find themselves caught in Beck and Cowan's earlier mentioned gamma trap.

Some years ago, Robert Spillane[5] argued that

> ... Stress is the result of personalities attempting to solve practical problems and distress is a result of attitudes about stress. ... stress is the result of demands made on people to change or adapt. Stress is the result of practical problems, distress represents emotional problems about practical problems.
>
> *(p.9)*

This helps us understand why, so often, trying to change individual bias is denigrated as being "political correctness" or being "woke". I feel my status quo is under threat and I am not willing to sharpen my mind "by increasing awareness of the consequences of different choices" (Spillane). My response is to become distressed about something that I feel is being foisted upon me – I have "emotional problems about practical problems" even if resolving these practical problems may actually benefit me and others. Rather than recognise the reality of the bias problem, I hide behind my status quo curtain.

The seminal work of Kurt Lewin[6] described change as a three-stage process. The first stage he called "unfreezing". Unfreezing involves overcoming inertia and dismantling the existing "mind set". It is a key part of surviving. Defence mechanisms have to be bypassed. In the second stage the change occurs. This is typically a period of confusion and transition. We are aware that the old ways are being challenged but we do not yet have a clear picture as to what we are replacing them with. The third and final stage he called "freezing". The new mindset is crystallising and one's comfort level is returning to previous levels. (In the earlier discussed change model of Beck and Cowan, this is the optimum move from an original alpha state to a new alpha state.)

It is now widely accepted that Lewin's concept provides a core model for any change process whether it be societal, organisational or individual. However, in many of the approaches currently advocated around cognitive bias, it seems this message may have been lost: all too often we seek to impose change by fiat – telling others what their behaviours should be and applying pressure until these are exhibited. No wonder people become distressed (Spillane) and oppose "political correctness" and/or "being woke".

So, what is the way forward?

The starting point is for each of us to fully acknowledge that we have biases – both those of which we are aware and those of which we are not aware. Most of us (at least when pressured) are generally prepared to acknowledge (some at least of) our conscious biases but acknowledgement of possible unconscious bias is far less likely. How often do we hear "I'm not biased, but …" or "I'm not prejudiced, but …. ". When attention is drawn to possible unconscious bias, we are far more likely to protest our innocence and to support such protestations with evidence such as comparing oneself to more egregious examples that can be observed. Our psychological defence mechanisms are fully engaged. It's along the lines of the old "insult card" that was widely used by children in my youth: "My mind's made up. Don't confuse me with the facts".

Lewin's concept of "unfreezing" starts with accepting that, no matter what and how we are currently doing, a better alternative might be possible. (As has been said, "whatever we are doing today, we are almost certainly doing in the most up-to-date, obsolete way possible"!) Sometimes it takes a very dramatic event to bring about this awareness, but dramatic events are not mandatory: a person with real self-confidence will always be open to the possibility of personal growth. Self-confidence doesn't mean being brash, aggressive, or offensive. Rather it means having a realistic sense of one's own strengths and weaknesses coupled with a determination to make a positive contribution to one's world wherever possible[7]. Self-confidence means knowing you are a person in your own right – a person to be respected – and who gives respect to others simply because they, too, are individuals. While physical growth is completed by one's late teens or early 20's, "self-confidence" recognises that the "expansion of one's mind" – mental and emotional growth – is possible throughout our lives.

The second step is to make an honest and balanced assessment as to the possibility of unconscious bias being present. This is hard.

Many years ago, in the movie "The Dead Poets' Society", the late Robin Williams played the role of John Keating, a charismatic teacher who inspired his class to "seize the day" (carpe diem). In one memorable scene, Keating tells his students to stand on their desks and look around. His point is that, when we look at the same scene from different aspects, we get different perspectives on the reality around us. We all have our individual "world views" or mental models. For many of us, this means that we tend towards a "black or white" (sometimes with some grades of grey) view of things. In Keating's terms, we may benefit by "standing on our desks".

The metaphor of a kaleidoscope may help us here. A kaleidoscope is an optical instrument with two or more reflecting surfaces tilted to each other at an angle, so that one or more objects on one end of these mirrors are shown as a regular symmetrical pattern when viewed from the other end, due to repeated reflection. It is as though different lenses are employed to look at the same feature. If we use only one lens, we get a far more restricted perspective than if multiple lenses are employed. Almost certainly there will always be some congruency between views no matter what lens is used but using them in a coordinated fashion will provide the most comprehensive picture.

The lenses we use will vary across a wide range of factors, and we are all capable of identifying those that are most appropriate for us. However, four common (and readily available) lenses are:

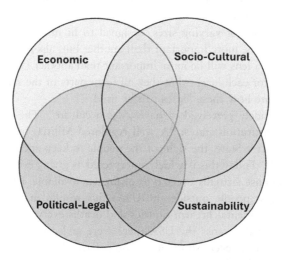

FIGURE 16.1 The Lens Kaleidoscope

Socio-cultural Lens – diversity of cultures: different beliefs, ways of living and doing things. Culture across different levels: Global and local culture and everything in-between

Political and Legal Lens – The basic structure of the contemporary global world: the world of nation-states. Rules and regulation and their influences on individuals and organisations

Economics Lens – Economic trends and fluctuations that shape economic behaviour. Economic development and growth; labour supply and consumption; fiscal and monetary policy

Sustainability Lens – The physical environment, interdependence and systems view that includes: "Ensure healthy lives and promote well-being for all at all ages" and: "Promote peaceful and inclusive societies for sustainable development, provide access to justice for all and build effective, accountable and inclusive institutions at all levels"

The thing to note is the overlaps that occur. There are some areas for each lens that are unique to that lens. There are some areas where just two or three lenses overlap. And there is a smaller area where all lenses overlap. The larger the area of overlap across all lenses employed, the lower the probability that we will allow unconscious bias to guide us because we will have identified what is held in common rather than focusing on what holds us apart. This can enable us to focus on a more comprehensive perspective than may otherwise have been available.

Along with the individual lenses themselves, it is also important to realise that, within these lenses, there is also a variety of levels, and these levels are a little like a traditional Russian doll (or "matryoshka doll") – a set of brightly painted hollow wooden dolls of varying sizes, designed to fit inside each other. Sometimes one lens will be more important than another but, also, there will be times when one level of a lens will be more important than another (and the levels may not be the same for each lens) – but they all form parts of the same set.

Let me illustrate how these lenses can be used.

The USA is widely perceived to have a "gun culture". The Second Amendment to the Constitution states: "A well regulated Militia, being necessary to the security of a free State, the right of the people to keep and bear Arms, shall not be infringed." Today this is widely interpreted as giving every US citizen the right to own and use virtually every type of firearm available. Far too frequently (at least for most people outside the USA) this results in large numbers of intentional and accidental firearm injuries and deaths every year. In the year to the end of May 2022 across the USA there were at least 269 instances where multiple people have been shot; 308 people have died (often including the shooter), and a further 1,114 have been wounded. Three of these shootings have occurred at a school or university and a further two have occurred at a place of worship. It is widely recognised that the USA has the highest level of shootings of any country in (at least) the Western world. All attempts to curb firearm ownership is thwarted on the grounds that individuals have the right to arms set in the Constitution. The Small Arms Survey[8] calculated that, in 2018, "the US ratio of 120.5 firearms per 100 residents, up from 88 per 100 in 2011, far surpasses that of other countries around the world". Pew Research Centre studies indicate "Four-in-ten U.S. adults say they live in a household with a gun, including 30% who say they personally own one"

Research by the Pew Research Centre[9] indicates that, as at September 2021, "roughly half of Americans (53%) favor stricter gun laws, a decline since 2019". This support (or lack of it) reaches across party lines. Despite this, the US Senate (dominated by Republicans and independents) refuses to allow debate of any bill that could have a negative impact on gun ownership. As at May 8, 2023, USA Today reports that there had been 221 mass killings in the USA in the first 4 months of 2023.[10] In the article, James Alan Fox, a professor at Northeastern University, stated that "all of the mass killings this year have been shootings, and 12 were among families. ... The number of annual mass killings in the U.S. remained largely steady from 2006 to 2018 but started to increase in 2019", he said. "Now, 2023 has seen more mass killings at this point in the year than in any other year," Fox said.

> We have seen a surge in the number of guns being purchased, and then you combine that with the impact that COVID had on people's emotional state and economic well-being. And of course, there's the political divisions that we have in our country, he said.

The four lenses provide a mechanism to understand why a group of 100 people are able to prevent any action relating to gun control. (The US Senate comprises 100 people and, as at March 2023, Republicans hold 49 seats, Democrats hold 48 seats and there are 3 independents.) As we use these lenses, it is important to note that opposition to firearm control reaches across the political divide – it is not just the Republicans who oppose.

> **Using the economic lens:** According to Forbes Magazine in 2018[11], "Gun stores had revenue of about $11 billion, IBIS World said in its 2018 report. Gun and ammunition manufacturers had revenues of $17 billion ..." Clearly firearms are a major source of employment and of small business enterprise profits. They are a significant contributor to the GDP of the USA. There are strong economic grounds for not limiting firearm sales.
>
> **Using the political/legal lens:** As in most other liberal democracies, politicians at all levels have a heavy reliance on donations to fuel their campaigns. The Boston Globe[12] in May 2022 reported that: "Since 2010, the NRA has spent more than $148 million on federal elections, nearly all of which has gone toward supporting Republican candidates in one way or another. About $91 million was spent trying to defeat candidates, according to OpenSecrets, a campaign finance watchdog. Former Democratic presidential nominee Hillary Clinton was the biggest target of NRA spending in the last 12 years, with $19.8 million being earmarked to defeat her. She was followed by President Biden at $12 million and former president Barack Obama at $10 million."

Clearly the National Rifle Association is a very powerful lobby group that seeks to influence votes relating to firearms.

Opposition to any form of regulation was further demonstrated in June 2022. Chris Jacobs, a Republican New York congressman who had recently voiced support of gun control legislation announced on Friday June 3 that he would no longer seek re-election after receiving backlash over his stance. Jacobs did not back any policy that would dramatically impact gun ownership. Rather, he expressed his support for several measures that would limit access to the particularly lethal weaponry used in recent mass killings. Following deadly mass shootings at a Buffalo, New York, grocery store and Uvalde, Texas, elementary school he said on 27 May: "A ban on something like an AR-15, I would vote for, so I want to be clear, I would vote for it. Individuals cannot buy beer, they cannot get cigarettes [until] 21," Jacobs said. "I think it's perfectly reasonable that the age limit, at least for these highly lethal, high-capacity semi-automatic weapons, should be 21." Seven days later the pressure had forced him to withdraw his nomination.

Despite lobbying from pressure groups advocating reform, using the political/legal lens shows there are even stronger lobby groups providing politicians with grounds for opposing any form of gun control.

Using the Sustainability lens: At first glance, the physical environment is a neutral factor. However, when considering this lens using the United Nations Sustainable Development Goals[13], a different picture emerges. Goal 3 states: "Ensure healthy lives and promote well-being for all at all ages" while Goal 16 states: "Promote peaceful and inclusive societies for sustainable development, provide access to justice for all and build effective, accountable and inclusive institutions at all levels". Even if one ignores the mass shootings of adults, then it is clear that shootings in schools such as the May 2022 event in Texas goes directly against these.

It is certainly true that "guns don't kill people. People kill people" – but ready availability and access to firearms makes it more likely that "bad people" will obtain and use guns against whomsoever they want. In countries where the rule of law (the restriction of the arbitrary exercise of power by subordinating it to well-defined and established laws) is weak there tend to be more gun-related deaths than in countries with a strong rule of law. The USA claims to be a country that abides by the rule of law yet, as already discussed, it has the highest rate of gun violence and mass shootings across all liberal democracies.

Using the sustainability lens, there is a strong argument in favour of increased restrictions around ownership of firearms.

Using the socio/cultural lens: The earlier mentioned Pew Research Centre report stated that "around half of Americans (48%) see gun violence as a very big problem in the country today" and that it rated fifth in the list of the top 15 concerns. They went on to say: "About eight-in-ten Black adults (82%) say gun violence is a very big problem – by far the largest share of any racial or ethnic group By comparison, about six-in-ten His-panic adults (58%) and 39% of White adults view gun violence this way." However, according to the same report, "Americans are split over whether legal changes would lead to fewer mass shootings, according to the same spring 2021 poll. About half of adults (49%) say there would be fewer mass shootings if it was harder for people to obtain guns legally, while about as many either say this would make no difference (42%) or that there would be more mass shootings (9%)."

This makes clear that the socio/cultural lens is capable of more than one interpretation. It makes clear that gun violence is a serious problem that people would like addressed but also shows that there is no overwhelming majority that are in favour of change.

We now need to move to the next stage of lens exploration – the levels.

At the Global Level: The NY Times[14] reports that "The world over, mass shootings are frequently met with a common response: Officials impose new restrictions on gun ownership. Mass shootings become rarer. Homi-cides and suicides tend to decrease, too."

(Perhaps the "the prayers and sympathy" so often mouthed by politicians in the USA need to be accompanied by some real activity.)

At the National Level: They go on to say "Britain, Australia, Canada, New Zealand, Norway: All had a culture of gun ownership, and all tightened restrictions anyway. Their violence statistics now diverge sharply from those of the U.S." It is clear that, in comparison with other liberal democ-racies and allies, the USA is an outlier.

At the State/Territory level: In the USA there is difference across the States in relation to firearm legislation[15]. 44 States allow licensed people to visibly carry a long gun (shotgun, rifle, etc) although 3 states (Iowa, Tennessee, and Utah) require that the weapon be unloaded. Thirty-one states allow the open carrying of a handgun without a permit or license. Fifteen states require a permit to carry a handgun. Five states (California, District of Columbia, Florida, Illinois, New York, and South Carolina) prohibit people from openly carrying handguns in public. No State pro-hibits ownership of firearms and there is pressure across the USA for more restrictions to be removed.

At the community level: Across the USA there is a variety of opinion about ownership of firearms and this is reflected in the slim majority of support for tighter regulations of any sort. However, almost everyone in the USA would agree that all people have the right to expect they can live and work safely. They would also agree that all students at schools and universities should have the right to be educated in safety.

At the individual level: For decades, individuals across the USA, from the President down, have consistently expressed their regrets following mass shootings and have offered "prayers and sympathy". However, this apparent support of victims is not consistently followed by advocacy of gun control. The more common response when individuals are questioned is along the lines of "Guns don't kill people. Other people kill people. The answer to bad people with guns is more good people with guns. We need to arm our teachers and to have armed police presence in schools." On May 24, 2022, when 18-year-old Salvador Rolando Ramos fatally shot nineteen students and two teachers, and wounded seventeen other people, at Robb Elementary School in Uvalde, Texas, this "good guy" vs "bad guy" argument was demonstrably false when the responding police waited outside for about an hour while Ramos was on his rampage.

It is possible to understand why, across the USA, there is ambivalence regarding any form of gun control but, when these lenses and levels are combined, it is clear that some form of restriction on firearm availability and ownership can be supported. Failure to support any form of further restriction is a clear incidence of (by now probably conscious) bias.

Using the kaleidoscope approach is a powerful way to make an honest and balanced assessment as to the possibility of unconscious bias being present. It forces us to confront things that we prefer to keep hidden and raises the possibility that unconscious bias could be overturned so that a more balanced approach emerges. It provides us with a tool to move from "red zone" brain dominance in which the amygdala sees threat from even the most benign shadows to "blue zone" dominance in which the frontal cortex enables us to act in a more measured manner.

However, as stated earlier, of itself, this awareness is insufficient. For change to be implemented, the environment must be not only conducive to change but must actively facilitate change. We may know the difference between "red zone" and "blue zone" mindset, and we may even agree that there are benefits in making the change. However, so long as "our world" is dominated by red zone thinking the change is unlikely to occur. In other words, we may acknowledge the reality of our biases and we may be able to recognise any negative impacts these have on others, but so long as we continue to find our support among communities that themselves actively promote or at least tacitly support such biases the probability of change is very low.

Making this sociocultural environment change is, of course, significantly harder to do than it is to say. Even considering it brings us back to issues around dealing with ambiguity and complexity. No matter who we are or where we are, increasingly we find ourselves living in an environment dominated by complexity, ambiguity and uncertainty. In order to survive, some element of cognitive bias is essential. No single person has the intellectual capability to consider every possible option when considering decisions – no matter how "low level" the decision may be. Accordingly, we need at least some reliance on heuristics but, as we have seen, one's cognitive bias is inherent in choosing these.

It seems generally accepted that complexity exists when multiple forces are simultaneously acting on something. This leads to difficulty in identifying critical issues and general confusion as to correct actions. Ambiguity is a further overlay in which reality becomes blurred and the potential for misreading it increases.

Although not addressing bias per se (they are addressing personal and organisational development), the work of Lisa Lahey and Robert Keegan[16] has relevance in addressing ways for managing bias. They argue that what we understand as "complexity" is actually the mismatch or conflict between two different complexities – that of the world and our own. They suggest that the way to deal with it is to make "adaptive" shifts – in other words, being fluid in our approach. They argue that there are three key mindsets found in confronting complexity. These are:

Socialized mind: the way you view the world is strongly influenced by shared beliefs and existing social norms. You will be either a team player or a faithful follower; and to navigate complexity and uncertainty you will seek direction or be reliant on "schools of thought" for ideas or beliefs and building "technical skills". Group Think (desire for harmony and conformity results in irrational decision making) is a common outcome of having a Socialized Mindset.

Self-authorized mind: is an advanced stage of dealing with complexity, where you are able to step back enough from the social environment to generate an "internal" set of judgement. As a leader, it involves challenging popular views and driving forward new agendas. The challenge with this mindset is the "filter" we create for ourselves and its alignment to our existing belief system makes it difficult to be open to conflicting views and values other than our own.

Transformational mind: is the ideal state to navigate ambiguity and complexity effectively. Having a transformational mindset allows one to step back and reflect on the limits of our own personal ideology and see that one system or ideology is in some way partial or incomplete; this helps us to alter, refine existing plans and act more inclusively, as we recognize that the world is inter-dependent.

Working from this model, they suggest the starting point is to recognise the power of social norms and then developing the ability to act independently without conforming to the expectations of both other people and of your surrounding environment – in other words, developing a transformational mindset. Given that our normal mindsets tend to be "socialised mind" and/or "self-authorised mind" this is difficult because it requires we examine and challenge our existing assumptions and internal filters. However, such action then enables consideration of system interdependencies and alternatives that are different from one's usual approach. Associated with this is cultivating more diverse networks and alternative viewpoints, then allowing yourself to be influenced by these. In other words, dealing with bias starts with one's personal acknowledgment of the reality that bias exists in me, then making a personal commitment to confront inappropriate bias in all its manifestations.

There are, however, additional steps that we can take to minimise bias problems for the next generation. If, as I suggest above, parents are genuinely concerned about facilitating the growth of children into mature adults who can make meaningful, positive contributions to society, then perhaps we need some modification of how we do this.

It is widely accepted that how we parent is strongly influenced by how we were parented. At the most negative end of the continuum we see this in the perpetuation of child abuse across generations. What we experience as infants and young children is, understandably, accepted as "normal". We have no other reference point and we are totally dependent on our parents (or equivalent). This is the point made by Miller[17] when she links violence perpetuated by adults to corporal punishment of children. She does not say that every child who experiences corporal punishment goes on to be a perpetuator of violence (inclusive of sexual violence) – that would be patently untrue – however she does argue that a clear link exists and posits that the probability of violence by any person may be increased because of such experiences. The possibility of such a link is endorsed by Lahey and Keegan's concept of the socialised or self-authorised mind. The allowability of corporal punishment of children warrants serious discussion and, as has been done in many jurisdictions across the world, potentially made illegal.

A second area of traditional parenting that warrants consideration is that of absolutism. Earlier it was argued that business, political and religious environments impact on all of us. We all tend to gravitate towards the elements of these that endorse the conditioning we receive when growing up and, as is graphically illustrated across many jurisdictions today, polarisations of societies (especially on political and religious grounds) is becoming more obvious.

Absolutism in any form adversely impacts ability to deal with complexity and ambiguity. It creates a "black/white", "either/or" choice in which only the one view advocated is acceptable and/or "true". This is especially obvious with extremist religious faiths and extremist politics whether "left" or "right". Any view other than "ours" is wrong and must be at least opposed and, preferably, eliminated by any means possible despite their legality. We will seek to reshape society to fit our mould and only what we espouse is culturally acceptable.

As commented on earlier, Stanford University's Carol Dweck talks of two mindsets[18] – a fixed mindset that believes that things like one's intelligence and talents are set and cannot be changed or developed and a growth mindset that believes we start with a basic set of such attributes and they can be developed through dedication and hard work. Although she does not extend this to consider resistance to or acceptance of change and she does not discuss bias per se, Dweck does consider the impact of a growth mindset on motivation, and productivity in business, education and sport. It also has relevance in relation to one's perspectives on politics, religion, and the like. Is it possible that a closed mind as to the possibility of developing things like one's own intelligence and talents also impacts on one's ability to consider the need for growth and development in such broader areas of life? Does a fixed mindset eventually lead (as was earlier stated) to the situation described in a popular "insult card" that was around in the 1950's: "My mind's made up. Don't confuse me with the facts"? It can – absolutism carries with it the seeds of a closed mind. Certainly, we should encourage the development of deeply held values in our young, but, along with this, we need to encourage genuine dialogue and discussion that fosters growth in understanding and expression rather than a mindset of "I am right and, by definition, you must be wrong."

Unwillingness to confront the reality of unconscious bias is a very real issue and an indicator of Dweck's "fixed mindset". Refusal to confront issues around conscious cognitive bias is a recipe for a regressive rather than a progressive society.

In every society across the globe, every individual and every organisation is impacted by biased decisions on a daily basis. Too often we pretend that, while bias is a reality, I, personally, have overcome it. Even for those who do acknowledge its reality in their lives, many are selective in acknowledging, confronting and managing the sources, reinforcers, and consequences that arise from decisions made using heuristics that are impacted by bias. Despite all evidence demonstrating that awareness of the reality of bias and/or of types of bias is largely ineffective, we continue to treat symptoms rather than causes. Then we wonder why nothing really changes.

As indicated above, studies across the world show that bias seriously impacts our choice of decision-making heuristic. Our choice of heuristic seriously impacts the quality of decisions that we make. Often, the implementation of these decisions has potential to impact even those not directly affected. Managing this entire process requires that in acknowledging, confronting, and managing the sources, reinforcers, and consequences that arise from such decisions we become leaders who facilitate development of environments that inform and are supportive of those who want to minimise the undesirable consequences of our biases.

As argued elsewhere[19] the core of leadership consists of creating an environment in which others can achieve success. If we can accept the reality of bias in our own lives; can learn to manage the impact of this on our decisions; and can facilitate this world-view growth process in others; we are well on the way in helping develop an environment in which the negative impacts of bias are minimised.

Questions for group discussion:

1.   "We are conditioned to demonstrate bias towards 'being decisive' or 'being in control' regardless of whether we are actually equipped for this – or whether the situation being faced actually requires this." Is this really

the case? Why? Why now? If it is, what practical changes can be implemented by people with authority to change this approach?

2. "The distinction between the person and their behaviour, makes it possible to deal with inappropriate behaviour in a manner which does not demean or bully in any way. It enables discussions in which all parties can learn and grow from the interaction. It enables a positive, healthy interaction no matter who the other person is or what they have done." What biases impact our willingness and ability to treat every person with unconditional respect? Why? How can we manage these?

3. "The conditioning from childhood has fostered a set of biases that have become the unconscious drivers of our everyday behaviour. Accordingly, when confronting the manifestations of bias, simply providing an intervention that highlights why our behaviour is considered to be inappropriate is unlikely to bring about any significant change. We need to return to first principles and create a new environment – one that is supportive and non-judgemental – to facilitate the change required." How can we create the requisite "new environment" for ourselves and others?

4. "While a behavioural intervention programme may argue that it is enabling a person to manage their biases, that person may not actually possess the 'real freedom to achieve' such change until their group affiliation and social conditioning environment provides a fertile environment within which the change can take place." How can any new supportive environment be provided for those seeking to address their biases and what processes could be followed to optimise personal development of "positive managed bias" behaviour?

5. "Despite all evidence demonstrating that awareness of the reality of bias and/or of types of bias is largely ineffective, we continue to treat symptoms rather than causes. Then we wonder why nothing really changes." How are you managing bias in your life? To what extent do you seek to identify and manage your (mainly) unconscious biases? How do you do this? How can you better identify and manage your biases?

Notes

1 Dobbs, Michael *To Play The King*, 1992, HarperCollins Publishers Ltd, London
2 There is some interesting discussion on this concept in Alice Miller's works ("Thou Shalt Not Be Aware", 1984; "For Your Own Good", 2002, Farrar Straus and Giroux, New York; "The Body Never Lies", 2005, W.W Norton & Company, New York)
3 An approach developed by The Centre for Creative Leadership, "The Situation-Behaviour Impact" (SBI) model provides a powerful way of demonstrating unconditional respect when addressing issues and/or giving feedback. https://www.mindtools.com/ay86376/the-situation-behavior-impact-feedback-tool See also https://www.ccl.org/leadership-solutions/leadership-topics/giving-effective-feedback-that-works/
4 Joydeep Baruah, 2014, *"Understanding Limits to Human Development: Group Affiliation and Social Conditioning"*, Paper presented at the HDCA Annual

Conference, "Human Development in Times of Crisis", September 2–5, 2014, Athens, Greece. (Session: 05PS3.6: Participation and Public Deliberation)

5 Spillane, Robert, 1985, *Achieving Peak Performance* Harper & Row (Australasia) Pty Ltd, Sydney

6 Lewin, Kurt (June 1947). *"Frontiers in Group Dynamics: Concept, Method and Reality in Social Science; Social Equilibria and Social Change"*. Human Relations. 1: 5–41.

7 The various works on Emotional Intelligence (EQ) have some relevance here. The two key aspects on EQ are, first, understanding ourselves (self-knowledge/awareness) and, second, understanding the impact of our behaviour on others. Each of us can always further develop our EQ.

8 https://www.bbc.com/news/world-us-canada-41488081

9 https://www.pewresearch.org/fact-tank/2021/09/13/key-facts-about-americans-and-guns/

10 https://www.usatoday.com/story/news/nation/2023/05/08/how-many-mass-shootings-in-2023-texas-shooting/70194519007/

11 https://www.forbes.com/sites/elizabethmacbride/2018/11/25/americas-gun-business-is-28b-the-gun-violence-business-is-bigger/?sh=32a4c2ca3ae8

12 https://www.bostonglobe.com/2022/05/27/nation/see-how-nra-other-gun-rights-groups-have-spent-money-political-campaigns-recent-years/

13 https://www.undp.org/sustainable-development-goals?utm_source=EN&utm_medium=GSR&utm_content=US_UNDP_PaidSearch_Brand_English&utm_campaign=CENTRAL&c_src=CENTRAL&c_src2=GSR&gclid=EAIaIQobChMImcqZyNHf_QIVxJlmAh169gpREAAYASAAEgIXcvD_BwE

14 https://www.nytimes.com/2022/05/25/world/europe/gun-laws-australia-britain.html

15 https://worldpopulationreview.com/state-rankings/open-carry-states

16 Lahey, Lisa Laskow & Keegan, Robert, 2009, *"Immunity to Change: How to Overcome It and Unlock the Potential in Yourself and Your Organization"*, Harvard Business School Publishing Company, Mass. USA

17 Miller, Alice, op cit

18 Dweck, Carol. 2017, *Mindset; changing the way you think to fulfil your potential,* Little, Brown Book Group, London. See also https://www.ted.com/talks/carol_dweck_the_power_of_believing_that_you_can_improve

19 Long, Douglas G, 2013, *"Delivering High Performance: The Third Generation Organisation"*, Gower Publishing, UK

SOME THOUGHTS ON DESIGNING PROGRAMMES ENABLING INDIVIDUALS AND ORGANISATIONS TO MANAGE BIAS ISSUES

During the 1970's and 1980's considerable work was done on understanding how to improve the probability that learning interventions would achieve their purpose of improving individual and organisational performance. Key researchers involved in this included Malcolm Knowles of North Carolina State University, Leonard Nadler of George Washington University, and David Kolb of Case Western University.

The late Malcolm Knowles[1] concentrated on what he termed "androgogy". He argues that there is a significant difference in the requirements for effective learning by an adult (androgogy) vis a vis teaching of a child (pedagogy). Knowles argues that pedagogy for adults is an oxymoron, because (although we may have lost sight of its origins) by definition, "pedagogy" is the teaching of a child. He posited six assumptions for designing adult learning: (1) Adults need to know why they need to learn something (2) Adults need to build on their experience, (3) Adults have a need to feel responsible for their learning, (4) Adults are ready to learn if training solves an immediate problem (5) Adults want their training to be problem focused, (6) Adults learn best when motivation comes intrinsically. This approach of building on experience and justifying the learning process is different from pedagogy (the teaching of children) which is an education method in which the learner depends on the teacher for guidance, evaluation, and knowledge acquisition. In pedagogy, the teacher is central and in control of the learning agenda even though the focus may be on the learner. In androgogy the learner is central, and the role of those providing the learning experience is to facilitate the learning process with the learner being in charge of the learning process.

Knowles fully recognised that both pedagogy and andragogy have certain similarities as teaching approaches in that they seek to register transformative learning among the students and, despite the age of the learners, the main objective of an effective teaching approach is to register transformative learning by creating a favourable learning environment. However, as he makes clear, the process by which this favourable learning environment is created is more complex for adults than may be the case for children.

Building on the early work of Knowles (with whom he had a long professional association), Nadler talks of the difference between experience (or incidental learning) and education (or intentional learning). He talks of behaviour or performance as being the sum of experience and education less the effect of any filtering done by our culture and personality. From here he goes on to speak of learning as being something that occurs independently of any structured or programmed learning activity. He stresses that education provides a framework within which we can maximise the benefit of experience. However, for adults, it is critical that the learning process minimises the possibility of learners thinking we are "remaking the wheel", "teaching people to suck eggs", or otherwise replicating teaching methodology mistakes that may have negatively impacted an adult's desire to be again involved in any formal educational process.

Nadler developed what he called "The Critical Events Model"[2] as a guide to optimising the success of learning interventions. The model has eight key stages surrounding a core of evaluation and feedback:

1. Identify the Needs of the Organisation
2. Specify Job Performance
3. Identify the Needs of the Learner
4. Determine Objectives
5. Build Curriculum
6. Select Instructional Strategies
7. Obtain Instructional Resources
8. Conduct Training

The key message from Nadler is that any learning intervention needs to start with the identifying of very specific needs of both organisation and individual learner, then end by detailed assessment as to whether those needs have been met through the intervention provided. By placing evaluation and feedback at the centre of his model, he emphasises that every stage of the model needs to be checked for congruency with the organisation's needs and to be assessed as to consistency across all elements. This is particularly important when addressing the issue of biases. Generic "anti-bias training" is unlikely to resolve specific organisational issues.

But being specific, on its own, is not enough. In Chapter 15, several instances of specific interventions were shown. The research by Denison et al focused specifically on professional rugby (under-18s and Colts (under-20s) team in Victoria, Australia) both two weeks before and two weeks after players from the Melbourne Rebels Super Rugby team had travelled around the state to deliver talks addressing the issue. Eberhardt worked with police in northern

California. Both interventions were well designed but, Denison is quoted as saying that the findings of their research into the effectiveness of this education intervention to stop homophobic language in men's rugby training were "very disappointing".

David Kolb[3], like Knowles and Nadler, has also sought to optimise the probability of adult learning being a successful process. Kolb developed a four-stage model that views learning as an integrated process. All four stages are mutually supportive because Kolb believes that effective learning is a cyclic process that involves experiencing, reflecting, thinking and acting. He argues that there are two ways of grasping knowledge. These are concrete experiences and abstract conceptualisation while the other two modes, reflective observation and active experimentation, help learners transform their experience into knowledge. Each of these stages acts as a foundation for the next stage.

As such, Kolb's experiential learning cycle highlights how learners change as a result of experience, reflection, conceptualisation and experimentation. According to the cycle, learning occurs when an individual comes across an experience and reflects upon it. This leads to an analysis and formulation of abstract concepts. Learners can then experiment with their hypotheses in various situations. For this to work properly, all those involved in the learning experience need to have input.

Steps 1 to 5 of Nadler's model address this issue of input from those who will be participating in the learning initiative. These steps focus on both the organisation and the individual by first ascertaining organisational requirements, second ensuring performance standards are clearly enunciated, third assessing individual performance against the organisation's performance requirements, fourth developing clear educational objectives, and fifth, only at this stage determining the curriculum and instructional strategies. This approach means, first, that all the Knowles' principles of androgogy can be applied and, second, that Kolb's experiential learning cycle can be fully utilised.

In Nadler's 6th stage (Select Instructional Strategies) it is important to ensure that those who will be participating in the learning initiative are adequately supported. This requires that, prior to embarking on any programme, all participants are fully briefed as to why they have been selected, what issues specific to them are being addressed, and what behavioural results are being sought by the organisation. This needs to be followed by ensuring that, while on the course, participants are able to give all their focus to the training initiative, and post course, they are fully debriefed and then supported and coached on their return to the work environment – in other words, recognising that providing a learning initiative does not mean that some magical process occurs such that behaviour change becomes immediately apparent and effective. The environment to which participants return must be supportive of implementing what was learned rather than being implicitly or explicitly resistant to this. As indicated throughout this book, the "in-group" vs "out-group" dynamic is powerful and, when seeking to implement learning, participants need to feel part of a new "in-group" – one in which implementing the new learning is actively supported – rather than feeling that they are now encouraged to act differently from their peers.

In today's work environment meeting these requirements is extremely difficult. Most 21st century organisations whether for-profit or not-for-profit, public or private sector, small or large operate on a business model in which expenditure on initiatives such as bias concerns is held to an absolute minimum. There is a preference for individual computer-based initiatives that minimise disruptions to work performance – despite any questions as to their overall effectiveness. The time, money, and resources involved in maximising the organisational benefits possible is seen as an expense rather than an investment. Human Resource Development personnel are pressured to address symptoms rather than underlying causes. Because of this, it may be necessary to find some way of providing this same level of involvement and, hopefully, of support through a computer-based initiative.

If an organisation can be persuaded to comprehensively address issues arising from biases, then, as discussed in this book, the potential benefits to both organisation and individuals are huge. Of course, the opposite also applies.

Notes

1   Knowles, MS, 1970, *"The Modern Practice of Adult Education: Androgogy versus Pedagogy"*, New York, Associated Press
    Knowles, MS, 1975, "Self Directed Learning: a Guide for Learners and *Teachers"*, New York, Cambridge Books3rd.
    Knowles, MS, 1984, *"The Adult Learner: A neglected Species"*, 3rd ed., Texas, Gulf Publishing Company
2   Nadler, L, 1982, *"Designing Training Programs: The Critical Events Model"*, Addison-Wesley
3   Kolb, D.A., Rubin, I.M., McIntyre, J.M. (1974). *Organizational Psychology: A Book of Readings, 2nd edition*. Englewood Cliffs, N.J.: Prentice-Hall.
    Kolb, D.A., Fry, R.E. (1974). Toward an Applied Theory of Experiential Learning

INDEX

Printed and bound by CPI Group (UK) Ltd, Croydon, CR0 4YY

01/12/2024

01797774-0005